Advance Praise for *Breakaway Learners*

"The book underscores the critical need for a high-quality college education; the significance of adequate and necessary postsecondary preparation; and the imperative for greater, deeper collaboration among higher education and K–12 partners, community support services leaders, and government officials. This book is a must-read for academics, policymakers, teachers, social service providers, police chiefs, and government officials."

—Martha Kanter, former under secretary, U.S. Department of Education

"We need to pay attention to what Karen Gross says; the challenges are real, the need urgent. In a policy landscape as contentious as that of education reform, many of Gross's observations and recommendations will be controversial, as she readily acknowledges. But however sharply one might dissent from one point or another, no one will come away from this book without a deep sense of reward. Read this book, then share it."

—Mark Huddleston, president, University of New Hampshire

"Karen Gross offers practical ideas based on her research and, more importantly, on her substantial leadership in assisting our nation's colleges and universities serving at-risk students. Gross's dedication to low-income students was clear when she was college president, and now she urges other leaders to commit to these students as well."

—Marybeth Gasman, University of Pennsylvania

"Karen Gross's new concept of *lasticity* fundamentally challenges the norms of our education system and seeks to create an authentic K–16 pipeline. She renames vulnerable students "breakaway students" and recognizes that the key to teaching these young people is by honoring that the act of learning requires trust. Her bold vision for education, grounded in real in-the-trenches experience, turns the current deficiency model into an interactive one, where trust is paramount and the educator is as much a learner as the student."

—Mary Frances Bisselle, head of school at Hathaway Brown

"Karen Gross asks schools, teachers, and administrators to change, because without change we cannot improve education or compete with other countries during the 21st century. It takes courage and tremendous effort to offer both a new paradigm and a new educational concept: "lasticity." The author deserves enormous credit for rocking the proverbial boat."

—Irwin Adler, public school principal

"This book should be a must-read for the educational establishment. Too much educational policy and methodology is driven by barnacle-encrusted thinking. Karen Gross lays the groundwork for some new and refreshing thinking that is long overdue."

—Wallace Altes, Altes Executive Consulting, LLC

"This book lays out a holistic set of solutions to a whole set of problems. Karen shows how to construct bridges for learning."

—Iván Figueroa, director of Mountaineer Scholars Program & Diversity Initiatives, Southern Vermont College

Breakaway Learners

Strategies for Post-Secondary Success with At-Risk Students

Karen Gross

TEACHERS COLLEGE PRESS

TEACHERS COLLEGE | COLUMBIA UNIVERSITY
NEW YORK AND LONDON

Published by Teachers College Press, 1234 Amsterdam Avenue, New York, NY 10027

Copyright © 2017 by Karen Gross

Cover photos: Ivy by Adnin Mayang under a creative commons attribution license. Student in library by Andersen Ross / Getty Images.

Library of Congress Cataloging-in-Publication Data is available at loc.gov

ISBN 978-0-8077-5842-7 (paper)
ISBN 978-0-8077-5843-4 (hardcover)
ISBN 978-0-8077-7577-6 (ebook)

Printed on acid-free paper
Manufactured in the United States of America

24 23 22 21 20 19 18 17   8 7 6 5 4 3 2 1

Contents

Preface

From the moment I became a college president in 2006 until I left my position some 8 years later, I always had a notebook in hand. Early on, that notebook was always the same—a small red leather journal. When one of these red journals became filled up with notes and speeches and documents, I'd start another. I dated and collected them and kept them in a safe place. People started to notice I always had a red leather journal in hand. I panicked if I misplaced a current journal—even for a moment.

I am not sure exactly when this started—whether it was Year 2 or Year 3—but people began asking whether I was writing a book about the college. They'd noticed the red journals. I answered truthfully: "Yes, I expect to write a book about this experience." Shortly thereafter, whenever something funny or serious or out of the ordinary would happen, folks would shout out, "She's got another chapter!" I'd smile. They were right.

At one point, after a particularly tough week, my assistant asked if she was going to be mentioned in the inevitable chapter concerning what had happened over the past several days. "No," I said, "you will get your own chapter!" And over the 8-plus years I was at the college, many people—faculty, students, staff, alums, donors, and even trustees—asked, "Will I be in your book?" My answer was always the same: "Yes."

Now, this book is the product of my experiences as an educator, before, during, and after my service as a college president at Southern Vermont College. For many years, I was a law professor at New York Law School. During the administration of President Barack Obama, I served as senior policy advisor to the U.S. Department of Education. Years ago, I was a teaching assistant in Spanish at Dartmouth College under the guidance of Professor John Rassias, and I student-taught and guest-taught in the Northampton Public Schools. All my many experiences and encounters in education have informed the contents of this book. While names have been changed and stories amalgamated to protect the innocence as well as the privacy of the many people who engage with a college or educational community, this is a book based on real-life events and my in-the-trenches experiences as a student, teacher, professor, and leader. It has also been informed by my work as a policymaker and my many conversations with teachers and professors across the disciplines. It is grounded in events and challenges from my own upbringing. It has been enriched by my son's educational experiences. It is a book about educational success. It is a book born from lived experience.

It is a story, a powerful one, I hope, about how institutions can better serve the students they enroll across the educational pipeline. And in this book, I launch and develop a new concept, and as if that were not enough newness, it has a name not currently in the lexicon: *lasticity*. I discussed, debated, and developed the concept of lasticity (and used the term) while at the college and at the U.S. Department of Education. So while both the word and the concept will most assuredly be new to many people, it is not new to a cadre of folks with whom I have worked. Lasticity—as a concept, a theory, a process, a quality—anchors this book, and its explanation starts (but is by no means finished) in Chapter 2. Lasticity, as explained, gives voice and an explanatory structure and framework to the many initiatives we launched at the college, the many students we helped, and the many extraordinary efforts extended to improve how to help students succeed. Its applicability, however, is not limited to the college or even to small liberal arts colleges more generally. It can apply to educational institutions throughout the entire K–20 pipeline.

This book is focused on students who are *not* bound for elite prep schools and equally, if not more, elite colleges, though lasticity can be applied to and benefit all students whose educational opportunity and pathway to success remain a deep challenge on many levels regardless of socioeconomic status, race, ethnicity, or gender. There are millions upon millions of students for whom lasticity has applicability. As later defined, I term these individuals "breakaway students," and I consider myself one among them, as will be shared more fully in subsequent chapters. Indeed, there are many of us—in education, in medicine, in the arts, in politics—who are breakaway kids, although unbeknown as such to many.

The book is grounded in this premise: Our educational pipeline from early childhood through adulthood is broken. Yes, there are pockets of true excellence along the way; there are promising practices, and there is growing research and data availability to inform decisionmaking. But the achievement chasm between Whites and minorities, between high- and low-socioeconomic-status children, between those within a stable home and those who are homeless and hungry, isn't shrinking. If anything, it is growing in most locations and across most age groups. That should worry us.

Surely we can do better, and we must do better. But words are not enough; they need to be supported by action—the time for talking has passed. Apart from the critically important arguments in support of equity, antidiscrimination, and equality, there are other reasons to care about our educational pipeline. In a nutshell and not to exaggerate, our collective future depends on it. When those of us who are baby boomers and even millennials are long gone, there needs to be a society in which a democracy can function—communities in which people give back and care about each other, where people vote and reflect on the critical issues of our time, where people can find meaningful employment for which they are prepared and paid a fair wage (regardless of race or gender or ethnicity), where people take seriously preventative health care for their own well-being and that of their families while ensuring that costs are contained and monies are available for the inevitable emergencies, and where people are not shooting each other in the streets as if life mattered little.

The pathway to this goal is our children—they hold our collective future in their hands. We need to do all we can today to ensure that their future is bright. As the saying goes, Time is a-wastin'.

I appreciate that some, perhaps more than some, of the ideas in this book will be troubling to people—educators, legislators, policymakers, parents. *Lasticity* is not only a new word that I hope will enter the lexicon but also a new concept, a new approach, a new way of explaining, describing, and improving the educational landscape. Something new can be disquieting, but it's worth observing that lasticity isn't new in any traditional sense; it is constructed from research and experience across a wide range of disciplines of which education is but one. Lasticity may be "new" in several senses but it is not constructed out of thin air. It can be seen as an "aggregator," bolstering our capacity to explain a complex world.

I get that there will not be universal agreement over the proffered approach, the explanations, the many suggestions, the calls to action, the push for changes. Agreement is hard when so many deeply held values, traditions, and habits are threatened with elimination or even change. It is hard when assumptions, both acknowledged and invisible, are shaken and even wrenched from their roots. I hope, though, we can agree to disagree respectfully, difficult as that is.

On one thing I think we can all agree: What is occurring now in education is not working. We are not serving all our children and adult learners well. We have not optimized opportunities, and we have become mired in political and educational debates at every level—from local school boards to state education departments to the U.S. Department of Education. We are not furthering the end game of better education. We may not agree on how to generate improvement in the educational attainment level of all who reside here in our nation. But surely, we know improvement is needed.

I do not want to undersell the importance of the prevention of poverty, homelessness, mental illness, addictions, food scarcity, abuse, and other wide-ranging stressors. But prevention is a lofty goal that we are far from reaching except in limited arenas in both the near and the longer term.

So at a minimum, I hope this book will cause readers from across the disciplines and across roles—educators, policymakers, elected and non-elected government officials, parents and guardians, trustees of schools and colleges, community workers and employers—to pause where they did not do so before. I hope it will foster reflection, and self-reflection, in ways that may not be totally comfortable. I hope readers can approach lasticity, in all its complexity, with a generosity of spirit—a spirit grounded in enhancing opportunity and success for children and adults everywhere. Perhaps ideas in this book will spark a reader's imagination and he or she will try them out or enable their use in a classroom or after-school program somewhere here in the United States or abroad. Perhaps teacher and faculty development workshops can wrestle with some of the strategies presented here.

As a nation, unlike many others, the United States can rightfully be proud that education is, at least in theory, available to all. We provide local, state, and federal funding; foundation and individual private donations meaningfully contribute to furthering the cause. Our legacy, however, is not built on good intentions. It is built on whether we can make our stated goals and world come alive in ways that are palpable.

This book provides more than a general definition of *lasticity*, although it certainly does that: It explains how the concept of lasticity is constructed, starting from the bottom up, detailing the nuances of its implementation and adoption. The book overtly links theory and facts with the real in-the-trenches experience of students, educators (broadly defined), and families. I have always harbored deep concerns about educational policymakers who have never been in a school beyond as a student. I worry about legislators who seem to be experts on education without having spent a month, let alone years, in schools in some professional capacity—as a teacher, an administrator, a security officer, a school nurse, a trustee. What happens in the trenches across the educational landscape matters. It matters a lot. This is because proffered change that doesn't reflect the real world—and real students and real parents/guardians and teachers—is unlikely to succeed.

Think about it this way: We do lots of medical experiments in laboratories with animals (for better or worse). But there is a vast distance between the laboratory and the use of new procedures and drugs on human beings. It turns out that humans are not homogeneous; they react differently to interventions from what we might expect; they show capacities to heal in ways we did not anticipate, and they fail to heal in ways that we did not imagine.

Education is similar. We can talk all we want, but we need to see, experience, and reflect on application in real life—the good, the bad, and the ugly. This book is by design in the trenches, sharing the stories and experiences of those involved in education. In many ways, this is their story, because it is their experiences that have enabled me to offer improvements to how we educate the youth and adults of our nation. For this reason, I am indebted to all the students, families, and educators with whom I have worked over more than 4 decades.

I can't think of any more important work than strategizing about improving our nation's educational systems. Join me in thinking about lasticity and taking steps to improve the future of our children—*all our children*, to use Robert Putnam's phraseology and plea. And to the members of the Southern Vermont community, this is your book—the one started in the red leather journals that accompanied me daily on my journey with you.

Acknowledgments

Most books cannot be completed without the assistance of many people, and this book is no exception. I am deeply indebted to all the students, faculty, and staff with whom I have worked over the past 4 decades. Special mention must be given to the individuals connected in a wide range of capacities with these institutions: the Northampton Public Schools, the Parkway High School (Philadelphia), Dartmouth College, Emma Willard School, the Ethical Culture Fieldston School, New York Law School, Southern Vermont College, Bennington College, and Molly Stark Elementary School.

My thinking on education has been influenced by many people, all of whom contributed directly or indirectly to the ideas, concepts, and examples contained in this book. Several have passed away, but most are still with us—although all are with me in my memories of educational excellence. These include but are not limited to Susan Abravanel, Irwin Adler, Wallace and Jane Altes, Debbie Bial, Frances Bisselle, Mary Botter, Neil Buckley, Greg Darnieder, Ivan Figueroa, Marjorie Girth, Trudy Hall, Gerry House, Irene and Susie Hunter, Sandra Jordan, Janet Judge, Martha Kanter, Lucille Kleiman, Sarah Knapp, Sue Lamontagne (Suela), Sonia Landes, Raymond Lenoue, Colleen Little, Lois Lupica, Richard Matasar, Chris Messina-Boyer, Barrye Price, Nancy Rapoport, John Rassias, Nancy Scattergood, Stephen Trachtenberg, Ira and Marcia Wagner, and Deborah Wiley. My deepest appreciation to all of you.

I also want to thank Brian Ellerbeck at Teachers College Press for believing in this book and understanding the pathway it suggests for improving our educational pipeline. Special thanks go to the entire staff at the press. And thanks go also to my amazing publicists, Deborah Kohan and Sharon Farnell, at Media Connect, a Finn Partners Company—we have been on a journey together, and I cannot think of two better people with whom to travel.

And on a very personal note, there are people in my life who enable me to do what I do; be who I am; and thrive, not just survive. Even in situations of extreme difficulty, they are there—even when they are not. While you know exactly who you are and what you mean to me, I gratefully acknowledge you here: SHC, ZNC, NH, GK, and PHR. No book of mine could or would be produced—ever—without you.

Please note: Images contained in this book do appear in color in the e-version of the book.

Breakaway Learners

CHAPTER 1

Can You See the Stars at Night?

It was not what I expected. The structure looked like a run-down apartment building but it could have passed for an old factory. There were bars on the lower-floor windows, some of which had broken glass. The building was situated on a street with row houses on both sides. There was no greenery—not a tree in sight. The edifice wasn't more than six floors high. It seemed oddly placed, in the middle of a block. No visible athletic facilities. No parking lot. No signage. No street number.

I was visiting a small public high school in Brooklyn, New York, a place where we wanted to identify high school seniors who could succeed at a private 4-year career-launching liberal arts college in Bennington, Vermont. That day I was meeting with five students, preselected by their principal as individuals whom she and her staff believed could succeed in higher education in a rural environment despite their low SAT scores and equally low grades. Actually, they had more than low scores and poor grades; they had the cumulative burden of a lifetime of adversity, and they were breaking away.[1]

My term for these students, who have accumulated negative experiences and curdled childhoods (the full impact of which are frequently better understood years later), is *breakaway students*. Rather than continuing to name such individuals *vulnerable students*, which I had for many years, I wanted a new term that reflects two ideas: These students have many strengths (often ignored and untapped and even undermined by educators) and are not weak; and the students are breaking away from the lives they have led and the people whom they love regardless of the quality of that attachment by taking steps toward their future, including through educational advancement. What makes one a breakaway student, then, is not necessarily "just" being the first in one's family to attend postsecondary education or living in poverty. It is a term that describes students who in their short lives have experienced toxic stress and abuse, as is more fully explained later. Breakaway students are moving (actually often wrenching themselves) away from where they were to where they can be. Some succeed. Others do not.

At the time when I was visiting this high school, I was a relatively new college president, and I wanted to change radically the college admissions paradigm. My unusual (some might say intrusive) involvement in collegiate admissions grew out of my frustration and dissatisfaction with our 1st- to 2nd-year retention rate of 42%; the number bothered me every time I repeated it on campus to faculty, staff, and coaches and to trustees, donors, accreditors, and community members. We lost more students than we kept between Year 1 and Year 2. We even lost some accepted and deposited students before the academic year began. Obviously, if you cannot keep students in this early period, there is no reason to expect high graduation rates. As the national conversation boiled over about getting more breakaway students to graduate from college, it seemed that we were missing the mark. It makes little sense to focus on the end point—graduation and graduation rates—if you can't get the beginning right.

Despite the fact that our retention rate was in line with retention figures at other open-access 2- and 4-year public institutions with many first-generation, Pell grant–eligible college students, we had to do better. How hard could it be to lift the retention rates of our students? How hard could it be to help these breakaway students succeed at a small college? Oh, how naive I was back then.

Here was the idea: Suppose we got the high schools to identify which of their low-income, Pell-eligible students they thought could succeed in higher education. Switch around the traditional admissions system and let high schools make the selection of who is admitted, since we do not seem to be doing such a good job distinguishing between those first-generation Pell-eligible minority students who could succeed and those who could not. Elite boarding schools had selected students for elite colleges decades ago with considerable success and little fuss; let's just flip it around, letting inner-city high schools and after-school programs select students for a non-elite college. Worth trying it as a pilot, I thought. Let's see if 10% of the college's student body can be selected by someone other than us and demonstrate improved success rates through this process.

At the Brooklyn school, I was greeted by an armed security guard, who asked where I was headed. I mentioned the name of the high school's principal. The guard shrugged and pointed me to an enclosed office area where the glass of both the interior and exterior windows was embedded with wire mesh. The space resembled a prison holding pen. "There?" I pointed. Once within that wire-windowed cage, I introduced myself and said I was looking for the principal. I was quickly informed that there were several schools in the building and thus several principals, and I wanted the high school principal on the fifth floor. They called upstairs, got permission for me to proceed, and sent me on my way to the stairwell. "No elevators," they announced.

I started walking up five flights of wide concrete steps. I saw middle school–aged kids in uniforms, some running but others in tightly formed lines. On each landing, there was an armed security guard; some were pacing, and some were leaning against the wall. The cement walls were bare; one floor looked like another. What if you broke your leg or were disabled? How exactly would a student, older parent, grandparent, or teacher actually get to the fifth floor? There had to be accidents on the cement steps, especially if it was raining or snowing out. Or if there was pushing. The experience of the place was messaging.

When I reached the fifth floor, the security guard there let me into the high school wing. No one greeted me, so I meandered through the halls, lined with cubbies meant for kindergarteners, until I happened upon the principal's office. A group of five diverse female students and a female school counselor were waiting for me, eating their lunch around a long plastic rectangular table. I said hello and explained who I was. They explained that it was lunchtime and there was no cafeteria, so they brought their own bagged lunches. There were chips and water on the table for me. The image of bread and water in the desert popped into my head.

I looked around at the students, each remarkably different from the others. One wore a hijab. Another was covered in tattoos, one of which, visible at the top of her shirt, read "Daddy." (I later learned he was in prison.) Another had an Afro. Yet another was a Latina student. Yet another had short-cropped hair and sported piercings everywhere visible (and I am sure some were in less visible places too).

Following introductions, I shared with the students that they had been chosen by their principal as candidates for admission to the college I led. I expressed how honored I was to meet them and that I wanted to describe some things about the college to prepare them for their first visit to our campus. I explained that we wanted them to see the school, ideally with a family member or two; they could meet professors, eat in the dining hall with enrolled students, stay in the residential hall (parents/guardians in a local motel), and attend an athletic event. Then they could decide if we were the right place for them. I explained that the costs of this visit would be entirely absorbed by the college. All they had to do was keep an open mind on the 2-day trip to our campus in Vermont.

After offering a few more details about the visit (the length of the bus ride to campus, the stay in the residential hall for students with already enrolled students, the individual motel for parents or guardians, the transportation to and from and around campus, the length of the various drives, the food options), I asked if there were any questions. I said, as I always do, that I would answer anything—as long as it was within the bounds of decency. Not even a chuckle. Nothing but silence. I waited. Nothing. No questions about the professors, the dorm rooms, the food, the academic support services, the required courses. I should have known that they would have few expectations; they had no sense that they even had a right to expectations. So I myself started asking a few questions: "How many of you have traveled?" A few hands went up. "Where have you gone?" "To New York City," a few replied. (Remember they lived in Brooklyn.) Another answered, "The Bronx." I should have known better; how presumptuous to assume folks had the time and money to travel. Work, illness, and living paycheck to paycheck were serious impediments to trips to close and faraway places, let alone different parts of one's homeland (safety concerns aside).

One student focused on her cellphone, tuning me out. "What interests do you have outside of school?" I asked. "Music." "Hanging with friends." "Music." We weren't getting very far. Clearly, I was not someone with whom they were comfortable. I mentioned that I looked forward to welcoming them to my home the first evening they arrived—signaling breaking bread together as a positive. They didn't seem to react as if this was such a favorable event to which to look forward. I got "the rich White lady welcoming us to her home" look, with smiles only because they knew that smile was what they were supposed to do. They understood "passing" and could do so if required, but I was hardly making them feel comfortable.

To be sure, these students had no clue that my childhood was not vastly different from theirs in many respects, despite my being White and coming from educated parents with money. They didn't know I had experienced toxic stress and abuse. They didn't know I was a "breakaway" kid too. Surely I did not look on the outside like someone to whom they could relate.

So I switched topics and asked what they thought would be the differences between their current school and a college outside the city. Answers: "My little sister won't be there to annoy me." "There will be bugs and snakes." "It won't be safe to walk around campus after dark, because there are no lights in the woods and bears will come out." "There aren't any places to eat on the street corners." "There will be nothing to do at night except sit." "I won't be able to go home for months." "I won't see my friends." Not exactly the answers I would have anticipated; the challenges were coming into sharper focus.

In these interactions (they hardly qualified as conversation), there was no mention of academics. Nothing about majors. Nothing about the cost of college. Nothing about the future—at least not in a positive sense. Nothing about college readiness. Nothing about grades. Nothing about careers. The elephant-in-the-room questions—Will I fit in? Will I succeed?—went unmentioned.

As I listened, it started to sink in—in a different way—how difficult it would be to go from this brick-and-cement school building without greenery to a 360-acre campus on a mountainside in Vermont; from a community where people lived together in small spaces to a place where there were few boundaries, other than those one created by oneself; from a place with acknowledged diversity to a state with little diversity of any kind; from a place of no expectations (or of expectations thwarted) to a place of limitless expectations, both personal and institutional.

Then one student, who had not previously raised her hand, quietly said she had a question that she wanted to ask. I nodded for her to go ahead. She asked, "Can you see the stars at night?"

I was stunned, flabbergasted. Of all the questions I had ever been asked or thought about, this was not one. It was a remarkably telling question on many levels. It had never dawned on me that in an urban environment, the stars are often obscured by pollution and city lights and buildings. I had never thought about this reality, of knowing that there are stars, the symbol of the possible, but never seeing them. I thought about how the Vermont sky lights up so brightly, even with no moon; I thought about how you can see the constellations and count the stars; on some nights, you can even see the space station. Really. Hard to know something exists—something so ordinary in one sense and extraordinary in another—if you cannot see it.

How do you answer that question and do it justice?

A simple yes didn't seem enough. I was sure that later, as I drove back to Vermont, I would come up with a wise answer, perhaps a line of poetry or some image to share. That's how it usually is; the wisdom or the right retort comes later. I could disclose that I, too, had lived in the city and had then adjusted to a rural environment, but that perhaps wasn't helpful: Where I lived in New York City, some stars still shone. And where I was raised, stars abounded in the sky.

That simple seven-word question revealed the distance between these students' lives in Brooklyn and their prospective experiences in Vermont.

The students just as well could have been going to the moon. In some sense, they were. It was not just the physical change; it was moving from their inner-city high school to a college environment, with everything that that entailed—separate buildings, residential halls, a different professor for each subject, athletic opportunities, new people, a new culture, open expanses of space, little security, abundant views, different expectations, lots of White folks. It was leaving family, howsoever defined. It was leaving the familiar. It was going from a place that was their normal now, however difficult or "abnormal" it was, to a new normal. It was traveling with baggage—lots of baggage, perhaps even steamer trunks filled to the brim. And they were going to a place where they didn't know if the people there could help them unpack, let alone carry, that baggage with them.

Little did I know at that time how these students' sense of normalcy had been shaped by their life experiences in their homes and communities—fights, drugs, alcohol, shortage of money and food, tiny shared apartments with an intergenerational presence, physical abuse, gangs, sexual assault, rivalries. Homelessness. The effects of poverty. Exposure to serious mental and physical illness in those around them. Enormous family caretaking responsibilities, demanding both time and earnings. Experience with death. Experience with a different tempo of life. Vastly different cultural, religious, and ethnicity-based norms. I did not fully grasp that getting *to* college was just the first step. Getting *through* college was yet another. Succeeding *after* college was a step beyond that. How little I had reflected on these three crucial transitions and what to do to make them a success. How I underestimated the many positive attributes that those who have experienced trauma and toxic stress, however defined, possess. And the often ignored positives within these breakaway students lay fallow. I assumed, too, that there had to be some positive life experiences in there; how else would they have landed in this get-together and been so forcefully recommended for admission to college?

And so I answered that seven-word question—and it is an answer that stays with me still: "Yes, we have stars—stars in the sky and many, many stars on the ground, students like you."

The just-recounted story is about just five of the millions of first-generation, low-income individuals who could both gain access to and succeed in postsecondary education.[2] This education is not limited to approved Title IV–eligible 4-year colleges and universities; postsecondary education extends to 2-year-degree-granting institutions and technical training programs. The goal is to increase high school graduation rates and then enable most (not all) of these graduates to progress to and through postsecondary education and enter the workforce as thoughtful and productive contributors to our communities, our economy, and our society. As a nation, we are lagging behind other developed countries in postsecondary degree attainment. That does not bode well for our collective future. The time for improvement is now.

There has been no shortage of academic work and media coverage seeking to explain the shortage of degree attainment, particularly among first-generation, low-income, diverse students, a growing population in this nation. Hardly a day goes by when there isn't some story about flaws in the pre-K–20 educational landscape: Common Core principle adoption (or lack of adoption), testing quality and its predictive capacity, teacher education, teacher quality, and elimination or redefinition of tenure. Debates rage about the costs of higher education and about the questionable behavior on campuses of students and sometimes of faculty, staff, coaches, and administrators—and trustees. The failures of accrediting agencies to identify poor-quality institutions are an overhanging cloud. Collegiate athletics offers up its own set of challenges, ranging from the inspirational to the frightening: cheating scandals, lack of degree attainment by "student" athletes, revenue made from players but used by the institutions they attend and a host of corporations engaged in the "sports" business, traumatic injuries from football and other contact sports, and sexual assaults by athletes (although surely they do not stand alone as aggressors). And then there are drugs and alcohol and the accompanying addictions and failures of judgment and unintended consequences.[3]

In addition, the challenges of the workforce of the future and the readiness of students to meet its needs postcollege have caused a front-and-center conversation, exacerbated by the debate over the aims of an undergraduate education, as if one had to choose between a liberal arts focus and career readiness. That is such a false dichotomy, and it is one that engenders (unintentionally or not) disparities between the haves and have-nots. The haves go to elite liberal arts institutions; the have-nots go to state universities or community colleges or job-training programs. This is an antiquated vision of both education generally and liberal arts education in particular. Who wants a nurse or police officer who is not a thoughtful problem-solver, a good aggregator of information, informatics savvy, and a quality thinker in a crisis? And who can become a quality airplane mechanic or industrial toolmaker today without understanding the rapidly changing and sophisticated developments in technology?

That said, we are producing graduates who seem ill equipped for the workforce of today and tomorrow. Whatever the skill sets are that employers seek (skills in, for example, teamwork, creativity, initiative, continued learning, and communication), there are complaints that our graduates do not possess them. Employers are speaking up and out, as well they should. So are parents. So are graduates. So are politicians and policymakers. So are educators. So are the trustees of institutions.[4]

Despite the growing need for college-educated workers, including in the disciplines of science, technology, engineering, and math (STEM, though I think a better acronym is STEAM—with an *A* for *art*), our efforts have not led to enough improvement over the past decade. Some even suggest we have "deproved." This signals that key jobs of the future will be filled overseas, where there are workers able to handle the designated tasks. Our failing educational system, then, has serious economic consequences for our nation.

One of the constant refrains, and laments, in the media and among local, regional, and national political pundits of all stripes concerns the growing divide between rich and poor—in education as well as employment, wages, housing, and health care. In the educational realm, this is exemplified by disparities in test scores, the lower quality of schools and higher high school dropout rates in low-income areas, and lack of access to college preparatory courses and other enrichment opportunities. In short, the achievement gap among most age groups is widening. It has created a chasm that has led Robert Putnam to suggest that because we have been "bowling alone" for so long we are focused on our own kids and kids like our own kids to the exclusion of other people's kids.[5] The Horatio Alger story is losing or has lost its punch for many breakaway kids. Going from rags to riches and living better than one's parents are becoming increasingly common challenges.

Putting some data to these issues allows us to see the challenges in the numeric equivalent of neon lights. There are approximately 8 million students who receive Pell grants, which are given by the federal government to provide financial support to low-income students seeking educational advancement in eligible programs. The vast majority of Pell students progress to non-elite institutions; the number of these students in highly competitive colleges and universities amounts to less than 20% of the overall student demographic on average. And even if these institutions doubled the number of Pell-eligible students that the "elites" enrolled, there would still be more than 7.5 million Pell students attending other institutions. (Forget, too, that these are elite institutions that could afford all interventions that could benefit these students.)[6]

The amount expended on the Pell program is approximately $30 billion annually, and that sum will increase as a growing number of prospective students seek government educational support. Indeed the form, known as the FAFSA (Free Application for Federal Student Aid), that needs to be completed to gain access to these monies is sufficiently complex, despite improvements, that students who could become eligible fail to complete it, a situation that folks are trying to remedy through programs like the American College Application Campaign, currently under way in most states. Until a solution is achieved and there is better symmetry in information, there will be more possible Pell recipients entitled to but not receiving federal educational grants. The Pell figures also underestimate government largesse, as they are not reflective of monies allocated to veterans and their families and other government educational grant opportunities. The Pell dollar amounts also fail to account for the billions of dollars in support to both institutions and academic researchers.

Now, for a government investment in education of this size (and the government is a direct lender too and forgives certain loans on the back end), one would expect positive returns in the form of degree attainment. But sadly, the data do not support that outcome. Fewer than 40% of Pell grantees who are enrolled at bachelor degree–granting institutions receive a BA or BS degree within 6 years. This compares with 60%–65% degree attainment among non-Pell-eligible students, not exactly a stunning success either but certainly better than the fate of low-income students. The success in 2-year programs and certificate programs is even lower than 40%. Stated most simply, our money is not producing the desired results.

We have proceeded as if the solution to the problem of postsecondary degree access and attainment rested largely on the shoulders of the students. If we could only get these breakaway students to persist at their educational institutions, we would solve the problem. This effort misses the mark in myriad ways. Basically, other than at the level of superficiality, we misunderstand the achievement gap problem and its causes. Those profound errors lead us to develop solutions that are not effective.

Consider the following flaws as exemplars.

For starters, we homogenize Pell-eligible students. They are not all in the 18- to 24-year range and attending 4-year private residential colleges with ivy on the walls. Pell-eligible students vary in age and attend a wide array of institutions—some that are brick and mortar, some that are online, many that are nonprofit, and some that are for profit. Some students are commuters; some are residential. Some Pell-eligible students have dropped out or stopped out along the way. Some have maxed out their Pell eligibility. The students of both today and, more clearly, tomorrow will range across a wide landscape in background, life experience, languages spoken, cultural exposure, and race. Minorities will be the majority. For these reasons, there is no one-size-fits-all solution for student success. Would that there were a singular prototype; it would make things simpler.

Then, reflect on this reality: The majority of the current student-focused attention is targeted at those who have failed and what we need to add to their tool box of skills. We employ a deficiency model. The approach runs like this: These students have major gaps, both academically and psychosocially. We need to fix these students in many ways. We should provide them with better alignment between high school courses and college academic standards. We need to foster grit, resiliency, and growth mindsets in these students. If we teach such strategies to students (some of whom already intuit them), the argument goes, we will have students whose progression across the educational pipeline is vastly improved. Thus, the students need to do things to improve themselves.[7]

This is where *lasticity* comes into play, and it offers an alternative to the deficiency model just described. Instead of shouldering the responsibility for their success, students need shoulders to *learn* on. Lasticity isn't about lowering standards and creating a pity party. It isn't about pampering or pandering.

So what is lasticity and how does it differ from how we are currently approaching student success? And why should we have confidence that this new concept—emboldened by a new word—will change the trajectory for breakaway kids? Why don't these breakaway kids just do what we all did, work hard and pull themselves up by their bootstraps? Isn't that the American way? Why can't they be like we were (as if those of us from generations ago were a paradigm of excellence)?

This book provides answers to those questions. The promise of a better future rests with the stars—the five mentioned in the story here and the millions of others on the ground whom we need to help to become visible and to shine brightly. We begin by getting a better understanding of lasticity—its meaning and its many dimensions. That is where the journey begins.

CHAPTER 2

Anchoring Lasticity

Lasticity is, to be sure, a made-up word, but its impact is anything but made up. Before I detail the meaning of this new term, engage with me in this wee experiment: Close your eyes and say the word *lasticity* several times aloud or in your mind. With your eyes still shut, ask yourself: What does this word sound like? Is it a positive word? Is it a word that reflects something I want to be? Repeat the word again: *lasticity*. Ask yourself: Is it a soft word or a hard word in its sound? What other words does it sound like? Does saying the word conjure up its possible meaning?

This exercise, playing off the linguistic literature related to sound meaningfulness or sound symbolism, points to this reality: The very word *lasticity* conveys meaning, even if we do not know exactly what it is—yet. Certain sounds, particularly if spoken and emphasized, produce understanding. By way of example, in one experiment, people were told they were about to land on a foreign planet and would be greeted by two tribes of people, one that liked other species and one that was mean spirited and destructive. The tribes were named the Lamonians and the Grataks. From the sound of the names alone, folks were asked which tribe was friendly and which was not. This isn't a trick question. Most people thought the friendly tribe was the Lamonians, because of the sound of their name. This experiment indicates that we associate sound with meaning, and not just within the English language. As beautifully expressed by Roa Lynn, "Sound unlocks an imagined scene, the sound puts me in the action, tells me what to be suspicious of and what to believe in. It's not just onomatopoeia. . . . They are 'sound glimpses,' perhaps into a room that has no fourth wall."[1]

And so it is with *lasticity*. The word, which sounds real to many people, evokes positive feelings; it's not a "mean" word. People sense endurance (as in the *last* of a fabric). Some sense movement (as in *elasticity* or *plasticity*). The last three letters, *ity*, are a common English-language ending to a descriptive noun, as in *authenticity* or *veracity* or *tenacity*, so people get that the word defines a quality of some sort. While linguists can and do debate whether sound symbolism or sound meaningfulness is verifiable as a valid approach to an understanding of and across languages (absent other intervening variables), there is value in just free-associating when hearing the word *lasticity*. As it turns out, those free associations provide a gateway into understanding this made-up word.

Stated in its simplest form, *lasticity* describes the set of express conditions (related to qualities, processes, approaches, values, and interconnectivity) that, if met and satisfied, operate to facilitate breakaway student success across the educational pipeline. So if lasticity's five building blocks—elasticity, plasticity, pivoting right, reciprocity, and belief in self—are present and animated, then the desired outcome—student success—can be fostered. If the conditions are not all present or not all met, then lasticity's capacity is diminished in terms of outcome. But there remains value even if only some of the conditions are present and met.

One way to conceptualize the fluid nature of lasticity (with its conditions that must be met) is to think about a legal contract that obligates people to each other. In a contract, there is often a set of conditions that must be met to animate the agreement between Parties A and B. If earnings are Y and interest rates are Q and if person R agrees to be employed, then party A will sell widget W to party B for dollars X. The failure of any one or more of these preconditions means the sale of the widget at the designated price will not occur. As with lasticity, some of the conditions in the described contractual agreement are within the control of the parties, while other conditions are not.

In a sense, we can view lasticity as a bargain between students and those with whom they engage within and outside the educational arena, and that bargain is mediated by the happening (or nonhappening) of certain conditions. We can, and I would argue we should, make that bargain both explicit and required; others may differ. But in society, we have lots of implicit and important bargains among and between people. For example, if you see someone standing on the railing of a bridge, you will not push him or her over into the river below. If a person is crossing in front of your moving car, you will stop to let that pedestrian through even if he or she shouldn't be stepping into the street just then. If you are in an elevator, you will not make loud, offensive noises or jump up and down to see if you can get the elevator to stop. The bargains we make reflect our values, and a breach of those bargains has consequences on a personal, legal, and societal level.

Lasticity may be present without our knowing it or having labeled it. Or lasticity can be nurtured and fostered by identifying its key elements and then enabling those elements to coexist, intersect, and interact.

Lasticity can be present in a person or an organization or the people within an organization. While descriptive of approaches that benefit breakaway students, it has utility for all students. Indeed, the term could be expanded outside the confines of education, although surely that is a topic for another day and another book.

There presently is no umbrella term that encompasses the process and characteristics and behaviors we seek to foster in our students and the institutions that service them. *Lasticity* is meant to fill that gap. Consider the word *grit* for a moment. As Paul Tough and others have described, grit (tenacity, stick-to-itiveness) is a quality that we want to nurture in children so that they can better navigate the hurdles before them. *Grit* is not a term that is focused solely on breakaway students; it is quality we want to teach all kids (and adults, for that matter). And data show—with some notable exceptions, as Angela Duckworth notes—that grit is beneficial in bettering student achievement because students with grit will keep at it, will keep trying, despite mistakes and the need for repetition and practice. In short, we want to be gritty.[2]

However, grit is not enough to enable student success, particularly breakaway student success. That is because the hurdles these students face are not overcome through just student tenacity and stick-to-itiveness. In fact, I might argue that breakaway students are grittier than nonbreakaway students given the impediments that stand and have stood in their pathways. Indeed, these students have survived toxic stress and trauma.

Resiliency, another concept that has caught the imagination and attention of many educators, focuses on developing—pre- or post-trauma—the capacity of individuals (or even institutions) to bounce back, to recover. I appreciate that the idea of recovery—whether from physical or psychic illness—is important. Resiliency education can make individuals better prepared for the trauma ahead and better able to navigate their return to a less or nontraumatic life. It could improve how we respond to microaggressions too. But, and this is key, the premise of resiliency presupposes that people can bounce back. Perhaps some can, but I suspect that most people who experience trauma are forever changed in ways that make it impossible to return to the status quo ante. Brain sciences support this conclusion too.[3]

By way of example, suppose a person loses a parent. We can talk about resiliency, but there will always be an absent parent. While we can help a child adjust to a new normal, that parental absence is not going away, even if the surviving parent remarries. When that child later marries and has children, the absent parent will reveal him- or herself again. At graduations, at proms, at Parents' Day in schools—these are all moments when that death will reappear. Resiliency cannot bring you back to where you were. That place no longer exists.

Both the literature surrounding growth mindsets and the importance of belief in self are valuable tools in the educational tool box—and belief in self is one of lasticity's five building blocks, albeit described and created somewhat differently. We know from research that belief in self is central and without it, it is hard, if not impossible, to take the risks that are involved in all learning. If the core of one's being is shaky, why keep undercutting the little stability one has by trying new things? And we know that breakaway students often have had their self-worth physically or psychically beaten out of them. So strategies to scaffold the sense of self of students—to enable them to believe in themselves and the capacity of their brains to change—are valuable. But how we do this matters. We need to know our students to do this.[4]

An image published on an education blog that depicts how students can climb the ladder of success based on increasing engagement (a feature of growth mindsets) begins with the assumption that students start at a first rung labeled *compliant*. It is followed by these words to elaborate the meaning of the term, and I quote (linguistic flaws and all): A compliant student "is not talking about their learning," "follows directions from teacher," and "learns about goals and objectives for learning from teacher."[5] Is that really where most students start? That is the assumption made explicit in the image (which includes a ladder that shows the progression from teacher centered to learner driven). But, and this is a critical *but*: Many students don't start as compliant; indeed, many start by being the opposite: *non*compliant. Many breakaway students do not listen and follow directions. Classroom disruption is common, not uncommon. Yes, many breakaway students do not talk about their classroom learning; consider instead what they talk about—life learning and life experience. Many don't even know about goals and learning objectives, however they may be proffered. In short, the ladder's lowest rung totally misses who breakaway students are, and if we presume our students are compliant, we will miss how to help them grow their mind(set)s.

Further, not only do we need belief in self; we also need to recognize that our growth continues through life, an invaluable quality. To maximize this growth, we can't be passive, waiting for personal change and development. We need to embrace and work for the next level of understanding or the next level of achievement or the next success. We are lifetime learners, whether we recognize that capacity or not, but some folks need help to awaken this learning. We can, the argument goes, get into the habit of learning, and this can be taught to us.

The three traits described above—grit, resilience, and a growth mindset—are strategies for helping students acquire a capacity that's missing or not honed fully. In other words, to return to the concept of how we treat students today, these traits presuppose a deficiency in our students that can be remedied. Sort of an add-and-stir approach. Breakaway students (perhaps many other students too), the assumption goes, are not gritty and resilient and have not established growth mindsets. So our job, as some see it, is to eliminate or lessen these deficiencies. Character education has a similar feel to it; our students are not displaying sufficient character in how they treat others, how they see their commitment to the larger world, how they handle the privilege they have inherited. Again, the focus is on filling up the deficient student—as if he or she were a beaker into which we need to pour traits or characteristics or even "character."

I have most assuredly nothing against trying to help students navigate life more easily and become better people. And I think educators can contribute positively to that effort. And I do not think the three qualities—grit, resilience, and a growth mindset—represent passing fads. But at the end of the day, that is *not* what lasticity is all about. Lasticity is vastly broader than any of the three identified terms, although belief in self is one key aspect of lasticity. It is not, by itself, enough to solve all that ails our educational pipeline, but it provides a rich architecture based on student success—not deficiencies. It meets students where they are and asks—demands—that institutions do vastly more to understand and respond to the students now enrolled in our educational system. And it provides a set of foundational principles that guide the development of lasticity—where grit, resilience, and growth mindsets can find a comfortable home.

Lasticity differs from existing approaches such as growth mindset training and resiliency education in that it does not deposit something into or onto students—even if the deposit requires some teacher action. Lasticity's power starts, for me, with the connection it bears to the work of Paulo Freire. In his now-classic book, *Pedagogy of the Oppressed*, he laments that education is usually conceived of as banking: Teachers make deposits into students just as people make deposits into a bank account.[6] I always have had this image of the head of a student with the top lifted and someone literally pouring information (or grit or resiliency or improved mindsets) into the student's head. We know that this approach, except in rare instances, does not work; engagement is needed for true learning and enduring growth. It requires the students to participate in the learning and for the teacher to be both a teacher and a learner. And we know that no 1st-grader can learn to read if he or she is hungry or hasn't had any sleep or has been physically abused in the morning. This is because, according to the psychologist Abraham Maslow's hierarchy or theory of needs, higher needs such as realizing one's potential can be reached only if basic needs for food, sleep, warmth, and safety are met. Maslow's point is that certain fundamental survival needs are in essence prerequisites to what could be termed "growth" needs. And there is no reason to focus on "higher level" needs if the basic needs go unmet. While we can criticize the rigidity of Maslow's hierarchy, it is difficult to argue with the reality that if we can't eat or sleep or breathe, we can't focus on other activities such as self-reflecting and engaging with others effectively.

And lasticity is not something static that one acquires in a given situation and then can "have" or "showcase" on a go-forward basis. Instead, lasticity is fluid and ongoing, and it rests fundamentally on reciprocity, a continual give-and-take from individuals in and outside education and students. This reciprocity is grounded and nurtured through trust, and it implicates more than one person to make it work. It requires something vastly different from *offering to*. Rather, it requires *engagement with*.

Lasticity embodies, in a sense, the educator as learner and the learner as educator. The educator is learning on several planes—including learning about his or her students. Students are learning on several planes too—including learning to trust their educators and the institutions that are enrolling them. Lasticity isn't about sages on stages; it is about guides on the sides.

In addition, lasticity is invoked to improve decisionmaking and to foster a better choice architecture in students of all ages. To be sure, the decisions students make along the educational pipeline differ dramatically from infancy through adulthood, and the risks of erroneous decisionmaking grow as a student grows older. But make no mistake about it: It is not enough to be resilient or gritty. One can make hugely bad choices and have these two traits or characteristics well in place. Drug dealers are gritty. Gang leaders are resilient. Neither is lastic.

Thinking about physics gives us additional understanding of lasticity. Traditional thinking in physics is Newtonian. Newton's third law states that for every action there is an equal and opposite reaction. Phenomena are measured, in a sense; they are predictable. They operate based on a pre-set number of rules. By way of contrast, think about quantum mechanics—which is not necessarily linear but instead tries to address a different set of issues in our universe, such as waves. They undulate and move.

Lasticity is less like Newtonian and more like quantum physics. It is a process, in essence, of trying to first recognize the positive and negative effects of trauma (toxic stress and abuse) on students who have had those experiences and have been forever changed by them. Then, lasticity uses that reality to develop a culture that is nurturing, that creates a sense of possibility and the power of the possible. Lasticity is, then, a reality-shifting, transportive approach that enables students to transition from their known sense of normal to a new one. And that's a substantial—some might say seismic—shift. While there is individual change, there is also bigger and broader change—namely, institutional change and, as a result, and even broader still, cultural change across many institutions in the educational pipeline and across our communities.

Changing culture is not automatic either. It calls for recognizing what was and the need to alter that state. And changing culture means changing both people and places. In education, a cultural shift is not moving a widget—it is reorienting roles, places, and spaces; it involves changing stereotypes, whether recognized or not. It calls for making the invisible visible, even if difficult. It begs for people to work together for each other rather than just adopting a sink-or-swim mentality for those in school.

Think about lasticity, then, as a constellation of ideas composed of individuals and institutions engaging with each other differently. Patterns are changed. There are new cultural memes. Lasticity's five foundational components—elasticity, plasticity, pivoting right, reciprocity, and belief in self (similar but not identical to growth mindsets)—are what will facilitate success and enable cultural change.

One other key observation: Lasticity is all around us. Now. We may not have seen it as such. We may not have had a label for it. We may not know the conditions that animate it. But we have seen breakaway students who succeed and institutions that facilitate their success. This book is, then, making visible that process that is now largely invisible, and we are naming what we see and what students and others working with those students experience. In so doing, we are creating opportunities for lasticity to grow, because now others can see and name its parts and consider implementing them.

So one benefit of this book is that it gives us a previously nonexistent word—not to create something new but to describe and explain and expand on some approaches, strategies, research, medical findings, and empirical data that already exist. Lasticity's gift is that it isn't an invention made out of whole cloth. It is not an invention at all. It is a rich, nuanced descriptor, as occurs in physics, as noted above, of what is occurring in real life, on the ground, in the trenches, with students and institutions. It aggregates what we know in important ways. As with physics, it is not easy to explain our complex world.

Lasticity is undergirded by the development of a vastly more nuanced understanding of the students who are entering college today and those who will do so in the years to come. We need to know and understand the parties to the contract, that contract between students and institutions that is filled with conditions. How else will institutions know how to engage with these breakaway students and determine what will help them flourish? And we need to disabuse ourselves of antiquated notions of who we *think* our students (those "deficient" students) are and replace those notions with the *reality* of who our students are—an honest assessment of who they are in terms of their remarkable strengths and capacities (which often go unrecognized) and a better appreciation for and understanding of their shortcomings. Once we develop this understanding, we can pursue ways to build lasticity, including increasing reciprocity. Lasticity is a door opener: It opens us up to the reality that we can, indeed, do better for our students, our communities, and our nation. The precursor to animating lasticity, then, rests on answering a seemingly simple question—Who are our students?—for which we have a ready, although perhaps unexpected, response, as will be seen.

CHAPTER 3

Who Are Our Students?–
Now and into the Future

The refrain is so commonplace that if I had a nickel for every time I heard it, I would be a wealthy woman: Educators across the pipeline from early childhood through Grade 20 keep articulating some version of this statement to administrators: "Get me better students." Graduate school professors lament what they perceive to be the absence of quality, well-prepared students and they blame inadequacies in undergraduate education for this situation. In turn, college faculty insist that the ability of students to write and think has been in steep decline, and they blame the high schools. The high schools blame the middle schools for student shortcomings; the middle schools blame the elementary schools; the elementary schools blame the preschools and the parents. In short, we have a litany of blame running up and down the educational landscape.[1]

Another frequent lament that gets at the same issues, although through a different lens, sounds something like this: "It was not like this when I was a student." Or "I always did my homework when asked." Or "In my generation, things were different; students listened." Or, finally, "These millennials; they don't get it. What's with these students?" These comments are heard across the educational arena and are often uttered with accompanying distain and most often spoken as if the assertions were proven statements of fact.

We also tend to homogenize students and their learning styles. We know that as a matter of both theory and practice, different students learn differently. And, in an ideal world, teachers and professors would adopt a wide array of teaching modalities to ensure that their students find a personalized entry into learning. Sadly, that rarely happens, in part because we tend to teach the way we were taught and we try to replicate in our students the way we ourselves learned and learn even now.

So if current educators had had teachers who fostered auditory learning and they (the current educators) were auditory learners, that is the

approach they are likely to take—or have dominate—their own work
with students. When a student doesn't learn the teacher's way, the teacher
in many instances can't figure out why that student can't learn the same
way the teacher did. To be sure, many students and their teachers are also
unaware of the students' (or their own) precise learning style, although
there are diagnostics that help people evaluate how they learn best. This is
particularly true at the college level.

Consider the concrete effects and implications of the sentiments and
approaches just described. One example involves Concordia University, in
St. Paul, Minnesota, which offered summer orientation but explicitly stated
that it was mandatory for students of color, forgetting for a moment who
"qualifies" as being of color and whether that is an institution or prospective
student definition. (Dr. Henry Louis Gates Jr. would also add the complexity of whether race and ethnicity is defined based on outward appearances
or based on our DNA, as evidenced by his remarkable work on identity,
exemplified by his books and his television series, *Finding Your Roots*.) A
not surprising outcry ensued, with one prospective student stating, "Guess
this is a class on how us po negroes should act in massas school." Ouch.[2]

Moraine Valley Community College offers a course designed to facilitate student transition to college-level learning. More recently, the college
is piloting two sections of this College 101 course for African American
students, noting how important it is that successful students create effective support networks—which they presume means networks of students
of one's same race. Another ouch. Wouldn't it be wiser to enable students
to develop networks among a wide range of students rather than implying
that comfort can and only does occur within one's specific race? Seems to
me to be an odd effort with the potential to encourage or reinforce isola-
tion of students.[3]

Finally, at the graduate level, Smith College professors complained that
they were teaching minority students who were unprepared for Smith's
School for Social Work. As one letter from a professor said, and I quote
intentionally at length, "The core of the problem is that the admissions
process of our School has been tainted for a number of years—we have
admitted students who did not have a reasonable chance of success in our
program. This is very problematic and it is an issue that seems to be somehow displaced onto the field department. Why is that?" Yet another ouch.[4]

These approaches all suffer from the same flaw: They fail to reflect
an understanding of our students at every age and stage. And as will be
addressed later, there is an implicit challenge to the notion that we really
do want to educate, and we care about educating, all students. At the
most basic level, the students of today and tomorrow are not the students

of yesterday or yesteryear. Full stop. We can complain all we want, but the clock is not moving in reverse. Many of today's students are the first in their families to attend college, let alone graduate; many are immigrants; many are low income. Many have experienced trauma or toxic stress.[5] Many have attended schools that were not exemplars of excellence. Today, we are not supposed to be segmenting higher education so that it is available only to those who are the landed gentry (or children of that gentry in some instances), who attended elite prep schools or selective public high schools and are White, Protestant, and male for the most part. Ostensibly, that restrictive era is in the past.

The problem, simply stated, is that many educators want to educate (whether consciously or not) their clones, rather than assessing how to educate the students before them. We need to leave aside whether we are doing a good job preparing our teachers across the educational pipeline—not just with respect to the quality and sophistication of how they cover the substantive material they are delivering but also in their pedagogy or andragogy, as the case may be.

Before turning to a more in-depth assessment of who our students are, let's circle back to the frequent laments about millennials. We can complain about them, but if truth be told, most of the students now entering school are not, in fact, in this category. The last millennials were born circa 1995—meaning the "last" of the millennials are already in middle school. What we have now, whether accurately defined or not, is Generation Z—individuals born from 1995 through 2020 give or take. Some have termed this the "iGen," given their propensity to use iPhones, iPads, and iPods. They are a tech-savvy generation, even those who are not of upper socioeconomic status. These are our students. Those of us teaching them are largely, but not exclusively, baby boomers.

For its wonderful annual overview of the students entering college (although an elite liberal arts college), Beloit College gathers information and produces lists that would startle even millennials. Here's the college's lead-in to the Class of 2020: "Students heading into their first year of college this year are mostly 18 and were born in 1998. Among those who have never been alive in their lifetime are Frank Sinatra, Phil Hartman, Matthew Shepard, Sonny Bono, and Flo-Jo." Yipes. Another yipes for Beloit and others failing to recognize that at most colleges, entering students are not 18 and many are not at their first higher ed institution.[6]

If our teachers fail to see our students for who they are, we are in trouble. For educators who are not tech savvy and don't tweet or use Instagram or Snapchat or instant messaging and who perhaps even view these forms of social media with some disdain (or fear), how exactly are they reaching their students? What worked decades ago in delivery of material and attention span and forms of engagement (if any) does not work today for most students. And many of today's teachers (the boomers) were themselves taught by members of the Silent Generation. Sure, there are students who can sit quietly in their seats and do worksheet after worksheet, even if it is busywork. There are students who can listen to professors lecturing from afar, including with PowerPoint slides that often replicate what the professor is saying or that are too dense with text to be read while they are on the screen.

As a participant in a three-leader swap between a college president, the head of a high school, and the head of an elementary school (I went to the high school to be "leader for the day"), I was struck by what we uncovered in the debrief we held. To a person, the three leaders noted that the teachers had not kept pace with the speed of technology and that their use of it in the classroom was not fluid or generally dynamic—except in the elementary school that was involved in project-based learning, and particularly the kindergarten teacher, who was using iPads with her students to teach math.[7]

How good would it be if we lived in a world where such kindergarten teachers received sufficient respect that they could lead workshops for high school teachers and college math professors on how young people are learning and processing math? Imagine workshops where attendees actually used iPads to test out the learning approaches of kindergarteners and perhaps even visited classes or Skyped into classes. Why not enable teacher swaps in addition to offering mixed-level professional development? (I know some readers will be muttering, "Yeah, that will happen when pigs fly.")

How can you teach well and engage effectively with your students if you do not know who they are?

The answer to that question, on the simplest level, is that you cannot. Consider this example: If a doctor does not know a lot about his or her patient, how exactly is the doctor going to divine a treatment that will actually work and be adhered to by the patient? The physician gets some information from taking a history. Some information can be garnered by looking at and examining a patient in person or via a computer screen (albeit this is not exactly the same in terms of "feel"). Added information can be garnered by listening to patients and viewing medical-knowledge graphs. Surely we have all experienced physicians who fail to understand what ails us and as a result do not treat us effectively.

Not to be outlandish here but I have always been especially fond of veterinarians. These doctors have patients that cannot speak (although they vocalize, to be sure) and give a history. Yet these doctors can detect what is wrong with their patients with remarkable accuracy. They read expressions. They assess body language. They examine the pet. They ask questions of the owner, if there is one. In short, because of these qualities, I want to go to a vet for my health care.

So teachers across the educational pipeline need to know who their students are—without homogenizing them and without wishing them to be better. Imagine a doctor who said, "I wish I had patients who weren't sick," or a lawyer who said, "I'd love the law if it were not for the clients." The sentiment in "I want better students" has a similar ring and feel to me. It sounds like "I would succeed at and love teaching if I had different (better?) students."

In an essay that appeared in *The Chronicle of Higher Education*, a professor tried to explain what the faculty–student relationship was all about. As I read the essay, my blood began to boil. The piece, sadly, also reminded me of some of the things I had said and thought when I was a young professor 4 decades ago. That wee selfie wasn't pretty.[8]

Trying to be hip and help his students, the professor refers to the need to "DTR" (define the relationship), because students do not accurately perceive the role and boundaries of faculty and other "authority" figures. Here are some of the article's proclamations: "I don't work for you. You're not a customer and I am not a clerk. I am not a cable or streaming site. I'm not a high school teacher. I'm not your BFF." The piece then continues to talk about what the professor "is," as opposed to "is not," but to be frank, I was so turned off by then that it left me cold to read the remaining statement: "I'd like to be your partner."

Now, it seems to me that this professor, although explicitly asserting that he was trying to be helpful, misunderstands his role and his relationship with his students. Partnering (his desired end) requires trust, among a host of other essential qualities. The harsh conclusions, such as "I don't work for you," when students and their families are paying buckets of money to be educated, seem to be ignoring the financial strain of an education. Yes, the professor is correct that we do risk commodification, but canceling out reality doesn't change that. In addressing not being a website or its equivalent, the professor added these words in the body of his article: "Consider this official notice that I have opted out of the on-demand world. My office hours are listed on my syllabus. If for some reason I can't be in my office during those hours, I'll let you know beforehand if possible or post a note on my door. But I'm usually there." He then went on to add, "As for email, yes, I have it and I check it often, but not constantly. I do have a life outside this classroom—a wife, kids, hobbies, other professional obligations. That's why I don't give out my private cell number. If you need me after hours, email me and I'll probably see it and respond within 24 to 48 hours."

How wrong this all is on so many levels! Yet many of the comments in response that were published online were deeply supportive of this professor's approach. It reminded me of how many people were so supportive of Yale's husband-and-wife Silliman College house masters Nicolas and Erika Christakis. These individuals were publicly derided by the students for being insensitive to and dismissive of student concerns. But many people agreed with the nonapologetic professors, commenting on how pampered and coddled and fragile the students of today are and demanding, How dare these students shout and protest given their place of privilege? After all, they were attending college—in fact, Yale. The argument, taken to its logical extreme, is this: If you go to an elite institution, you park who you are at the door and you need to become the student and person the institution is used to serving and has served for generations. You need to "buck up" and "fly right." You need to be grittier and more resilient.[9]

The students of today—the ones that I term *breakaway students*, as described in Chapter 1—have had myriad experiences that have shaped who they are, how they feel, and how they respond. Indeed, the brain's hardwiring for breakaway students is likely changed because of their early life experiences, some of which had unimaginable impacts on their sense of identity and safety. Some of these students live in poverty. Some are homeless. Some go hungry at night. Others can't get a good night's sleep. Others are exposed to outbursts or other violence in their home or on the streets of their community. Others have witnessed excesses, including of drugs and alcohol. Some have experienced, and others have witnessed their loved ones experiencing, physical and sexual abuse. Some have a medical condition, such as asthma; others have dealt with the illness of those close to them. They have been yelled at or ignored or both. They have observed and felt the impacts of mental illness, including depression or bipolar disorder. They have seen post-traumatic stress up close, as the result of military service or of lives lived on the ground in their homes and communities.[10]

Here's an important reminder: While poverty can be a prominent factor in students' experiences, many of the described issues are not a matter of socioeconomic status (SES). Whether rich or poor or anything in between, young people can be exposed to conditions and people and situations that are damaging, a point recognized by Robert Putnam in his book *Our Kids*.[11] Often without an outlet through which to escape or respond or even understand, these kids muddle along—some better than others.

For children with curdled childhoods like mine (where SES and race were not directly implicated), the pathway through the educational pipeline is fraught with hurdles. Teachers may not even be aware of the experiences of these children and may assume them away or assume the presence of issues wrongly. But we all know, and Maslow, mentioned in Chapter 2, made this abundantly clear, that unless certain basic needs are met, it is tough to teach kids who are tired or homeless or hungry or stressed or physically or psychically damaged. The problem is that these stressors are borne internally, and many teachers and administrators (among others, including even pediatricians) do not see them (or perhaps do not want to see them).

Sadly, the reality is that more and more students entering the educational pipeline have had curdled childhoods. One has only to look at the data in Putnam's *Our Kids* to appreciate the level of poverty affecting youth in America. Over 8 million college students receive Pell grants, which were created, as noted earlier, for students in the lowest-income quartiles, and there are students who are eligible for these monies but (unfortunately) do not complete the needed paperwork.

Ponder these data points: In the United States, 15.3 million children live in households with food insecurity. Approximately 2.5 million children were homeless for some part of the past year. Some 8 million children live in a household where at least one parent has an alcohol or drug addiction, and more than 14% of these children are under the age of 2. Each year, 5.5 million children are the subject of reported child abuse, and much abuse goes unreported. More than 400,000 children are in foster care. And we are not counting here students with physical and mental disabilities, whether mainstreamed or not.

One method for reflecting on these data points is to look at the adverse childhood experiences, or ACE, assessment calculator—a "quiz" (although that is something of a misnomer when one realizes what it uncovers) to determine the number of negative experiences one has had as a child. As in golf, one wants a low score; sadly, many children from all walks of life receive a high score, confirming that they have been living with toxic stress and trauma, the impacts of which are without question negative and have a lifelong impact on health, well-being, and success, both academic and personal.[12] (Adverse experiences can also produce a different set of positive attributes that often go unnoticed and unrecognized, as discussed later.)

Two key points before turning to ACE test questions and the meaning of the results: Just because one has a high score does not mean one lives a life that is doomed from the get-go. That's an important point. Even those with high scores can, with various successful interventions, learn from and experience success in spite of, or perhaps more important, because of, their early years. The key here—and this is critically important from an educational standpoint—is that there is much that can be done by educational institutions to improve the quality of the outcomes for children with high ACE scores. In other words, birth is not destiny. Helping students with high ACE scores is one of the aims of lasticity—the new concept developed in this book. Some people seem to be lastic, but others can be aided if we focus on enhancing their lasticity through our own behavior, actions, interventions, and cultural norms. And we would do well to ferret out and emphasize the positives of the negative experiences, a new way of reflecting on trauma.

The 10 ACE quiz questions focus on whether before the age of 18 a person was exposed to the mental illness or addiction of a household member, to personal psychological or physical abuse or danger, or to sexual assault within or outside the household or was witness to the abuse of a mother or stepmother or the imprisonment of a household member. In the original quiz, conducted with White middle-class individuals, approximately two-thirds of those questioned ticked off at least one "yes" answer, and of those, 87% ticked off one or more "yes" answers. Those who tick off four or more "yes" answers are at greatest risk. You can include me in that number, sadly. Stated another way, huge percentages of children are exposed to toxic stress, trauma, or abuse, producing the increased risk of many hazards as they mature in terms of well-being.[13]

To put numbers to all this, more than 34.8 million children have at least one "yes" answer on the ACE quiz. Nearly one-third of all children aged 12 to 17 have experienced at least two "yes" events. While the rates do vary according to SES, between one-quarter and one-third of all children under age 6 experience at least one "yes" answer on the ACE quiz.[14]

If there ever were a clarion call to respond to the abuse and toxic stress of our youth in America, this is it. Further, the absence of abundant mental health programming (and funding for it) across the K–6 educational pipeline doesn't help one bit. Nor, to be sure, are most elementary educators trained to address these issues. Courses and strategies on classroom management are not the answer.[15]

For educators at every level across the pipeline, this means we need to rethink how we address the needs of the students we have. Some faculty and staff and school trustees may even have a deep understanding—because of their own background and experiences, including being first-generation or breakaway students themselves. They, too, may have had low standardized test scores; they may have struggled with "fitting in," even after getting a PhD. Some may even intuit the challenges. They may have been shown to have high ACE scores had they taken the quiz. Some may be minorities, which can help students identify and form relationships with them; but it is at once an ambitious and a long-range strategy to overhaul the teacher corps across our nation. And such an overhaul would encompass who becomes an educator in the first instance (and we cannot hope or expect that they will all be breakaway kids themselves) and then what information, knowledge, and experience these educators need to have before they enter classrooms unsupervised.

In the absence of a massive revamping of the teaching corps in our nation, we need a different approach. For educators and those working with children within and outside schools now, we need a set of implementable strategies that will help students excel. We need to create environments in which these breakaway students can thrive despite the plethora of "yes" ACE responses.

Breakaway students, then, have a certain set of mental attributes (some that can be very positive and mined for strength) and hurdles that may not be present in other students. Importantly, to repeat an earlier point, it is not poverty per se that distinguishes these students; rather, it is having had a childhood burdened by one or more of these experiences: hunger and exposure to or experience with drugs, alcohol, abandonment, frequent moves, abuse, or self-harm or harm of others. Some students have experienced or watched others suffer from serious health conditions—diabetes and emphysema among them. Some students believe that the world in which they live is "how it is," and for them, the abnormal is normal. They have experienced "gaslighting," a distortion of reality and hence struggle to know (and normalize) the world beyond their confines.[16]

The need for understanding students' capacities is vital because breakaway students may not trust those within institutions where they are enrolled; nor may they trust their own capacities, even when these are obvious to others. If you have tattered attachments when you are young, your capacity to trust is weakened, if not broken, and has to be rebuilt. The act of learning requires trust. Learning asks us to change our paradigm: to take risks, to fail, to seek help. Learning environments must have reciprocal trust in actuality; students must trust their teachers and professors, teachers and professors need to trust their students, and eventually, students must trust themselves.[17]

How we build a changed institutional culture for the institution itself and for the individuals within that institution that can understand breakaway students and adapt to them is no small challenge. There is an assumption embedded here: Folks want to accept this challenge and are willing, as people and as members of institutions, to take the time and make the effort, to understand the students they serve. To be candid, although I tend to gloss over this reality, there is not a uniform desire either for cultural change or for understanding breakaway students. Sad but true. For lasticity to embed itself in our approaches, we need a willingness to change institutional culture, and that change is hinged on developing an understanding of the students we serve. A later chapter includes some strategies to address these hurdles, but make no mistake: Educational success can't and won't happen if we continue as we currently are. Equally bluntly, the assumption that the flaws rest with the students, not the institutions and teachers, runs deep and is firmly rooted in the psyche of many who work along and engage with the educational pipeline.

To return to and reflect on the importance of culture, keep this phrase in mind, as it highlights how central culture is and how little we do to measure it: "Culture eats strategy for lunch every day."[18] Stated differently, all the strategy in the world to help students (think multipage strategic plans as requested by trustees, mandated by accreditors, common in the business sector, and often proffered as a solution to all that ails an institution) will fall short if institutional culture does not support the strategy. Lip service doesn't work; unauthentic solutions written on pieces of paper don't have "stickiness," let alone the needed monetary allocations. It is vastly better and infinitely more effective to spend time creating a quality culture than developing and writing down a long-term strategy, as no strategic plan will trump culture, of that I am sure. For some, this may be a heretical notion, given the emphasis we place on strategic plans (and the time, effort, and money expended on them in part because of demands from accreditors).

Consider how the culture surrounding tattoos has changed over time—although some folks in the Silent Generation and among the baby boomers still view them askance. Tattoos were seen as evidence of a person's instability, of being marginal, of being powerless (but asserting power through a scary symbol on one's arm). The tats were seen as evidence of military service or of an act carried out in a drunken stupor. Tattoos intimated "low rent."

Today, students and young adults in general have very different views of tattoos and their meaning. They wear them proudly; they wear them to remember something; they wear them to provide inspiration. Look at the movement to create artful tattoos—amazing tattoos—to cover surgical scarring, including for women who have had mastectomies. A museum in Bennington, Vermont, actually had a "live" exhibit of tattoo art.[19]

There are still teachers and professors—usually of a certain age—who misunderstand tattoos. They see the tattoos as signaling trouble, as opposed to being evidence of strength or pride. But perhaps an example—if made known—might alter teacher thinking: There is a new movement centered on Holocaust number tattoos. Holocaust survivors often hid from their families and the general public the numbers tattooed on their left forearms. Those painful reminders of the camps and being objectified were not to be shared. The external symbol was to be hidden (tattooing is also prohibited in Jewish tradition), while the internal memories remained permanent.[20]

However, as this generation of Holocaust survivors is dying, their grandchildren see the need to remember the pain and discrimination that was suffered. So—and note the generation skipping that is generally happening—these younger people are tattooing their grandparents' concentration camp numbers on their own arms. And they are not hiding them. Indeed, keeping the exact number matters; some of the numbers have special meaning, as they represent the survivors who were in Auschwitz and suffered the most hardships (they number between 30,000 and 80,000).

So, at least for some, there has been a change in how we perceive and receive tattoos—a change in culture that needs to be recognized and, in many instances, lauded. For breakaway students, tattoos can have profound meaning—they reflect the past but some point forward to hope. Some represent and serve as reminders of loss. Others serve as inspiration—signaling a desire for a better future.

How we change culture in the context of education and throughout the educational landscape is the challenge to which we now turn. Perhaps the change in tattoo culture can alert us to the possibility of change as generations progress; perhaps we can—as suggested with tattoos—view people and situations through a different lens.

Chapter 4

Breakaway Students and Culture Change

For breakaway students to realize their potential and for us to create a culture in which this realization can not only occur but also have "stickiness," and for lasticity to take root and be animated with intentionality, we need to focus on what I term the six Ts. To be clear, these are not synonymous with the five building blocks of lasticity (a detailed discussion of which follows). The six Ts are the qualities that must be fostered to enable breakaway students to find educational success; they also foreshadow how institutions and those within them can develop lasticity. The six Ts, then, are like the necessary prerequisites (elements) that enable a human body to function: oxygen, carbon, hydrogen, nitrogen, calcium, and phosphorus. They do not, in and of themselves, explain or prevent or foster "wellness." This is what lasticity accomplishes.

Importantly, developing the six Ts is only the first part of a two-part equation; the second part identifies the often ignored strengths that can be tapped into among many breakaway students referenced earlier; these too inform and shape culture and enable lasticity to take hold. Consider these Ts, then, as precursors to enabling existing breakaway student strengths to be tapped and lasticity to flourish. These Ts are *trust* (including authentic and acknowledged trust, often referred to in psychotherapy as epistemic trust), *transparency, tranquility, teachers and teaching, tolerance*, and *temperance*.

Some may wonder why I am not adding a seventh T, namely, *trigger warnings*, given all the debate in academia about their usage and value. But trigger warnings are a response of institutions to breakaway students; they do not provide explanations of the students themselves. However, I will return to their use, as using them is a strategy to consider for improving the educational success of breakaway students, extensive controversy notwithstanding.[1]

Before I show how the six *T*s play out in real life, let me provide a further explanation of each term.

Breakaway students may not *trust*. They have lived in worlds where expectations are not met. Parents (assuming they live with their children) do not come home when promised. Children are not told the truth about key aspects of their lives (why they are moving, why an adult is behaving in a particular way, why a parent is no longer present). Only authentic trust works; it must be exhibited consistently. There must be object constancy. And an individual needs to develop trust in his or her own perceptions, which have often been distorted through gaslighting. Trust isn't a given for breakaway kids; it needs to be built. And we know, for sure, that since learning involves making mistakes and risk taking, the absence of trust inhibits quality learning. Recollect the absence of trust in the story at the commencement of this book; why would or should students trust a stranger in their midst?

Transparency, while related in some respects to trust, is a separate concept. Disclosing the truth—sharing the good and the bad—enables one to see more clearly what is occurring in one's life. If the disclosure is authentic and complete, people can develop a respect for the reality of the situation in which they find themselves. Even when that picture is not pleasant, we tend to do better with honesty that is grounded in disclosure. Kids are very quick to distinguish between those who are truth telling and those who are "BS-ing"—unless there has been so much gaslighting that what is abnormal becomes normal, something commonly seen and experienced in religious or other cults. Ponder stories of defectors from Scientology or the Amish way of life or Hasidic life; those who have departed are often considered "dead."

Tranquility is not intended to refer to a Zen-like state in which we can find peace (as beneficial as that may be). Instead, the term as used here emphasizes the need for consistency and predictability. Posit this example: A child spills a glass of milk at home. One day, the reaction from the adult present at that event is "It's okay; spills happen to everyone. No worries." But if the next time the milk spills, there is a parental outburst accompanied by comments like "What's wrong with you? Money doesn't grow on trees. Now we need to buy more milk. You're careless. You're a klutz." The first reaction does not diminish the child; the second denounces both the act and the child. When the same action produces such divergent and disparate outcomes ("it's okay" and "it's totally unacceptable"), there is stress. Kids start walking on eggshells, not knowing which reaction will be induced by their behavior. And prolonged stress of this sort (prolonged absence of tranquility) produces such high stress levels that they become toxic.

An additional *T*, evidenced in the preceding situation, involves learning and *teaching*, albeit not involving a classroom teacher. All engagements with young, and even older, children—including frequent time outside the classroom—involve learning. Educators, then, are not just those with a teaching degree. Teachers are people who help students grow and flourish in myriad locations and situations, including but not limited to the classroom: Role models are teachers; coaches are teachers; maintenance workers are teachers. We need to recognize and authenticate the many places and spaces in which teaching can and should occur. As I used to say repeatedly on the college campus: Education happens in many places and spaces, of which the classroom is but one.

To be sure, there are people in children's lives—in the home, in the news, in the neighborhood—who are not quality role models or teachers. But there are many folks who could be, especially if we recognized and respected the roles they can play in the lives of children. Relationship building is key. Mentoring is a concept worth lauding.

Tolerance speaks to the need to recognize that breakaway children may act out, may make unwise decisions, and may exhibit behavior that is outside the "norm" of acceptable—thus my earlier objection to the observation that kids are compliant. Instead of reacting with knee-jerk responses that amount to punishment, we need to better understand what is driving behavior. A description appeared in *The Atlantic* of a breakaway kid who engaged in a violent encounter in her 1st year of high school; instead of being kicked out of school, she was given a "time-out," a hand on her shoulder, and an effort to help her understand what had just occurred. And there were consequences (suspension), but she was in a community that demonstrated care; they "tolerated" her behavior, even though they did not want it replicated. And tolerance is not the equivalent of permissiveness (or coddling); indeed, tolerance focuses on the response to the offending behavior—expressing tolerance does not mean the behavior itself is excused.[2]

The final *T* is *temperance*, and most assuredly not in the sense of alcohol abstention and the movement to promote it! Temperance has to do with decisionmaking and impulse control, creating environments in which thoughtful decisions—not snap judgments—can be made. It is easy for breakaway kids to make unwise choices—occasionally choices from which there is no return. That is because their choice architecture has not been well constructed or well developed. Breakaway students are often unaware of the options available to them and cannot effectively distinguish—at least at certain moments in time—between good and bad choices, including the impact those choices may have both narrowly and more broadly. These students need to be in environments that regularly and consistently showcase how to decrease stimuli so that there is the needed space and place to make good decisions. Think about it this way: Chaos doesn't lead to pausing and reflecting. Imagine making key choices in the midst of the equivalent of a rock concert.

The six *T*s represent behaviors, attitudes, and cultural norms that are institution focused. It is not students who need to be "given" or "inculcated with" the six *T*s. Rather, the people and institutions that serve these students need to create environments and relationships that foster the six *T*s. This is a critical paradigm shift, as we usually focus on ameliorating or "curing" student deficiency.

The six *T*s, then, are not premised on breakaway student deficiencies. Quite the contrary. They refer to strategies and states and behaviors that will allow breakaway students to succeed. If there is a deficiency, it lies with the individuals and institutions that are not fostering the six *T*s day in and day out. And to be sure, students, teachers, and families may not even know how critical these six qualities are. What one needs is a culture that is receptive and adapts to the needs of breakaway kids. That calls for a changed paradigm. Instead of shoveling skills onto and into students, institutions and those within them need to create the fertile soil in which the students can do more than survive—they can thrive. Lasticity rests on this shift from student deficits to institutional behavior (by the institution itself and those within it).

Pause momentarily and reflect on how these issues manifest themselves in educational settings. Suppose, for example, that a teacher in the K–6 pipeline asks his or her students to get signatures from parents or guardians on documents the teacher sends home with the students. If information letters are sent home, a teacher often asks for signatures to show that letters have been read. If a student is acting up, a note might go home that has to be signed by a parent or guardian. There is an assumption that the parent or guardian is there and will meet the designated deadline set by the teacher. There is also an assumption that parents or guardians have reading skills in English sufficient for them to comprehend what has been given to them to read. But what happens if a teacher does not know his or her students—what if there is no parent or guardian to sign (for any number of reasons, such as a mother is absent or working or drinking or deceased)? What if parents are non–English speaking and it is the student who is their conduit to engagement in American society? Consider the note from a student that is shown in Figure 4.1—it says it all.[3]

Figure 4.1. Handwritten note by a student, explaining why it would help if the teacher knew the student's situation.

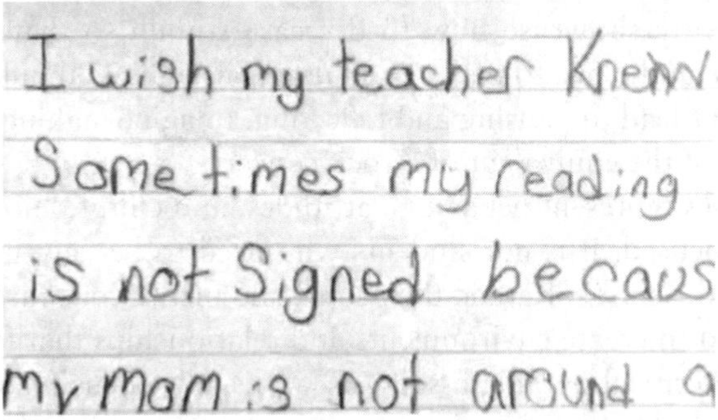

I wish my teacher Knew. Sometimes my reading is not Signed becaus my mom is not around a

Here's another example. I started my presidency at Southern Vermont College during orientation in late August 2006. My early education as a leader commenced immediately. We had already had several students return home because of homesickness and another student's mother screamed at me over the phone, declaring that her son was starving—she'd never seen the campus and had no knowledge of what was offered in the dining hall. Two weeks into the fall semester, when grades from initial quizzes were being handed back in various courses, a student notified the dean of students that she had decided to withdraw from the college. The dean asked for a reason. The student reported that she had received a D on a math test and when she called home, her mother had said to her, "I told you college wasn't right for you."

Upon hearing this story, I practically shouted, "Wait—let me speak to this student." Breaking away is not accomplished by simply walking out the door and onto a campus; the effects of leaving home, leaving one's neighborhood, adjusting to new academic standards, are tough. I asked the student to come visit me in my office, making sure my invitation did not sound like I was ordering a mandated visit to the principal for the breaking of some school rule. I shared how awful it feels to get a D. I noted that when I was in college I got a score of 42 out of 100 on a quiz in Introduction to Biology. (More on this experience in Chapter 10.) I remarked that virtually everyone I knew had struggled in some course along their college pathway, often encountering hurdles in several courses. And if each of us had left school, none of us would be where we are today.

This one incident invokes all six *T*s, most particularly transparency, tolerance, and temperance. For the record, this student did not return home and completed the course in question satisfactorily.

However, here's what I missed about the students at Southern Vermont College. Despite my personally being a breakaway student, there was always an expectation that I would go to college; there never was a parental response that resembled "I managed fine without college; so can you." Or "You need to go to work right after [if not during] high school; we need the money." If one's belief in self is shot to smithereens and one's parents have no confidence in one's capacity to live a life different from theirs (and in fact don't want their child to "leave"), how exactly can that student survive poor grades without feeling like a failure? Who is there to tell that student and all those in similar situations that it is okay to get a D on a quiz?

Institutions that serve students who lack self-confidence and have incomplete attachments need to handle student failures and mishaps in college differently. I appreciate that personal engagement between a student and a president when a bad grade in a course is received is not possible in most institutions, whether they have 1,000 or 10,000 or 30,000 students. In many institutions, students don't even know who the president is, let alone where that president's office is. And in most institutions, the president would not even know about the student's leaving because of a bad grade on an early quiz.

In practice, then, we need much better explanations of grading before the first grades are handed out to new students. We need to talk to parents and guardians so they understand that a bad grade in college does not mean a student lacks "college capacity." We need to find ways to reward students who show increasing competency; we need to evaluate students based not on where they start but on where they end. It means we need to help faculty understand how destabilizing a poor grade can be and what alternatives might exist—not to lower standards (and that's important, because this is not about making college simple and giving false trophies) but to create opportunities for improvement.

Consider dropping lowest test scores. Consider weighting the later, more comprehensive tests more heavily. Consider ways faculty can show belief in capacity even in the presence of low grades—saying things like "Let me help you," or "I know you can do this," or "I have taught this course to hundreds of students and I am sure I can teach you—work with me here." Let's be clear too: It is not as if our tests are so scientifically designed that they are perfect measures of learning. We can try other measures of learning too. Why are we so reluctant to let students show competence through an oral test or a video or a technological invention? Perhaps we need to give some thought to having no grades in the 1st semester of college or in the 1st month of college; what about just using comments as an evaluative tool?

An added point on grading and comments on student work: Across the educational pipeline, we would be wise to do away with red pens and pencils when we make corrections (this problem is lessened with online work and online grading). Red is a "hot" color and surely signals to many students that they did something very wrong. Why not use another color? Why not let younger students select the color they want for the corrections on their papers? Perhaps kids would select a color that would not make them turn off to the teacher's suggestions. One related point is that, whether marking is done in red or any other color, the amount of corrections on written work needs to be limited. The goal is not to rewrite the paper for the student and have him or her simply copy a teacher's corrections; it is to help the student rewrite the paper him- or herself. And if a paper has more red (or any other color) than student writing, perhaps the issue is that the student actually did not understand the assignment—and all the corrections in the world would not fix that. Why not have a teacher sit down with the student and talk about what the assignment called for and how the student paper (not the student) could be improved upon to meet the designated goals? I can already hear in the background the whispers of readers—"What teachers or professors have time for this in their already busy day, whether they are teaching 30 elementary school kids or 100 college students?" And what pandering, letting students select the color of the criticism placed on their work.[4]

Despite the practical implementation issues to which I'll return, I know the value of such meetings with a teacher from personal experience. Many moons ago, in middle school, I wanted to write a paper in a more sophisticated writing style. After producing my initial draft I went to a thesaurus and basically replaced all the words I had used with "big" words. To say that the paper must have made the teacher laugh is an understatement. Instead of correcting the paper, the teacher put a note on it: "I understand this effort; come meet with me so we can make it work more effectively." The teacher and I met and she gently shared that she would happily help me improve my writing and guide me in how to use words with more power. She showed which of the words I had chosen were powerful and which seemed out of place. And to complete the story, she actually taught me again years later, when I was a high school senior, and, no doubt attesting to her efforts years before, I won the school's English prize at graduation. Later still, I guest-taught her class when I was a college student. And I never, ever used a red pen for corrections.

Some view the red-pen-or-pencil discussion as trivial. Why focus on such a little thing when we have deep issues in education? That very question misrepresents the problem. There is nothing even vaguely trivial about correcting a student's work. What is key is to grade the work—not the student. Why not optimize critiques and corrections by offering them in a way that is less threatening and less confrontational? Not seeing the hotness of red is like not seeing microaggressions. Just because one does not see a problem does not mean it does not exist. Think about it this way: It does not really matter if *the teacher* thinks the color of the pen is important or unimportant; the question is whether *the student* thinks the color matters.

Lack of belief in self is not the only issue. Youngsters (and adults, for that matter) who have been abused or have witnessed abuse or the consequences of the overuse of alcohol or drugs have problems establishing nontoxic relationships; they haven't had the luxury or the benefit of a lot of experience with quality engagements. They might have relationships based on dependency as a result of family illness. While it is easy for outsiders to say, "Step away from your past and move ahead," terminating dependent or even toxic relationships, particularly with a parent, is profoundly difficult. That is why these students are often drawn back to their homes (or never leave them), even if they know their situation there is suboptimal. This is especially true if the student's income is needed for family support or if the student's time is taken up with the caretaking of younger children or parents or grandparents. That is why their romantic relationships and friendships and even engagement with college personnel are often fraught with drama and dysfunction.[5] A drawing by a student conveys how painful such an experience can be (Figure 4.2).

Institutions can help with enabling a quality separation in two ways: They can help students learn to develop healthier relationships by role modeling quality engagement, and they can demonstrate consistency and trust in their encounters with students. Also helpful is enabling students to feel they are welcome in the college community; it is easier to move away from a community if one has another community to join. In short, a campus needs a culture that signals acceptance and the ability to identify and live a "new normal."

Here are two examples of these approaches in action. When students (vulnerable or not) arrive on campus, it is hard for them to settle in— exciting, yes, but hard, even overwhelming. They leave behind old friends and struggle to fit into their new environment. That happens at several levels—among peers and between students and faculty/staff and administrators. The first example of the approach is to offer midsummer orientation. This is a partial solution because it starts the ball rolling in the right direction early on and creates added opportunities to transition. It is akin to the organized way in which corporate borrowing occurs, in tranches

Figure 4.2. Artwork by Jailene Gonzalez, a breakaway student, of two people connected together and trying to separate simultaneously.

of debt that are prioritized; this differs from the sudden pain that results when an adhesive bandage is suddenly pulled off.

The second example shows how a situation can be further eased. The dean of students and I brought freshly baked cookies in the evening to the room of every residential student; we did this during the 1st week of classes, over 2 nights—walking up and down the stairs of the residential halls. Over time we got better at it, learning to carry a notebook during our cookie delivery to jot down reminders of things that needed repair or concerns students had voiced that needed attention. Concrete evidence of trust and transparency in action.

I always asked this one question: "Is there anything we can do to make your life better?" My question took many students aback. I could see them thinking, Is she really asking? Does she want an answer? Sometimes, I'd tee up follow-up questions: "How's the food? Anything broken in the dorm that we can get fixed? Who's your favorite professor so far?" What is amazing is that students appreciated the questions themselves (and the cookies, of course). Trust and transparency in action again.

And many students could not believe that the president and dean were actually visiting their suites. Some students thought they had to pay for the cookies. This was no-strings-attached outreach, and it was new for many students. I remember one turning to the dean and saying, "Who are you?" The dean offered her title, described her role, and gently reminded the student that she had seen her at orientation. (Hard for students to remember whom they have seen and met early on.) Then the student turned to me and said, "Who are you?" I said, "Hi. I'm Karen Gross and I'm the president of the college," to which she responded, "No really. Who are you?"

Point made. But let's pause and reflect on how these suggested approaches can be replicated and scaled for larger institutions—including community colleges and large state universities that enroll many breakaway students. For a large nonresidential student population or a campus with tens of thousands of residential students, cookie delivery isn't going to work, forgetting cost for a moment. There isn't the time, let alone the person power, to deliver cookies on campus; and home delivery of cookies (like pizza delivery) to nonresidential students isn't happening. Second semester would roll around before all the cookies were handed out!

Ponder some alternatives. Why are we so wedded to one orientation? Cost? Time? Custom? Why do we expect that students will need just one event (whether 2 days or a week long) to get to know all they need to know to adjust to college life and navigate college/university systems? For all of us, it sometimes takes repeated get-togethers to understand something. And orientation is "wasted" on new students in the sense that one could really appreciate orientation several weeks into the semester, when one knows more and has more questions and has found the way to the bathroom and dining hall.

As an analogy that may be useful for faculty, think of your colleagues who are not computer savvy; it might just be you too. Think about how a one-shot introduction to the new course management system isn't sufficient; a faculty person actually wants his or her own personal tutor to help with the transition. In fact, the best interventions come after one has started to use a new system and struggled with its features. And the whole experience is disquieting. So why not have more than one orientation, perhaps relabeling it? And one orientation should be after, not before, the semester gets under way. Indeed, I remember a program for new college presidents I attended after I had been in office for 10 months; the program made sense to me in ways that it never would have had I attended before I took the job. And it was clear that yet-to-be presidents had takes on issues

very different from the outlooks of those of us who had already confronted (and struggled with) issues.

Consider this suggestion to address these orientation issues: On the
first day or two of classes, all senior administrators across an institution
(president; provost; dean of students; dean of the law school, the medical
school, the business school, the engineering school) keep an open calen-
dar. And rather than sit in their respective offices, they walk their campus,
including dining halls and registrar offices and cafés and student lounges.
They stand outside classrooms and in other areas where students congre-
gate. They greet students (and faculty and staff) and they carry a notebook
and ask individual students if there is anything they can do to make the
student's life better. They introduce themselves (no name tags.) They go to
places leaders may not normally go to (unless they are used to leading by
walking): the athletic facilities, the student offices for organizations, the
laboratories, the career center, the tutoring center. On larger campuses,
they might need a golf cart to get around. They could go in pairs. The bottom line is that these senior administrators need to engage with students,
welcome them, and make them feel that they are in a place they can and
will learn to call their academic (or more than academic) home.

No doubt some senior administrators will find this awkward and perhaps even trivial. What a kerfuffle over nothing. I can hear some saying
(either aloud or silently), "I have more important work to do today and
appointments to keep and meetings to hold." But what work would that
be exactly that is more important than setting the academic year off on
a good footing for students, faculty, and staff? And for those breakaway
students, how powerful is it to have a president or provost or dean greet
you and learn your name and ask you if he or she can improve your life
on, or off, campus? This may not be cookie delivery, but it qualifies for
sure as "human delivery" in the very best sense of that phrase. Call me, to
use the words of the Bill and Melinda Gates Foundation, an "impatient
optimist"; I still believe that this "day in the halls" could actually happen
on hundreds, if not thousands, of campuses.

Consider also this second, all-too-common example: Many institutions have many student support services, ranging from professional
tutoring to difference-learning specialists to counseling centers for psychological support to peer mentoring to academic advising to workshops on
various topics. Most professors hold office hours, and many arrive early
to class and leave late, to make themselves available to students. In short,
institutions do offer to help their struggling students and, in many cases,
these services are of high quality and immensely helpful.

But many students who could benefit from such services do not partake of them fully, if at all. Many folks on our campuses complain that students will make an appointment and not show up or show up late or start sessions and make a schedule and then "slack off." Workshops can be poorly attended. Often the students who show up are those who are least in need of the proffered help.

Providers of the services get angry—or perhaps *peeved* is a more accurate word. They see the students as not fulfilling their part of the educational bargain; we offer the services, the institutional piece, and the students need to participate and engage. The argument goes that the students are not taking responsibility for their actions (their not attending) and their failures (the results of their not attending). College personnel take the absences personally. Professors especially lament the limited uptake and then feel little or no sympathy when the student fails to perform well in their classes. In other words, professionals within the institution assume that the absence of uptake is evidence of a lack of interest, lack of commitment, lack of effort. (Forget for a moment whether the services would, in truth, help.) The same reaction is felt by professors when students are late to class. Faculty and staff take such student behavior as an affront and respond accordingly. Once, early in my academic career, I even went so far as to say that students who were more than 10 minutes late were not welcome and the doors to the classroom would be locked. Really.

But here's the flaw in this argument: Why would a student who has trust issues want to share his or her weaknesses in support programs, however excellent these offerings may be? How do these students know that if they do trust these people who are helping them, it will not come back to haunt them in some fashion? Perhaps what they share will not be kept confidential. If being on time was not important in one's home, why should it matter so much now? For students with absentee issues in high school, just getting to class is an achievement—even if they are 15 minutes late. At least they are showing up. And by the way, I am not suggesting that being late is to be rewarded and encouraged and treated as an acceptable norm—whether in class, for a meeting, or in the workplace.

In other words, if one lived in a world where expectations were rarely met or were met inconsistently, why would one expect tutors or professors to be there consistently? Do they need the safe spaces and trigger warnings that are the topic of considerable debate these days in academic circles? For many students, it is an alien concept that people in positions of trust are where they are supposed to be when they are supposed to be there and do what they are supposed to do consistently and regularly. The importance of the student being somewhere on time and ready to engage is new, having never been part of their cultural norm. Why not help them ease into and gain comfort in this new environment?[6]

So consider these approaches: A professor can walk a student down to the tutoring center and introduce the student to the head tutor—engaging in a conversation about needs and wants. Yes, that is difficult on a large campus where the services are in a location far from the professor's office. Consider a professional tutor who reaches out to a student who does not show up with this response via text, email, or phone: "Where are you? I missed seeing you today. Please pop in tomorrow so I know you're okay." Or what if a support provider who realizes a student did not show up to a group workshop engages with that student in the dining hall, sitting down with him or her, breaking bread and asking why he or she did not appear? Is the student okay? Is there something bothering the student that he or she wants to share? What if professors took late students aside and shared how disruptive it was for them and other students when students come in late? One loses one's train of thought, and it is hard enough to concentrate. Explain why being on time matters. What if we ensured that the learning environment was safe, not by limiting free speech, but by forewarning students that some topics may be difficult and raise anxiety? Ah, the trigger warning debate. Forewarned is, in a sense, forearmed.

These kinds of faculty and staff activities are counterintuitive; they call for a different, proactive kind of professional engagement that some may consider maternalistic or paternalistic; the approaches are most assuredly nonpunitive. Some faculty might be tempted to respond, "Not my job." Or faculty can lament the need to be so cautious and sensitive to student sensibilities and triggers. That leads to articles like the one titled, enticingly, "The Coddling of the American Mind." But these new approaches recognize that trust needs to be built and that the onus is on the institution to create that trust so the vulnerable student can find his or her pathway to success. To be clear, this is not about excusing behavior or lowering expectations. It is about building a rationale for behavior; it is about constructing trust.[7]

Some institutions serving first-generation minority students are starting to see the benefits of changing institutional culture. Reflect on this statement from William Franklin, vice president of student affairs at California State University, Dominguez Hills, a large institution that has seen considerable improvement in graduation rates: "More campus leaders should be asking, 'Is the university ready for the student?'" Spot on.[8] The six *T*s are what enable an institution to create the environment in which breakaway students' learning can be optimized. They call for a reorientation of how institutions and those within them view their roles.

Total faculty and staff buy-in is, of course, an impossibility. There will always be naysayers and nonbelievers. But if more staff and faculty alter their behavior, if there is a shift in culture, and if enough people change the ways in which they engage with students, there could be a tipping point, to use Malcolm Gladwell's term from his book with that title.[9] In other words, cultural change doesn't require 100% participation; it requires some considerable participation and also requires that others who are nonparticipatory do not hold their oars in the water to impede progress.

It may be helpful for some educators (and family members) to recognize that some of what has been described is actually developmental—having to do with how the younger brain develops. Students in their teenage and early college years are not always ready, willing, and able to engage in the whole preparation for and attendance at college, a point thoughtfully detailed in Mandy Savitz-Romer and Suzanne Bouffard's *Ready, Willing, and Able*.[10] They would view these breakaway students as "assets to be developed, not problems to be managed." That's a critically important change in focus and one that readies us for understanding the many positives of breakaway students.

One last point: Much has been studied and written about *nudges*, actions that encourage individuals to make wiser choices or decisions. The use of nudges in education has been shown to increase college enrollment and improve student retention, for example. Tweets work—across the educational pipeline. Short programs on brain development (and the brain's capacity for continuous learning) and campus navigational skills—learning who the registrar is and how to select courses—enable students to settle in more effectively and develop a deeper belief in self. Nudges have real power and tend to be low cost and short term, making their successes replicable and scalable.[11]

To be blunt, however, adding nudges across the educational pipeline is not a substitute for changing institutional culture to respond to the students we enroll today. Nudges are only part of a solution (we will return to their real effectiveness in a later chapter) and do not eliminate the need for deeper change. Think about it using an analogy provided by David Kirp in a *New York Times* op-ed.[12] If going to and graduating from college is like an airplane's taking off and then landing, then nudges are what facilitate your getting on the plane and staying in your seat without freaking out. But nudges are not the plane or the pilot. One still needs the plane (college) and the pilots (educators) to move the students from where they were to where they are going. Best not to consider nudges as universal answers to all that ails our educational pipeline.

We can acknowledge the challenges of breakaway students and we can develop some effective strategies for addressing them—even on large campuses with thousands of students. But we can do more. To play off the approach of *Ready, Willing, and Able*, mentioned above, we can look not at the challenges but at the strengths that breakaway students bring to the table. Those strengths are there—even if we often neither see them nor make any effort to maximize them. We now turn to those strengths and how they can be mobilized for our collective benefit.

CHAPTER 5

Yes, the Positives of Toxic Stress and Trauma

Thus far, we have been focused on optimizing the educational environment to foster breakaway student success. There is another major piece of this effort, namely, identifying the positive attributes of breakaway students—those kids with curdled childhoods and bent lives. Lasticity requires that we understand and apply not only the "downsides" of breakaway students but the upsides as well; indeed, lasticity incorporates these positives when determining the conditions that must be met to get this doctrine activated and active.

Our analysis begins with identifying and distinguishing between behaviors of breakaway students that are self-hurtful and those that are self-protective and even empowering. The positive qualities are ones we often either do not see or do not perceive as positive. We focus on what is missing or broken (that deficiency model again) instead of the remarkable qualities that emerge from tattered childhoods. Shame on us.

A unique way of reaching and understanding these positives is to understand and then visualize a Japanese form of pottery called Kintsugi and then to reflect on its accompanying philosophy (Figure 5.1).[1]

In Japanese culture, when a piece of pottery breaks, it is repaired with gold such that it looks as good—or even better—than the original. The philosophy behind the artwork is that there is real beauty in things that have been broken. Rather than discarding or recycling the broken chards, this pottery approach (which is also a life approach) "upcycles" the pieces. As observed by artist Teresita Fernández, "Often, we try to repair broken things in such a way as to conceal the repair and make it 'good as new.' But the tea masters understood that by repairing the broken bowl with the distinct beauty of radiant gold, they could create an alternative to 'good as new' and instead employ a 'better than new' aesthetic. . . . Because after mending, the bowl's unique fault lines were transformed into little rivers

Figure 5.1. Kintsugi dish repaired in gold.

of gold that post repair were even more special because the bowl could then resemble nothing but itself."[2]

The dish shown in Figure 5.1, reflective of other Kintsugi pieces, showcases the power of this approach. Indeed, I have given Kintsugi pieces to people who had recently experienced a struggle or had helped me overcome my own struggles. The reaction to the pieces, whether or not one is a breakaway kid, is universal: how amazing, how beautiful, how so unlike the discard culture in the United States.

Those who survive the challenges of curdled childhoods, including toxic stress and trauma, carry with them (often unrecognized by the individuals themselves) these qualities, among others: courage; a finely tuned antenna that focuses on situations and people's reactions (technically, and I think pejoratively, termed *hypervigilance*); and the capacity to solve problems or do workarounds, namely, achieving desired ends through nontraditional routes and deep responsibility for the well-being of those close to them (family, relatives, friends), even if those receiving such care are undeserving in some sense.[3] To be sure, not all familial relationships of breakaway kids are defective or damaging; yes, there can be a parent or relative who "gets it" and who is deeply supportive in ways that are "belief in self optimizing." But that support is not the norm, sadly.

It takes courage to break away from one's home, friends, and community. And there are immediate consequences. College changes you, and when you return home, you will feel different, and the folks at home will have different feelings about you. Not easy. For students who go home often, it is hard to navigate one's new world and the world one has left all in the same time frame. And the pull home is not always a positive one. Parents or grandparents may need caretaking or there may be a local job to generate extra funds for the family. We often don't acknowledge this difficulty or the courage that students need to make profound personal changes. We don't voice or acknowledge the possible guilt that these students feel. We don't speak to them about the difficult transitions they are experiencing, exacerbated by advances in social media that keep people connected even when physically separated, something that could be leveraged for the positive. We don't foster comfortable transitions with them.[4] One could say there is reciprocal blindness.

Students often don't share these experiences. I don't think that I shared with a single person (other than perhaps someone I was dating) that I never could go away during spring vacation because I was taking care of my four half-siblings; that was the only time my parents felt comfortable going on vacation far away (such as to Europe or the Virgin Islands). So there I was parenting a host of kids while my parents luxuriated. There was some help to be sure from an au pair, among others, but I was transporting younger kids from place to place, going to school events and athletic games, shopping for food, visiting the emergency room or a doctor. No evenings with friends. No time to decompress from school. No opportunity to say, "What about me?" In fact, I never questioned the arrangement. I wasn't aware of any jealousy of my parents. It was my normal. It was the price I paid for going to college and having my tuition paid by my parents. It was how it was. Period.

Consider this example drawn from another context: When people go off to serve our nation in the military and head off to war, we know they need courage and we know they will be forever changed. When they return home after months away, things are not the same; not only are they different but their families are different too, having navigated without them often for extended periods. Such transitions are difficult for everyone and, until recently, we did not work hard enough to understand and help folks understand and handle these changes; all parties—those returning and those who remained at home—need help if we are to make such changes smoother and more successful. It takes courage to enable these transitions. And getting help—whether asked for or simply needed—isn't easy for many people. It is seen, particularly in the military context but in other realms as well, as a sign of weakness, not strength.[5]

Tapping into the courage of breakaway students has potential for institutions seeking to facilitate the success of these students. For starters, learning involves mistakes, and you need courage to try, dust yourself off, and try again. Breakaway kids may not have used their courage in an academic setting, but they could if they were encouraged to do so; we could say to a struggling student, "I know this is hard but I also know you can do this. You have courage." Instead, we often say something quite different, something that resembles "You are not concentrating or working hard enough. Come on here. You can practice free-throws for hours but you can't practice math problem sets." I have to admit it took me years to realize why these skill sets are not easily transportable because we assume that a skill like tenacity is fungible. I thought rigor in one setting could just be applied to another situation. But that is true only if one sees potential as being equal in both settings and as providing the same pleasure and success in both situations. Students who excel at basketball hoops may feel totally out of their element in a classroom. We can facilitate a greater capacity for success in academic settings if we can navigate the differences that account for why a student is comfortable in one setting and not in another.

In terms of being hypervigilant, breakaway students are often able to read the dynamics of a room; they are quick to sense what they need to do to fly below the radar. They can take offense at something when the other person is totally unaware that they have been offensive. For minority students, they can sense what White society wants and they can mimic the expected behavior. There's even a term for this: *passing*; another is *fronting*. They can detect what another person wants or needs, often before the person even asks. They can tap into where others are coming from emotionally and either avoid them if they sense danger or approach them if they sense warmth. They can mediate their actions to avoid a catastrophe; in other words, they can be chameleon-like, changing as needed to keep the proverbial peace.

With all the testing we do, including for what is badly termed "non-cognitive" skills (they are cognitive, in my view—they don't emanate from one's liver, do they?), we do not look for or identify hypervigilance; we do not develop strategies that leverage this capacity for the students' benefit.

If we are aware of this tendency, we can better explain why some students sit at the edge of a group rather than engaging with it. They are watching the others, sensing the dynamic, figuring out how to avoid trouble or enter the fray without risk. They sit at the back of the class-room, not because they are not paying any attention but because they are paying too much attention. They respond to strange and new sounds. New experiences are overstimulating at some level because they cannot control the environment. Perhaps lateness to class can be tied to this too; it is quieter once class starts and students are in their seats.[6]

We habitually make mistakes when we ask and expect students to par-ticipate with each other easily during orientation or even class or team proj-ects, especially when we leave them to pick their own partners, at least early on. We fail to realize how even the slightest comment in a residential hall suite can send a hypervigilant student into what appears to be an overly dra-matic reaction. Indeed, we often hear people commenting that with break-away students, there is "so much drama." However, that drama is the result of hypervigilance, which is a byproduct of abuse or trauma. The musical *Poster Boy*, about the life of Tyler Clemente, a gay student who took his own life after being spied on by a roommate, makes this point eloquently by showing people in a chat room engaging with each other—creating live what is usually typed and sent over the Internet. Here's what emerges when we see the engagement: We underestimate the depth of the behaviors of hypervigilant people because we do not actually see them.[7]

But if you ask a hypervigilant student to share with you what his or her classmates are feeling or thinking, if you ask the hypervigilant student to reach out to others and find out what they are interested in doing on campus, they can do this remarkably well. They can read crowds; they can read rooms; they can read individual people. In a literature class, ask such students why a character in a book is behaving in a certain way and they can answer. Ask them to explain when a character is scared or insecure. They can dissect a problem into its many pieces, and they can come up with solutions that are often outside the proverbial lines, because they do it all the time in their lives. They know whether their teachers/faculty like them or dislike them. They can sense which students are the teacher's/faculty person's pet. They can even sense discrimination when it is invisi-ble and would be denied by the person discriminating.

I recall one incident when a student did not return to school at the start of the semester. She seemed to fall off the map. Her home address was no longer valid. Her cellphone was not working. Her mother was in a homeless shelter. Where was this student? As an institution we tried to find her, to welcome her back to school. But we didn't have the right antennae to find her. We tried the only methods we knew. Here's who found her: her hypervigilant friends, who figured out where she was, why her cellphone was not working, and why she feared returning to school. The good news is that at least someone at the college, a breakaway program director, knew enough or sensed who would be able to solve this conundrum.

Once her fellow students found her and assured her she was welcome to return, even if she had no money and no clothes and no home and no phone, we arranged to pick her up. I was waiting for her in the security office to express to her that she had a home here on campus and to say how delighted I was to see her. Yes, I appreciate that on large campuses, it might not be the president, provost, or dean who would be waiting. But surely an institution can provide some "adult" person to welcome a student back to campus, showing that that the institution—qua institution—cared.

It is worth observing—as an important aspect of hypervigilance—that it can work against an institution if it does not pay attention to details that matter to a student, such as his or her name. The University of Michigan may have lost a football recruit because they sent him a thank you note for attending an event he had not attended and misspelled both his first and last name. In decommitting, the prospective student athlete for 2017 said, "It was just a little heartbreaking, for me to supposedly be so high on their list, for them to confuse me with someone else. Plus they spelled both of my names wrong after I told them, but that was not the main issue. I guess they do not have tabs on me." Yup—hypervigilance can come back to bite an institution.[8]

There are other attributes our vulnerable students carry with them, including creative problem-solving skills. Having lived in environments where traditional modes of thinking do not work or lead to positive results, they are excellent at developing workarounds—both acceptable ones and ones that are outside the bounds of the social norms to which we are accustomed or even outside the bounds of legality. Their solutions to posed academic problems will seem odd to some professors and often mischaracterized by faculty for being off point or missing the mark. And they fight the posited classroom hypothetical because it is too far outside their reality. While hypervigilant individuals are nimble (as earlier noted), they also can avoid situations that stress them: writing papers, studying and taking tests, asking for needed help.

In a children's story I wrote, I tried to bring these very points home to youngsters—the positives that can come from negatives. In the story, the protagonist has to overcome myriad hurdles to fulfill her dream of becoming a Knight of the Round Table. Her family, the townspeople, and the Knights are most assuredly not in her corner. Each challenge she is given leads to her coming up with a solution that is unexpected, creative, and imaginative. She sees solutions others do not, in a way reminiscent of Edward de Bono's lateral thinking. These out-of-the-box approaches account for why the story has such appeal for breakaway readers: They can relate to solutions that don't follow a linear modality. As one adult, who was without question a breakaway student in her youth and who had read the book, remarked to me, "I get it. She thinks differently and I wish I had known that that was okay when I was younger. I never solved things the way others did, but that was not recognized as a plus." How well described.[9]

Breakaway students are, unfortunately, often searching for their own voice, not the voice they have developed to protect themselves. They often do not see their own strengths; if anything, they deprecate the very skills that enabled them to survive. They have been so chameleon-like that they don't actually know who they are and what voices in their heads are theirs. That's why their behaviors are often inconsistent. Perhaps all this is because they don't want to see how much they have had to bend to compensate for their lived lives. Perhaps the processes that saved them were only intuited and hence not obvious to them.

This might account for why choosing a major is so difficult. What is it that one wants for oneself, as opposed to what is it one wants because of one's family or society? We pressure students to select a major, underestimating the challenge of the task. And we lambast students for taking "extra" courses, ones they did not need for graduation, as if those courses had no value and reflected bad choices (their own or the institution's). Identifying that one's selection capacities are limited isn't easy. You have to fess up to (at least) two things: informational deficits and an absence of a clear direction in one's mind of what one wants for oneself (which is because that seems too selfish). Breakaway students may well be asking, silently, to be sure, Do I even know and understand what is out there in terms of courses and careers? If you haven't been exposed to sociology, how do you understand what sociologists actually do in real life? If you've never met an accountant and your family hasn't used one (think H&R Block), how would one get a sense of the variety of opportunities for accountants (which don't include pocket protectors and dark shades)? Finding one's voice is a considerable challenge and requires vastly more information and experience than many breakaway students have early in their college years. Whatever happened to the mantra "Explore, find your passions, see where you excel, test out different options"? It may not have been intended for breakaway students, but it would serve them well.

At Southern Vermont College, in furtherance of the importance of voice, I had an open-door policy. The only time my door was closed was when there was a confidential meeting, and that was relatively rare. People could just pop in—students, faculty, and staff, as well as prospective students and their families. In addition, outside my door hung an amazing piece of art that said in big bold letters: SPEAK. There were swirling cloud formations around the word SPEAK, as if the artist knew that speaking could launch a storm or a brouhaha or an argument (Figure 5.2). It was an invitation to all to speak about whatever was on their minds—whether pleasant or unpleasant, or positive or negative, or angry or calm.

Here's the point: Even if no one came into my office (they did, in fact), there was value in students' knowing that they could voice what was on their mind and that that was openly encouraged, not discouraged. Sure, it made for some difficulties for administrators, faculty, and staff who saw normal chains of command circumvented or meetings temporarily disrupted. Yes, it was a tad hard if I was trying to meet a deadline. But it allowed students to have a touchstone, a place to go, a place to check in, a

Figure 5.2. Artwork by Rachel Kerwin with the word *SPEAK*.

place where someone knew them and valued them. And by the by, it was helpful for faculty and staff as well when they had a need to share. Importantly, other people on campus started to do this too—though not all administrators, faculty, staff, and coaches. For those who kept their door open, it messaged—powerfully.

I understand that open doors may not work on extremely large campuses where a president's role is often not defined as involving day-to-day engagement with students, faculty, and staff. Consider the architecture of where leaders house themselves—often walled off (literally) from others with an antechamber and doors and walls. Indeed, for some presidents, their time is spent with their senior leadership team across the vast institution and with donors, alums, and outside constituencies, including state government officials who are responsible for sizable portions of the institution's budget (except in Vermont and New Hampshire, incidentally).[10] And a college or university president may see his or her role differently from the way I saw mine, on a small liberal arts campus.

But the importance of valuing speaking up and out is an issue on all campuses, brought into the light of day by wide-ranging student protests and the refusal by professional athletes to stand for the national anthem. It is an issue when speakers invited to campuses have views that are venomous or hurtful, even if their legal right to speak is most assuredly in force. So, while the artwork *SPEAK* (Figure 5.2) may not be at every college or university president's open office door, openness to speech and voice pervades campuses, and institutions have an opportunity—I might say, obligation—to help students find their voice and hone their voice as part of the educational process.

Later in my college presidency, I came upon Kimochis, which are small stuffed toys that have both a word and an image of emotion on them—like joyful or sad or scared or happy or worried or afraid or excited or hurt. Originally they were intended for young children so these children could learn about different types of emotions, with their accompanying facial expressions. I ordered buckets of them. Each was paired with a carabiner, and after I met with a student or if a student just ambled by, I'd take him or her outside my office and say, "Take one." Students adored them. They came back for seconds. I still carry one. I gave a set to someone who regularly deals with patients who are struggling with depression. They now sit in his office. It was and still is a way of acknowledging emotions and their impact. The makers of Kimochis are aware of the broader use of their products: They just developed a set to deal with separations in the military.[11]

To return to breakaway student behavior, as noted in the previous chapter, we often get our noses out of joint when students fail to do their work or to show up on time to class, tutoring, and events. We regard these students as not meeting their responsibilities—to the teacher, to their fellow students, to themselves. But I think we are missing something important here. How often do we ask a student why he or she failed to do the needed tasks? Do we ask what stood in the way of their completing assigned tasks? Many teachers would balk at even asking. "Not my job," would be the response; "students need to own their behavior." Teachers and faculty are remarkably focused on self and interpret student action (or inaction) as a personal affront. Really? Not everything is personal and focused on faculty.

I get the need for students to develop responsibility, but I would venture to say that many breakaway students actually have a deep sense of responsibility—just not to their schoolwork. If anything, they are hyperresponsible but not in a way that educators recognize or appreciate much of the time. Let me explain. Many breakaway students have had to handle outsized responsibility in their homes and communities. Many have had to deal with the illness of family members, caring for their parents or grandparents—taking them to doctors; helping them with basic functions; soothing them when they are in pain; translating and literally speaking for them in medical, work, and banking situations. Some breakaway kids have had to clean up the messes (literal) caused by rampages—empty bottles, open food packages, damaged dishware, collections of garbage. Many have had to navigate getting to and from school alone and arriving home without an adult there. Many have dealt with disruptions in their communities, whether gang related or not. Many have visited friends who have been injured by gunfire or knife attacks, seeing things well beyond their years.

Another concrete example from my own life: In a household filled with chaos, I was often asked to take a younger half-sibling (14 years my junior) with me on dates during the summers between semesters in college. With my date, I took my sibling with me out to dinner; I took him on weekends away. People would often come to our table at a restaurant and say, "Your son is so adorable. He looks so much like you." I am still shocked that the people I was dating did not speak up and out, saying something like "Why exactly are you acting like your brother's parent? Doesn't he have parents?" He did; they just weren't able to take care of him. And I did take care of him, parenting (well or badly can be debated) before my time, so to speak. And as remarkable as it is that my dates did not question this situation, neither did I. It was what it was. I was responsible for my brother's well-being. Period, full stop.

So many breakaway students act responsibly in ways that are totally age inappropriate. It is not a shock, then, that while a student's not handing in a paper may seem dramatic for a teacher, it is not such a big deal for the breakaway student. And when a teacher or professor questions students' sense of responsibility, it is no wonder students don't appreciate the comments or even listen. It's not like they disconnected their mother's oxygen tank or forgot to refill it in time. These students know about responsibility. Might they be rebelling a tad too, enabled for the first time to be totally irresponsible without dire consequences?

Perhaps we need to reconsider how we respond to students who fail to meet our expectations. Perhaps they had other responsibilities to attend to that seemed more important. Perhaps they were distracted from all the responsibilities they had, and a school obligation did not seem a priority. Perhaps they could not handle one more task. Perhaps they could not handle one more responsibility.

It is easy to mistake teacher sensitivity to noncompliance as caving in to students, to lowering the bar, to giving them a pass, to failing to adhere to standards, to enabling lower expectations. That is one lens through which to assess student behavior or shortcomings. But consider this lens: What accounts for student inaction, whether the students or the educators recognize it, is a response to too much responsibility, not to too little or nonexistent responsibility. Knowing that, might we react differently to the student who does not turn in work, who does not show up on time, or who even skips an exam? Might we be more accommodating? There is a vast difference between indifference caused by overresponsibility and indifference that occurs because students don't care or because they believe the assigned material doesn't matter.

A research project on which I worked looked at what is helpful to breakaway students in their effort to succeed in college. One unexpected (and unfortunately unreported) finding was that the students appreciated the opportunities to write for and read blogs from members of their scholarship cohort that cut across many campuses and to reflect on the prompts sent by the sponsoring organization. Initially, I would have dismissed the power of blogging, thinking, Why would it matter? Students were on different campuses across the nation, they had much to occupy their time and attention, and they were trying to connect with students and faculty at their home institution.[12]

But that is just the point. Many breakaway students need to connect with others who understand their situation, their hurdles, their challenges. And what better way than sharing, whether through writing or reading or self-reflecting on prompts? These students, then, are not ignoring college requirements because they are careless or misguided or flighty or even defiant. Instead, they are trying to figure out how to fit in, how to get comfortable, how to find their way in new situations and new settings. They are trying to balance their responsibilities to "home" while making a new home. Indeed, what many see as weaknesses are, in reality, enormous strengths.

Try it this way: We ascribe meaning to student behavior that may not be accurate. We make assertions about why students are acting in a certain way, and we lament their failure to follow our rules. We argue that students need to come up to our standards, and we cannot lower standards because of who they are and from whence they came. Really? Is it lowering standards to understand students and help them grow and flourish even if that calls for some gentle (or not so gentle) bending of traditions, routines, and deadlines? I get the risks, including the possibility of opening the proverbial floodgates. Students will repeatedly ask for extensions (as if they don't now); they will try to explain that their grandmother died (for the third time); they will try to press the limits. And yes, they will claim they were ill or a family member was ill. True enough. That will happen. For sure.

But the alternative, denying our students a level of compassion that enables them to explain themselves and their action, is not better. Why not help them become their best selves rather than punishing them into compliance? What we are doing, just as a point of reference, isn't working optimally. Can we step out of our own traditions, our own backgrounds, our own sense of right and wrong long enough to see the breakaway students for who they are and for the strengths (and struggles) they bring with them across the educational pipeline? Showing flexibility and understanding is not synonymous with becoming an enabler—something these students also know about in many instances from personal experience. Augmenting understanding does not mean we, as institutions and people, like certain behavior and want it to continue unabated. Let's not mistake helping someone see the light with valuing the absence of light.

Two other observations on the importance of the focus on positives in children are relevant. First, there is a growing movement to create compassionate schools. One might say these are schools that exhibit empathy through their culture. The Center for Developing Children at Harvard points out the science backing the impact of toxic stress on kids. School systems too are starting to respond. Dr. Pamela Carter founded the Turnaround Center, based in New York City, to help schools understand the impact of trauma, such as from 9/11, initially, on their students. The organization sends teams of trained personnel into schools that have students who have been traumatized, and they stay there for several years. Addressing toxic shock and trauma and curdled childhoods requires more than a one-off intervention or a nudge here and there. In short, we are making progress on a wider scale. We now need to ensure that it can be replicated and scaled.[13]

Second, empirical data are newly emerging on how to educate children with learning differences—even profound learning differences. The answer starts with the notion of *neurodiversity*, namely, recognizing the brain's wiring in some children. The effort seeks to focus on the positive skills of these neurodiverse students and to build on those skills. In this approach, instead of complaints being made that a child cannot do something, "positive learning niches" are created. This occurs through mapping a student's strengths and weaknesses and playing off the strengths. Applying this to a breakaway student, suppose that for the student anger control is difficult but the student is an excellent artist. When that student gets angry, instead of punishing him or her, ask the student to draw what he or she is feeling (the student might make an angry drawing) and then share that drawing with the people affected by the student's behavior.[14]

Such positive approaches lead us into lasticity—itself a positive approach. Before turning to lasticity and elasticity, it's worth pausing to contemplate that there are many people who do not see or recognize breakaway students for their strengths or who do not understand their behaviors. What has been described thus far in this book is alien or invisible to them. Or both. In fact, a book by Julie Lythcott-Haims titled *How to Raise an Adult* speaks about overprotective, overcaring, overhandholding, overconnected parents of students all across the educational landscape. These parents do their children's schoolwork for them. They go on job interviews with them. They rent apartments near the schools and colleges their children attend. They call school administrators in a panic if a student who is traveling abroad in a college-sponsored program does not answer his or her cellphone immediately (notwithstanding that the parent has a GPS tracker). And the students themselves panic: If they get a cold they run to the ER; they let their parents speak for them at school or college meetings, complain for them, fix nasty situations for them. The cellphone is referred to by Lythcott-Haims as the longest umbilical cord in existence.[15]

Lythcott-Haims provides strategies for building resiliency in children and offers a list, yes, a list, of mistakes all kids must be allowed to experience before they are 18. Here are some of the items (with my commentary in parentheses): experiencing the death of a pet (what about death of a parent or a friend?); breaking a valuable vase (seriously? That assumes there are artifacts of value in one's home, assuming one even lives in a home); having a car break down away from home (which assumes that one has not only a car but also a license, which many inner-city kids do not); and being hit by another kid (how about the uniqueness of *not* being hit, or shot, for that matter?).

Lythcott-Haims describes parents and students of privilege. In a sense, the book can be seen as the opposite of the present book. It is addressing a different universe, a parallel one, but it is treating it as if it is the dominant one, the one for which we need solutions. This is not the only education book that has decried a problem that applies to a limited pool of students (privileged ones) and then proffers the findings and suggestions as if they have universal appeal.

It makes my blood boil and my skin itch—in part because such books not only work counter to lasticity but also reinforce a false norm of who our students and their families are in real life in most educational settings. Studying at Stanford or Berkeley or Harvard or Oxford hardly sets up a prototype that describes the thousands of institutions and the millions of students who would beg for a helicopter parent, who would be thrilled (though scared) of an opportunity to study or simply to travel abroad, who would not complain even in the face of growing frustration and fear.

I was particularly struck by a checklist of what 18-year-olds should be capable of accomplishing. It would be comical if it were not being proffered for real. Among the examples are that 18-year-olds must be able to talk to strangers, must be able to find their way around a campus without parental help, must be able to contribute to the running of a household, must be able to handle interpersonal problems . . . and the list goes on. Use an "orphan" model, the author suggests, to help these kids get independence and prevent them from suffering the harms of overprotectiveness. Virtually all breakaway kids can do what is on the designated list of needed skills when one turns 18, and they do these things regularly.

Here's the point: There are overprotective parents and there are privileged students, but the latter are not the majority—not even close to the majority—of individuals now attending schools or seeking to enroll or enrolling in colleges and universities. Our institutions are not populated by the elite. They are populated by breakaway students. Not only do they not have the longest umbilical cord in the universe, some of them have no umbilical cord at all. We may want to ignore this population; we may want to pretend these breakaway students don't exist. We may falsely believe they are a tiny minority of the student population. We may not want to deal with messes that are vastly harder to stomach than those overprotected kids with overprotective parents.

It is this group of students—breakaway kids—that the present volume addresses, and for a good reason: They are our students, like it or not. Ironically, Lythcott-Haims's book begins with a quote in Spanish (translated, too) that actually describes how to help breakaway students, and it provides a lead-in to lasticity's five foundational elements, starting with elasticity. It is a quote that somehow seems, at least in my mind, to fit *Breakaway Learners* vastly better than Lythcott-Haims's *How to Raise an Adult*. First in Spanish and then in English, here are the words of Antonio Machado, a leading Spanish poet at the turn of the 19th century: "Caminante, no hay camino, se hace camino al andar" (Traveler, there is no path; the path is made by walking).[16] For breakaway kids, I would alter the quote this way: Traveler, there is no one path. The path is made by walking, and we are here to help you learn your way on the path you make.

CHAPTER 6

Elasticity: One of Lasticity's Building Blocks

There is no magic order for developing an understanding of lasticity's five fundamental and foundational building blocks: elasticity, plasticity, pivoting right, reciprocity, and belief in self. Two of these five building blocks—elasticity and plasticity—are centered on the breakaway students themselves and often occur without intentionality and design. Reciprocity and belief in self, two of the remaining building blocks, involve engagement between both the students and the institutions they are attending. Pivoting right centers on student decisionmaking, but it requires engagement of others (whether or not they are within educational institutions) for it to be animated fully.

The interaction between these five building blocks is not linear. In other words, you do not start with one specific foundational block and "master it" to progress to another block. Instead, the elements of lasticity coexist and are fostered, inculcated, intuited, learned, or developed in different ways and at different times along a breakaway student's educational experience. The same holds true for institutions. As a result, there is no single recipe for developing lasticity. Instead of picturing lasticity as a straight-line progression, then, reflect on it as a web filled with conditions, as noted in Chapter 2, and as demonstrated visually in the concept mobile that appears in Chapter 11 (see Figure 11.1). Each of the five identified elements forms a part of the web and then there is engagement among and between the elements, the intensity of which changes over time.

Another way of reflecting on lasticity's building blocks is to think about each of the five identified elements of lasticity as a different musical instrument. Each has its own timber, yet several of the instruments can be played together and the combinations can shift. So can the volume. But if the piece of music is to reach its full potential, all five instruments need to be playing (all five conditions need to be satisfied, to refer to what is noted in Chapter 2), but that playing does not need to be synchronized; some of the instrumental voice can be prerecorded. There is an ensemble, then, of students and institutions—with all five elements—some live, some recorded, all creating music. That ensemble varies from student to student, institution to institution.

Recognizing that there is no precise order to the five building blocks, one can, in essence, cut the web at any spot to start developing an understanding of the elements. Because the word *lastic* is derived in part from and linked linguistically to the word *elasticity*, it makes sense and seems easiest to start off there. It's a relatively comfortable starting point too.

The basic premise is this: Breakaway kids are (and need to be) elastic. The obvious question is, What does that actually mean? Elasticity relates to how an individual responds to adverse events; the response can occur over seconds, minutes, hours, days. It is "permanent" in some people. It is invoked repeatedly over a lifetime.

The traditional definition of *elastic* or *elasticity* refers to the capacity, usually of an object or material, to return to its original state after being stretched or distorted. It also refers, secondarily, to the capacity of some individuals to overcome or deal with adversity, as in the phrase *my elastic spirit*. And one more relevant meaning: In the business world, we can have elasticity of demand or of price, meaning that fluctuations (stretching) can occur as a market response to events. And this can happen repeatedly.[1]

Ponder for a moment a rubber band. It can be stretched and relaxed. But note two features of what can happen. If a rubber band is stretched way too far, it can snap—and snap it does, often with a sound. It can hurt you physically when the snapped piece hits your skin. If a rubber band is stretched too often, it frays and its edges start to disintegrate; it can no longer snap back to its original form. With each stretch, the rubber band experiences wear, even if not visible or devastating to its functionality.

Turning to the human dimensions of elasticity, we often speak of the strength of the human spirit, its capacity to endure hardship and deprivation. We find it remarkable when individuals are capable of responding well to crises and can move forward. A child is killed in a school bus accident, but the parents move forward, honoring the child's memory. Parents lose a son or daughter in war, and they stand up for the values of our democracy and the precepts embedded in our Constitution, even supporting protesters who sit or kneel during the singing of the national anthem. These people are elastic; they can be stretched and then they bounce back to something that resembles their original, undistorted shape. The rubber band stays elastic, though at some unseen level, changes are happening to it—to the people represented by that rubber band. More on that in the next chapter.

Note, though, that some events that individuals, families, or groups of individuals experience are so traumatic and stressful that their effect is devastating; people are so hurt they break. Think about people who lose many family members in a fire. Sometimes, like an overused rubber band, folks who have experienced repeated traumas fray. Or they become like a rubber band that hardens and loses its snap. These individuals lose their elasticity; their capacity to return to their prior state is impaired. Think about soldiers at war, seeing human carnage day in, day out. Like a rubber band they have been stretched to their breaking point.

These observations indicate that while elasticity is evident in many individuals who succeed despite trauma, the concept does not protect all the people all the time. That is why, for example, some individuals can never recover and move forward from their past. This is not a sign of weakness; rather, it demonstrates the level of stressors on the symbolic rubber band. To offer an educational analogy, despite the power and presence of elasticity, some students along the educational pipeline will not move forward successfully, regardless of efforts to provide assistance and support at every juncture. While this can be viewed as an individual or systemic failure, it seems that what it really represents is the reality that some events are so devastating that nothing can remediate the consequences. A 100% success rate is simply not realistic. And it isn't worth the time or effort to achieve it; we need to live with the impossibility of perfection. As in health care, not every patient—even with the best care—is cured.

For breakaway students who succeed, there are some common ways elasticity is exhibited. Breakaway students have the capacity, as noted earlier, to be chameleon-like; they can read a situation and adapt to it to survive. Picture animals that know how to camouflage themselves for self-protection. Breakaway students can do that too—flying low to preserve their well-being mentally and sometimes physically. Breakaway students also need to be able to withstand bruising that is mental and physical, compartmentalize the harm, or repress or defuse the harm and then move on. They have developed (or just innately possess) the capacity to "love despite." In other words, in spite of the harm flung at them by parents or other caregivers or siblings or gangs or others in their community, they can see the good in those who are harming them.

This quality is different from optimism, which many psychologists and educators, among others, believe is central to psychic well-being and success. Whether true or not, "love despite" is not premised in or reflective of optimism. Rather, it is a reflection of capacity—the capacity to care in the face of noncaring by others. It is a form of self-preservation, not necessarily reflective of a positive approach more broadly.

Elastic breakaway students also exhibit this quality of "love despite" through their capacity to defer gratification. In other words, they can keep hoping and expecting that things will improve. There is a Don Quixote–like quality to their behavior. In a famous experiment, children were given the choice of having one cookie immediately or waiting and receiving two. A child who can wait in exchange for getting a second cookie is elastic (assuming of course that hunger is not an issue). That child can be stretched. The child who immediately takes the cookie will not necessarily be able to withstand the deferral of love (i.e., gratification) that comes from a curdled childhood.[2]

There is one final example of elasticity and the rubber band analogy. There is a Caribbean game called Lastic.[3] It involves rubber bands that are thrown against a wall; depending on where they land, different players can collect them. Apparently, the more rubber bands collected, the better. You can't make that up. More elasticity—just like in the game Lastic—provides a greater likelihood of "winning."

For those for whom the rubber band analogy doesn't work all that well, try this analogy with respect to elasticity: Reflect for a moment on tennis rackets and their strings. For the amateur, occasional player, this is not an issue. You play with whatever racket someone hands you. But for serious tennis players, how a racket is strung—how elastic it is— makes an enormous difference. And elasticity is not simple. There are different kinds of tennis strings and different levels of pressure on them; strings of different fibers can be combined. Professional tennis players show up at tournaments with different rackets, many strung differently to enable them to better respond to their opponent. For our purposes, here are two key points, at least one of which seems counterintuitive to me: If a racket is strung too tightly and is met with a strong shot coming over the net from an opponent, the strings simply break. The racket becomes unstrung—kind of like a person who is hit with too strong a tragedy or harm and simply falls apart. Unlike with rackets, it is not so easy to restring people.

Professional players who want to increase their power and gain some control over their shots string their rackets more loosely, I'm told. They also use strings made of natural fibers that are more responsive than chemically created strings. By loosening the tension on their racket, they can hit the more powerful shots that come across the net. In part, as a scientific matter, it is because there is more time (as in milliseconds) for the racket to respond to an incoming ball because the racket can move. That extra time gives players the flex they need—the time they need—to return the ball back with power.

Think about this in the context of breakaway kids (and people more generally). If you are too tightly strung, you can break. We even have expressions we use for what we perceive as overly sensitive people—they are too highly strung or too tightly wound. They are high maintenance. Elastic breakaway kids are "softly" strung; they have a bigger sweet spot, to use the tennis term; they can and do take that extra second to respond, and they do not become unstrung by what hits them, literally or figuratively; their capacities even gain in strength over time. They are strung, then, like a professional tennis racquet, with enough looseness in the strings to be able to withstand the hardships flung at them from across the room and exhibit power.

However, as valuable as elasticity is, there is a price to pay for it. That is where plasticity enters the picture. Before we turn to this building block in the next chapter, there are questions worth both asking and answering: How often are kids asked or forced to be elastic? And for those who deal with breakaway kids, how does elasticity manifest itself in real-life situations?

Elastic kids do progress along the educational pipeline in many instances. But access to higher education, in and of itself, is a challenge on many fronts for the breakaway students who progress even that far. But we all know there are students who do progress into postsecondary education despite the many intervening hurdles.

Once within a college or university, however, the level of challenges ratchets up. If we can get breakaway students to college but can't help them both obtain a degree *and* enter the workforce successfully, then we are failing them. To be sure, they are failing themselves too. When students stop out or drop out, there are numerous consequences, not the least of which is debt without a diploma. Add to this reality that many jobs of today and tomorrow require some form of postsecondary degree, not uncommonly a bachelor's degree. Folks keep asserting that a college degree is the equivalent of what a high school diploma was decades ago. Some even say that a master's degree has become the new floor for many jobs. Consider the apt title of a new collection of essays: *The Convergence of K–12 and Higher Education*; Grade 12 is not the end point. (I would add, though, that college is not Grade 13.)[4]

The data on the number of students reaching high school graduation and then progressing to college in the United States are not heartening when examined in depth. Nationwide, the high school graduation rate is approximately 82%, but that data point masks inequities buried in the amalgamated percentage. Looking at high school graduation across different groups of students, we see distressing gaps, both between the states and between students from different demographic cohorts. The high school graduation rates among minority students are double-digit percentage points behind those of their White peers.[5]

Of those students who do graduate from high school, the progression to college is far from 100%. In my home state of Vermont, for example, the high school graduation rate, at over 91%, is one of the highest in the nation. Before we start celebrating, note that the rate of progression to postsecondary education is vastly lower, lower than in many neighboring states, at approximately 52%. Ouch. That percentage varies widely across the small state. By way of example, Burr and Burton Academy—an independent school in Manchester known for its high quality—has a postsecondary progression rate of 72.7%. Not all that far down the road in Bennington, the postsecondary progression rate is 54.3%. Winooski High School, located not far from St. Michaels College and the Vermont Student Assistance Corporation (VSAC, an organization that ironically gives out state monies to enable students to pay for college while also serving as a lender), has a progression rate of 43.2%. Don't get me started on why those VSAC monies are portable, meaning that students in Vermont can carry their state grant dollars into another state, where they can attend college. Just ask, Don't most states want to grow their own workforces with the dollars they expend?[6]

There are lots of ways to slice and dice these data based on income, gender, race, disability status, English-language proficiency, and ethnicity. Not surprisingly, across our nation those who hail from high-income families are more likely to graduate from high school and progress to college. Further, the best predictor of college success may be whether your parents went to and graduated from college.

There has been a concerted effort to help more and more students not just progress to college but also graduate. Barack Obama's White House, and particularly First Lady Michelle Obama, championed this effort (although I perceive its focus largely to be on progression to elite colleges, sadly). Surely the overall effort makes sense. It is not enough just to start college or any other postsecondary program. The issue is whether the students can complete the programs in which they are enrolled. The task is hardly easy or simple.[7]

Currently, those reflecting on these challenges to progression and success across the higher education landscape focus on three basic strategies to foster success: improved academic alignment between high school and college (a by-product of the Common Core and dual-enrollment programs, both of which are not without controversy and concerns about quality and effectiveness); development of resiliency or grit or growth mindsets within the students themselves before or when they enter college; and pre- and postcollege entrance support programs (bridge programs, nudges) that enable students to navigate more effectively and succeed in the collegiate environment.

These efforts have value and do benefit students. If there is improved alignment, academic challenges related to content knowledge will be lessened. The need for remediation may decline. (Leave for later issues of admissions and testing pre-college.) Students with the capacity to study hard, manage their time well, stick to their goals, and respond to frequent bumps in the road to a degree (tough courses, roommate issues, poor professors, homesickness, decisions on majors, change in majors, disappointments in athletics, failed romantic ties, questioning of sexual identity) are more likely to succeed.

Indeed, I think we recognize the degree of difficulty of college progression when we somewhat flippantly remark, "College is wasted on the young." By this statement we mean, Imagine college if the personal challenges of growing up (including those pesky hormones) were already solved when one enrolled and all one had to do was enjoy the academic richness and, like a sponge, absorb all the offerings on a campus. Ironically, in a terrific little book called *Racing Odysseus*, a former college president returns to college to see what it is like, and to his shock and amazement, some of the tendencies of an 18-year-old returned. So perhaps we are too optimistic when we say that returning to college would be a bed of roses.[8]

But even with all the current strategies deployed (and even if some are handled optimally and supported by data), we still see remarkable failure rates among breakaway students. The needle is not rising in the ways we would anticipate with all the time, money, and energy being poured into their success. To use business terminology, our return on investment is suboptimal. Yes, there are smaller programs demonstrating remarkable success, but these efforts turn out to be harder to replicate and scale than we thought. Look, for example, at the programs at the City University of New York, including their COPE program. Look at Single Stop, available on a range of campuses across the nation. Look at the Center for Student Opportunity Scholarship programs with additive supports (now merged with Strive) but sadly now on hiatus. Look at Southern Vermont College's Pipelines into Partnership Project.[9]

There is another gap that affects outcomes. Many of the breakaway students do not stay connected to their high schools except in idiosyncratic cases or in schools with the resources for post–high school graduation support. Even if we inundate breakaway students with increased capacities to be gritty, be resilient, and have expanding mindsets, the transition points are impeded when our institutions act in silos and do not work together or remain connected with students after they leave their buildings. Think about the impact of this. Those who know these students well, ideally, and have vouched for their capacity to succeed in postsecondary education then vanish, leaving the students to settle into their new environment alone. Ironically, when the need for continuity is greatest, the presence of familiar faces within schools disappear.

Given that many breakaway students, as already noted, have separation issues with insecure attachments and an absence of easily created trust, we need to do more to keep connections across the educational pipeline. Graduation at any stage and on any point along the educational pipeline is about completing prescribed requirements; it does not necessarily mean severing ties. Ask yourself: How many people stay in touch with one or more of their elementary school teachers? How many readers of this book have stayed in touch with a high school teacher? And conversely, how many teachers have reached back to students to ask how they are doing? If there was continuing connection, were these students at public, private, or parochial schools?

At Southern Vermont College, I attempted to institute a program in which our graduates would reach back to their favorite high school teacher to thank him or her for the support and to share their successful completion of college. We provided the letterhead and even a certificate of appreciation. All the graduates had to do was give us the name of that favorite teacher. The impetus behind this pilot project was multifaceted. We wanted our students to share their progress; we wanted high schools to see how much the college cared about its students—in the hopes that they would direct more students our way. We wanted teachers to realize what they had done for their students—with tangible evidence—and literally feel the joy of the success of their former pupils.

The program was an abject failure. For starters, most graduates did not provide the name of a favorite teacher, despite repeated prompts. Perhaps they were too busy with graduation rituals; perhaps they did not have a favorite teacher with whom they wanted to stay in touch. For the students who did supply names, the outreach appeared to fall into a deep sinkhole. To my knowledge, not a single ongoing mentorship emerged. As an institution, we did not hear back from a single teacher or school. I could say the post office lost all the letters (in both directions) or the letters were lost internally within schools and named teachers had left. But I suspect none of that is even a tad true.

We can work hard in high schools to encourage progression to postsecondary education, but surely our efforts would be enhanced if there were continuity as students progressed along the educational pipeline. This is not to suggest that we eliminate efforts to improve the psychosocial capacities of students; it is to say that, except at the margins, no amount of grit, resiliency, or growth mindsets will remedy what ails students. That's because what ails students doesn't have to do with what is missing and can be filled in; it has to do with what is present and how to deal with and process complicated, often toxic, lives. It has to do, to return to the rubber band and elasticity, with the state of the rubber bands and how frayed and broken they are.

A work titled *Building Authentic Confidence in Children* by educator Spencer Taintor suggests that the quality named in the title is the needed missing ingredient and that our job is to build true confidence in our students. Wisely noting that confidence, as compared with self-esteem, is external, the author proceeds to offer suggestions for building confidence across the educational pipeline. Sadly, as with many efforts toward school improvement, he homogenizes today's students. He focuses on nonbreakaway students without even realizing it. He cites the characteristics of millennials, including that they are sheltered. Bemoaning the fragility and false confidence of many students, to exemplify this generation, he quotes a story told to him by a dean of admissions at a well-ranked institution. The dean had reported that the biggest complaint from professors was that students lacked alarm clocks. The reason: "Highly successful students usually had parents telling them when to get out of bed . . . and once mom and dad were gone, they [the students] didn't know what to do." This book can be filed on a shelf near *How to Raise an Adult*, discussed in Chapter 5.[10]

The only example worse than that, to show how *Building Authentic Confidence in Children* posits a complete homogenization of students and reveals a total failure to understand the experiences of breakaway students, is a story told about National Football League quarterback Steve Young. The quarterback's father, ironically named Grit (yes, really), responds to his son's desire to leave Brigham Young and return home, at a time when the athlete was a 1st-year student and struggling, by saying, "Okay, Steve, you can quit. But you can't come home."

Perhaps the story makes more sense—and reveals how out of touch it really is with many of today's students—when one learns that LeGrand "Grit" Young was a well-known labor lawyer who moved with his family to tony Greenwich, Connecticut, and was the great-great-grandson of the founder of the Mormon religion, Brigham Young (also the name of the college that Grit and his sons attended).[11]

This example, touted as if it had universality and was sending a message, is really all about a Hobson's choice and is hardly the typical situation—a future NFL player (for sure and that's a rarity) with a legendary legacy at a college (and religion) named after his relative. Come on. Find me a breakaway kid with that story.

With the failure of high schools and colleges to foster success with their current students in terms of retention and graduation rates, there is a new cadre of providers of services to breakaway students, some of which are not intimately connected to the colleges that these students attend. In a sense, they are intended to accomplish what I'd call elasticity preservation efforts. I have to say that initially these programs bothered me; it seemed as though colleges and universities were outsourcing some of their key functions or relying on others to do their work, even if they were paying for it. These organizations work on course advising, navigational skills when problems arise, and issues of adjustment to life on a campus. When I was a college president, I kept thinking, Isn't this work we (or other colleges) should be doing? Why are others doing our most important work?

Consider these examples: In one such program operating in New England, the "mentor" meets with students on the students' campuses but rarely engages with the institution or its personnel; the "mentors" and their "mentees" operate outside the college, smoothing the pathway. They meet in the dining hall or the student center. There is no comprehensive effort to engage with support systems on campus.[12] If this works, why be so critical? Some high schools have organized themselves in ways that enable continuity with their students when they enter college, including visits and regular contact. KIPP is a prime example, and if this keeps their graduates in college, perhaps it deserves more plaudits. To be fair, KIPP and some other high school–grounded programs work hand in hand with college personnel.[13]

Ponder the benefits of the services of an organization called Persistency Plus, which provides personalized email nudges to students to improve their academic and psychosocial success in colleges. One organization that formerly offered scholarships sent students emails, offered students advice by telephone, hosted online get-togethers, and sent some care packages too. Compsych, which provides counseling services to help students overcome problems while in college, was hired by the Dell Foundation to serve Dell's scholarship recipients, with early positive results.[14]

Not all is rosy for these outsourced efforts. Some are costly. Results are not always as positive as expected or desired. And there is the larger philosophical question of what should be outsourced in the first place; if one outsources core academic and psychosocial functions of the institution (as opposed to, say, payroll or purchasing or technology or transportation or food services), what is left of the institution and its values? What about outsourcing mental health counseling or advising or health care or tutoring? What about outsourcing admissions? How about outsourcing online learning to a nonacademic for-profit provider that produces set courses and materials? What about outsourcing campus security? Surely outsourcing challenges campus culture and its maintenance and consistency.[15]

In the midst of this debate, some institutions have backed off outsourcing. For example, the University of Akron just terminated its relationship with Trust Navigators, an organization that assists students; the university cited cost and lack of results as the prime reasons. Ironically, outsourcing is and was often seen as a cost-saving measure. The University of Florida recently terminated its contract with Pearson Embanet, its online course enabler. Chapman University curtailed its use of InsideTrack, a company that provides student mentorship and advising. Other institutions create "alternative pathways" into their institution to ensure that foreign students in particular are prepared for the rigors of college. These prospective students attend "special college programs," often within a larger college community. Cambridge Education Group and Navitas are examples. These two examples are not exactly outsourcing; it is more like "outplacing" until a prospective student meets certain eligibility standards and is "ready" to enroll full time in college.[16]

Instead of outsourcing what could be considered core institutional obligations, institutions need to look inward and think differently about breakaway student success. Consider these two approaches: (1) Institutions need to focus on those breakaway students who succeed rather than fail and look at the attributes they possess (either naturally or through some programmatic interventions along the way) and (2) we need to look at and study those institutions that serve breakaway students and develop their readiness and capacity to serve students ably. We could also improve the connectivity between their prior and current institutions all across the educational pipeline.

We can call these efforts a search for elasticity. But elasticity, standing alone, is not enough to enable breakaway student success. The numbers tell us that. So do the stories. With that in mind, we now turn to the second of lasticity's foundational elements, plasticity.

CHAPTER 7

The Untapped Power
of Plasticity

Plasticity is the second building block we'll address. It is a concept with roots outside education but impactful when applied in education. In a nutshell, plasticity explains what happens to those who experience toxic stress and trauma; it is what happens when the elastic band gets partially or totally frayed.

Plasticity is an immensely complex concept that cuts across many disciplines, including physics, biology, medicine, and neuroscience.[1] At the most basic level and without oversimplifying to the point of inaccuracy or absurdity, *plasticity* refers to the capacity of an object to be altered in shape, to be molded into a new shape. In biology, it can refer to the capacity of organisms to adjust to a changed or changing environment. For example, the mandibular muscles of grasshoppers change based on what the insects are eating in the locale where they are at any given point in time. Fireflies demonstrate behavioral plasticity by changing their light signaling system depending on the environment, the presence of danger, or their willingness to mate.

In physics, *plasticity* has a more dramatic meaning. There, it refers to the capacity of an object to change completely as a result of some exterior force, such as heat or pressure, without rupturing. The object remains in its new shape. In a phenomenon often referred to as *plastic deformation*, the resulting object is not actually "deformed"; I think it is preferable to say that it is forever changed. Take a lump of metal that is heated and pounded and rolled into a tube—the making of steel is plasticity in action.

In medicine, *plasticity* often refers to the body's capacity to find alternative pathways when nerves or other structures are damaged; the body finds alternative ways to enable digestion or breathing or motor and sensory skills to develop again. In neuroscience, when there is a brain injury or other forced changes or even retraining efforts, the brain is able to reroute certain functions. Although the actual process of rerouting is complex (involving axonal sprouting, among other processes), the results are amazing as the brain responds to changed circumstances and, in essence, refashions itself, within limits, of course.

Here's one shared point regarding plasticity, in science or medicine or any other field: A person or object is changed by intrinsic or extrinsic influences. The intervention or accident or trauma causes negative, positive, or neutral change. People who have experienced brain trauma may look and act on the outside as if there has been no change, but their brains are different and are functioning differently. The wiring and firing of the brain are altered.

Stated another way, our capacity to be plastic means we cannot return to where we were before. We are, and not necessarily negatively, altered from a functional perspective. But keep this in mind too—our brain is not static, and even if the hardwiring is changed, the brain can and does continue to change and adapt based on new stimuli. True, as we age, the speed of change slows, but change is still possible. Indeed there is research saying that even with changes, the human brain remains plastic and eventually we will be able to encourage it to work in certain ways. That's a positive development for brains that have changed in ways that are not producing positive outcomes. In the meanwhile, absent such scientific interventions producing change, we can already make inroads with respect to the changed brain of students and soldiers, among others.[2]

Consider plasticity in the context of assisting service members who return from deployment. We talk about the need for these soldiers to be resilient and about their returning to their prior lives. We speak about helping their families adjust to their return—as if they all can just pick themselves back up as if nothing has changed. We provide predeployment resiliency training and postdeployment resiliency support. Government and private programs are growing.

But as observed earlier, much has changed for the soldiers and their families, revealing that the premise that soldiers can be restored to the status quo ante is flawed. Once exposed to the ravages of war, even soldiers who are not injured and not suffering from post-traumatic stress are changed. The experience of war changes you, plain and simple. Deployment changes you. Repeated deployments change you even more. There is no bouncing back to where you were; there is, indeed, a need to deal with the consequences of change rather than pretending there is none. Families have changed too in the soldier's absence; they cannot move back to where they were—too much time has elapsed; too much has happened.[3]

In the context of soldiers, Professor Nancy Sherman has made a remarkable contribution by pointing out that not all injuries suffered by soldiers are physical or psychological (as in depression or post-traumatic stress) in the traditional sense. She points to a different kind of harm: a moral injury. It occurs commonly when soldiers make decisions or face situations that run counter to their personal moral code but are inevitable in or mandated by war. The killing of innocent civilians, including children, is but one example. These moral injuries change a person forever and make it hard for them to adjust to civilian life. A valuable insight of Sherman's work is what enables soldiers to begin recovery from moral injury: sharing the story behind the injury and having a willing audience of nonsoldiers who can learn about these military experiences. Hold that thought for a moment: the power of telling and listening. We will return to it shortly.[4]

We know that not all traumas are the same. Contrast these two categories: big-T trauma and small-t trauma, referred to collectively as *relational trauma*, all terms used in the psychological and psychiatric fields. It is critical not to mistake the word *small* for *unimportant* or *nonimpactful*. Think about the following small-t life-altering events in the context of plasticity: growing up in an abusive household where there was physical and psychic harm, such as beatings with leather straps and constant, uncontrollable screaming or irrational behavior; experiencing sexual abuse or assault on an ongoing basis by a family member, a teacher, or a clergy member; being raised by parents plagued by addictions, whether to drugs or alcohol or both, where parental behavior is irrational or uncontrollable or where there are frequent absences caused by binges or searches for more substances or prolonged sleep or unconsciousness. Consider homelessness and hunger—not for one night but for days or months or years.

Then there are the big-T traumas that can cause change too—one-off life-altering events: watching the fall of the Twin Towers and experiencing its aftermath, living through a hurricane or flood and losing all one's possessions and perhaps family members, experiencing a plane or train crash and struggling to recover one's sense of safety, losing limbs or enduring the diagnosis of a serious illness.

This second group of tragic or traumatic events is not the focus of our efforts to facilitate success in breakaway students. To be sure, some students suffer one-off big-T trauma. Our focus, however, is on the small-t traumas, the ones that repeat, that tend to occur in childhood, that often but surely not always occur in the context of poverty. Small-t traumas are recurring stressful events or circumstances, the persistent exposure to physically or psychologically threatening situations. Wars contain both big-T and small-t events.

Science shows that these types of repeated occurrences, these small-t traumas, affect a child's brain and its development. Brain hardwiring is changed by repeated exposure to trauma and toxic stress. There are autonomic changes (say, to cortisol levels). Study after study confirms such brain changes in children, changes that lead to lifelong negative impacts such as an increased likelihood of adverse health outcomes.[5]

This has led to increased calls for prevention. Stop or lower the toxic stress so that children have decreased negative brain impact and can progress through their lives with less damage. I get the value of prevention, but I think the likelihood of systemic and systematic improvement will be hard to realize in the near and longer term. The history of efforts to eradicate or even curb poverty (that can lead to toxic stress) show they have not been a resounding success.

I think instead we need to acknowledge the changes that younger children incur—a hard swallow. And then we have to assess what can be done to mitigate the outcomes. Yes, the brain changes are there, but interventions can be developed that direct those changes in a positive direction and narrow the pathway to harm down the road.

We also know that, despite these brain changes, many affected children can and do surmount traumas without formalized interventions in schools or after-school programs. These kids are forever changed, yes. But they are not rendered dysfunctional, and they have found, or others have unknowingly perhaps helped them find, ways to rewire their brains. These kids, and those around them—and that includes pediatricians and school guidance counselors—aren't even aware of the notion of plasticity that is at work in most instances.

Before turning to these possible interventions (which are not teaching grit or resiliency), the first key point for readers here is this: We need to recognize that many of the children we teach have not "just" suffered toxic stress and trauma, as previously noted. These children have experienced brain changes that are hardwired and can produce negative long-term outcomes. They have psychological shrapnel that is not disappearing. The concept of plasticity, then, forces a recognition by the affected individuals and the institutions that serve them that early negative experiences have life-changing effects. (There is even research, albeit showing only correlation, not causation, suggesting that trauma actually may shorten a person's life by reducing telomere length.) If one acknowledges that, one is better prepared to respond to, address, and assist those who have been affected. Doing what we have always done is not going to help kids who have been changed by toxic stress and trauma.[6]

Think about it this way: Picture a house that has a weak foundation; I'd say it is a porous foundation, in that things can leak in and out. Now, we can fix the roof and the chimney and the shutters. We can redecorate the rooms and renovate the bathrooms. But none of those activities—even those that are aimed at more than cosmetic improvements—will shore up the foundation. It remains weaker than is ideal. We can abandon the house and look for a new one with a better foundation. Alternatively, we can look for ways to rebuild the foundation—even when or despite when there is a home on top of it. Surely that is not an easy task. But if we can do it, we will be doing critically important work that affects the longevity of the house. Our foundation effort has positive long-term consequences.

Similarly, researchers, among them psychologists, have observed that negative brain changes in young children can be mitigated by interventions—sort of like scaffolding a foundation to shore it up. These fall into two key categories, although more research is sorely needed given the prevalence of these problems among our youth.

First, children whose brains have changed can have those changes mitigated or even rerouted if they can develop stable relationships within or outside the home. There are cadres of possible adults who can help reroot relationships, and many now carry out that function without knowing what they are actually accomplishing. We talk about building mentorships, of enabling and facilitating the way teachers engage with students. We talk about grandparents or other relatives playing a central role in the life of a traumatized child.[7]

But here's something important: For this intervention to be optimized, it needs intentionality. Yes, it can happen by accident or good fortune or happenstance, something that occurred in my own life. Two babysitters, one domestic worker, one grandmother, and one unrelated couple in the neighborhood and one other couple filled many relationship gaps, and their collective scaffolding shored up (though not completely) my foundation. I am not sure if any of these remarkable people actually understood the role they were playing or its necessity in my life. Perhaps our neighbor Herb Benson (yes, the one who wrote early on about the mind–body connection) and his wife did.[8]

Here's one reason I know this is what happened: The man in one of the supportive couples, Arnie Mork, used to hold me on his lap (forget for a moment what that did to his own daughter). He was warm and comforting and cuddly. And he was always glad to see me when I came to his house, which was frequently. Then he was found to have cancer in his 40s, and as I continued to see him, I witnessed his decline. This father figure of 5 years was fading. Now, over my lifetime I have experienced many deaths—of best friends and family members and parents. But this death stays with me still; it continues to bring tears to my eyes. Somewhere, deep down, I know I owe more to this individual than meets the eye. He was there for me and helped rebuild my shattered foundation through the development of a stable relationship of caring.

Ways of toning down the autonomic nervous system are beneficial. Certainly, among adults, the most common approach is meditation, established as an effective mechanism for lowering heart rates based on the cutting-edge work of the just-mentioned Herb Benson. A similar approach has been tried with service members, and there are desensitization strategies that work on reducing the autonomic response system, say, in the context of a fear of planes or of heights. It has intentionality.

But meditation is something a child would need to do, and I am more interested for our purposes here in things that others can do with and for children (and even adults) who have experienced toxic stress and trauma. Strategies for creating calm and deescalating issues have real power for kids (and adults) suffering from toxic stress and trauma. Hint: trigger warnings.

Ponder the situation of a 1st-grade student who makes a mistake and is demeaned and then ostracized by the teacher, sent to the corner; her paper is ripped up and she is berated repeatedly. The irony of the student being sent to the "calm-down chair" shouldn't be lost. It is the teacher, not the student, who needs to cool down. This teacher is doing the opposite of what will lower the autonomic response system, and that system is not just revved up for the student who made the wrong decision but also heightens the stress response of the other students. Rather than improving the capacities of her students, this teacher has set back learning, and what was lost was an opportunity to affect the plastic brain in a positive way.

To see this situation in action, consider watching an online video of the teacher described here and her charter school students, if you can control your outrage.[9] As you watch the video, reflect on the possibility of creating "time-ins" instead of time-outs if we want to help our breakaway students overcome the impacts of their childhood stresses and traumas.

Think about another example, a common one on college campuses: There is a complaint that students in a particular dorm room are being too noisy; they are disturbing others, and it is likely that alcohol and drugs are fueling their evening. When campus security steps in to quiet things down, the students are not too keen to listen. That revs up the security team, who start to feel threatened, and words are exchanged. The "offending" students keep saying they are not being that loud—they have overly sensitive neighbors and it is only 11:00 P.M. and the night is still young.

Now, this kind of encounter can escalate; students can be slapped with citations and brought up on disciplinary charges; deans can be called.

There are negative feelings from different groups of students, those who felt there was too much noise and those producing the noise.

Forceful action to address this situation may work in the short term. The party will be quieted down for sure—at least for a bit. But isn't there a different and better way to lower the tension and the stress levels? For security teams entering a room of partying students, the autonomic response system—fight or flight—will be alerted. And though some students will leave the party to avoid conflict, others will get more aggressive.

Step back and see that for some students, given their childhood experiences with police and violence, this relatively innocuous series of events is much more than that. These students feel the need to fight back, to settle the score, to defend themselves. What if the security guards did not always wear uniforms that clearly signaled power? What if, instead of barging into the room, they used a different strategy? What if they knocked and asked a couple of the students to share with them what was going on and whether they thought there might be too much noise? In other words, the security team could engage the students, not rush in, threatening them (even with a seemingly tame verbal threat like "There's too much noise; cut it out now"). Deescalate and defuse, not ramp up and sanction. That's what we can learn from plasticity: When the hardwiring is changed, the responses need to be changed too.

Ponder several other key aspects of plasticity and the changes that occur in children. Earlier, we noted some positive attributes of breakaway students, those who have experienced toxic stress and trauma (and as a result, would have high ACE [adverse childhood experiences] scores), although these attributes are often unrecognized and untapped. Recollect that these students can be quality problem-solvers, having had numerous opportunities to solve problems in their homes at an early age. And they may be hypervigilant—yes, they may have short fuses—but they may also have the capacity to ferret out what others are feeling, to sense the dynamic in a room, to detect unsafe situations.

What this means in real life on campus is that for some students, events that seem trivial to others take on added meaning and raise tension levels. Having disagreements with roommates is one example. Sensing that a professor does not like you or views you as inferior based on your race (an altogether too common complaint of which the professor is often unaware) is another; feeling out of place and unwelcome is another. We can say, "You are overreacting. This situation is not that severe. Stop being overly dramatic." Or we can recognize that the intensity with which these students are feeling what they are feeling is real for them. The fact that they feel like outsiders and as though they are unwelcome is what matters; in a way, perception in this instance is reality.

For a poignant example of this, read Jeff Hobbs's book on his college roommate, Robert Peace, *The Short and Tragic Life of Robert Peace: A Brilliant Young Man Who Left Newark for the Ivy League*. Sadly, Peace never finds peace and always feels "left out" and "out of place" and "alone." For me, part of the tragedy of the Robert Peace experience is that he was not alone but did not know that. He didn't connect or hadn't connected with others who could validate his feelings or who were living through the same experience in their own space and place. He just kept *passin'* and that eventually killed him.[10]

Before we leave plasticity, two more points, which will reappear later in the book, need to be mentioned, remembering that it is in the nature of webs that things are interconnected and repetition occurs. First, it is critically important to distinguish plasticity from resiliency. The word *resilience* derives from the Latin for "leaping back." *Resilience* is the capacity to return to an original form or position subsequent to being altered. Those who are plastic are not returning to the status quo ante. In a central feature of resiliency and, I believe, one of its limitations, those who are plastic must bounce forward instead of bouncing back. They are so changed that bouncing back is not even possible—their brains are changed. Indeed, in the recognition that breakaway students cannot bounce back, an effort has to be made to understand the consequences of the changes that have occurred, to view them without negativity, to develop strategies that are affirming of the changes. Further, there are opportunities to enable brain changes because brain plasticity continues throughout a person's lifetime. (For proof, look at the capacity of those with brain injury such as stroke to recover, even in adulthood.)

Unfortunately, the word *resiliency* is often used when a term like *plasticity* or *lasticity* is meant. For example, in an article on how to treat the effects of toxic stress, a text that provides useful and powerful strategies, the author states, "Resilience is the ability to properly adapt to adversity despite the conditions." Not to create a nomenclature game, but this is not the definition of *resiliency* or *being resilient*. Apart from the word "properly," which seems misplaced (and is grammatically wrong too by splitting the infinitive), adapting to adversity despite conditions is what happens through plasticity and what creates lasticity. That is not resilience—which is backward looking.[11]

It is worth noting that there is an emerging effort to rethink resiliency, redefining what it is in practice. In a sense, the term as now used connotes hard work—keep at it, practice, strive to overcome. However, new studies suggest that developing resiliency is also about achieving balance, pausing, stopping to enable recovery. Toughing things out, although deeply appealing in our culture, isn't even scientifically verified as a strategy for resiliency. Grit Young, the quarterback's father discussed earlier, had it wrong. Resiliency is about knowing when to work less, not more.[12]

Ponder the observation that those breakaway students who are stressed and trying to adjust to new situations in college are "upregulating," and that is exhausting. They need to find homeostasis. Think about how well this new approach fits into the earlier observations about how to respond to kids who have experienced toxic stress and trauma—calming down, deescalating, lowering the cortisol levels. All across the educational arena, students are upregulating as we encourage them to demonstrate grit and resilience and growth mindsets. They get exhausted. We're not helping these students; we are exacerbating the effects of toxic stress and trauma. Yes, it is unintentional, but it is harmful nonetheless. Time to readjust our perspective.

The second point to mention about plasticity is that it is valuable, in the context of this concept, to reflect on the credo and approaches of the compassionate school movement and look at what compassionate schools are doing to deactivate the autoimmune response and enhance the relationship capacity of their students. The compassionate schools project describes these goals for their younger students as follows: "Elementary-school students will learn to cultivate the basis for focus, resilience, empathy, connection, and wellbeing as academic and personal success." They refer to educating the "whole" child, a concept surely not unique to the movement. The program in Washington State is clearer about the uniqueness of their effort, stating in reference to their handbook, which I have reviewed at length, that it is designed to "inform, validate, and strengthen the collective work of educators to support students whose learning is adversely affected by chronic stress and trauma." It continues, "This handbook provides current information about trauma and learning, self care, classroom strategies, and building parent and community partnerships that work."[13]

What a powerful expression of the effort of an educational system to meet students where they are, not where we want them to be. What an authentic statement about the need to change institutions to respond to students who have suffered toxic stress and trauma. And they are not wrong. Students who have experienced trauma and stress are not a small subpopulation of students; they are not the three foster kids and the one kid with a divorce. No. That is not who our students are today. Their baggage—their human backpacks—are filled with psychosocial complexities that affect their learning, their psychosocial behavior, their health. And those impacts do not end in elementary school or even middle or high school.

That is why those who teach students all across the educational pipeline need to understand their students as they are, with all the pluses and minuses of their backgrounds. One caveat: Some in the compassionate school movement zero in on mindfulness (distinguishable from growth mindsets), a strategy to lower stress levels and improve intentionality. This is important and valuable work, but it is surely not enough to solve the myriad problems facing our children today. In a sense, we are seeing strategies of which none alone will move the progress needle sufficiently but that used together and collectively and within a larger framework can produce change.

As a way to summarize the import of plasticity and how our understanding of it can change our responses to students in and outside the classroom, consider this situation: Many students simply cut school, at times without their caregivers even noticing. And what accounts for their nonattendance at school? Late for the bus because they overslept because their home was noisy until 2:00 A.M.? (Recollect the absurdity of the alarm clock example from Chapter 6 in this context.) Perhaps a student is avoiding school because he or she is being bullied there. Perhaps students don't think of school as a safe place. Perhaps they think no one will notice anyway. Perhaps they are not learning in school and feel inadequate. Perhaps their caregivers don't see school as such an important place and don't really care if they attend or not.

The causes of absenteeism are varied, to be sure. Quantifying the problem, Johns Hopkins University researchers suggest that between 5 million and 7.5 million students do not regularly attend school. Government data show that almost one-third of students in Washington, DC, miss 15 or more days of school annually. Something is up here, and it isn't good. Holding kids back a grade because of absences just punts the problem forward (or backward as the case may be).[14]

Chronic absenteeism, pejoratively termed *truancy*, is not an easy issue to solve. However, many options are on the table. We could punish the students who skip out by keeping them away from school for a set time period. Notice the irony of this: The punishment is the same as the bad act. We could punish the parents of kids who do not show up, and that type of punishment is, not surprisingly, a matter of some debate. We pay truancy officers to track down kids, and we levy fees on offending parents. We could ramp up the juvenile justice system. We could involve law enforcement. We could decrease funding for schools with high truancy rates, punishing schools for the behavior of their students. Some localities link truancy with maintenance of a driver's license; if you skip school, you can lose your license for a pre-set period. Some schools contemplate taking away cellphones as a punishment.

Consider more creative and potentially beneficial approaches not based on a deviance model. What about nonpunitive approaches? Think about what institutions can do to discourage truancy—and what they can do to see attendance as their responsibility by asking the question, What can we do to encourage attendance?[15]

Two educators in the Washington, DC, region seeking to address student absences suggest, "To turn absences into attendance, we must form supportive relationships with chronically absent students and their families."[16] These need to be authentic relationships, grounded in trust and executed with consistency, ideally with unchanged personnel in place. Other institutions are trying approaches based on restorative justice, focusing on empathy, a welcoming tone, and respect, and are seeing remarkable results—but not without considerable institutional pushback from teachers who did not buy in.[17]

Instead of using punitive approaches to deal with students who have suffered toxic stress and trauma and for whom there have been brain changes, why not offer reasons for children to come to school—from people in the school who genuinely care and will notice their attendance. Instead of punishment, offer the older truant child the project of helping younger students to care about school in afternoon programs, through art, athletics, or something else. Rev up the truant kid's empathy engine; create a school garden that he or she must tend to produce food eaten at school and available to bring home. Bring in stray pets and assign truant students to provide care to these pets and nurture them back to health. This can activate those all-important mirror neurons—the neurons that enable the help provided to others to redound to the benefit of the provider.[18]

As one commentator on truancy observed, "Schools definitely have a role in truancy too. The research shows that kids who feel that at least one person in the school cares about them in some personal way are more likely to go to school and make an effort at school. There are actually a lot of kids in school who feel like there isn't anybody at school who knows anything about them or care[s] about them." Ouch.[19]

And there is institutional responsibility and ways institutions can change to better serve the students under their watch. In a sense, we can say these institutions are "plastic" too; they are changing. And by being plastic, they are enabling themselves, with other behaviors, to be lastic. Relationships—later termed *reciprocity* in the context of lasticity—have the potential to be game changers because they focus on a key missing ingredient in the foundation of kids with curdled childhoods: relationships that matter and that are trustworthy. So ask these questions: Are institutions like compassionate schools revealing plasticity? Are the schools themselves forever changed by the students they serve? And if the answer is yes, then these schools have demonstrated one of the elements of lasticity—albeit in some instances by design as opposed to by biology that includes hardwiring in individuals, the hallmarks of plasticity.

In a sense, as we will see later, reciprocity hinges on acknowledgment by both breakaway students and their institutions of the existence of plasticity (and the underlying traumatic elements that lead to changes) in the students and of the implications of this. But, for sure, we want students themselves to make good and wise decisions. Cutting school is an example of not making a quality decision. We want to encourage decisions that will help, not hurt, them in the long term. That is the next element of lasticity to which we turn: developing the capacity to pivot right.

One noted caveat before we focus on decisionmaking capacities: Helping students to the extent suggested here in this book has consequences. Some wealthy alums (who were typically from privileged backgrounds and certainly are privileged now, since they have the capacity to give) who toughed it out are curbing their gift-giving to their alma mater. That doesn't go unnoticed. They think the institutions are pandering, and they do not want to support such efforts. The alma mater is being too soft, too lenient; the students are being too fragile and too needy and too entitled. Institutions are pampering their students; why not let them sink or swim or sink and sink further before bailing them out?

Recall when doctors wanted interns and residents to work for the outrageously long hours they did (part of the ritual, the argument went—I did it; now you do it) until they saw the consequences of such overwork: doctor errors and patient deaths. One case in particular got caught in their thought: 18-year-old Libby Zion, who in 1984 died shortly after an emergency admission to a hospital. The outraged reaction of her father upon his learning that medical residents had been treating not only Libby but also dozens of other patients, all at the same time and under inadequate supervision, led to reforms that included limits on hours of work for medical staff.[20]

I am wondering if alum impatience with current students is partly a product of alums' lack of awareness of the students their alma maters are currently educating. The students of today simply do not look like the students of their generation. And these alums look at their own kids as if they were all kids. Many of today's students at colleges and universities do not hail from Andover or Exeter or Milton or Deerfield. They don't have priv-ilege. Now, it is true, too, that some of the current students at elite institu-tions have overbearing, overcontrolling, and overinvolved parents, which contributes to the problem. But I suspect alums conflate breakaway kids with overprotected kids and in so doing damn supportive efforts for them all. In a way, the alums fail to distinguish between those in the student body who grew up with privilege and are not breakaway kids (although they could be) and true breakaway kids. There is one more, somewhat odi-ous possibility: Perhaps alums are not pleased with the students their alma mater is educating. Perhaps they don't want more Pell-eligible, minority, first-generation students in their hallowed halls. Maybe these alums walk on campus and instead of seeing themselves (or their children), they see other children and don't want those "others" there. How possible is that?

I am sure these same alums complain about the youth who work in their place of employ; they simply are not acting like they did. They are not stepping up in the ways they did; they are not obedient. They are protesting or complaining and exercising their voices. Instead, the alums believe these students/employees need to button it up and do as they are told and follow the linear, decades-old pathway set for them. I wonder how many of these are actually breakaway kids who may lack the net-works needed to land these jobs. Perhaps they are complaining about the children of their peers.

The solution: increased experience with the reality of who the stu-dents are, including exposure to how remarkable breakaway students can be. Not easy, especially for those who won't like what they see—literally. These alums (including alum trustees) need to visit campuses and evaluate what they see from a different lens. They need their own navigators to understand the changes on campus and in our nation in terms of demo-graphics and student enrollment. They need to see and experience how those changes can serve their personal best interests and the interests of their own families. Nothing like personal gain and personal benefits to alter perspectives—at least long enough for new ideas to be considered. We need these alums to pause where they did not pause before. We need them to understand what their largesse really can do. They need to catch up with the times. They need to be exposed to breakaway students and lasticity.

CHAPTER 8

Pivoting Right

We now turn to the third of the five building blocks of lasticity—the importance of all children (all people) making wise choices and exhibiting quality decisionmaking.

We are painfully aware of the challenges of quality decisionmaking among young adults. Indeed, research has shown that the youthful brain does not mature until age 25 or so, which accounts for why college-age students often exhibit serious errors in judgment and why they are willing to take what seem to adults to be unnecessary risks. And they get hurt—physically and mentally. The problem is, in short, that some bad decisions are life altering, inhibiting career choices (such as in nursing and police work) and leading to expulsion from school and criminal prosecution. Excessive drug use, drinking and driving, and sexual abuse are just some of the examples of risky behavior. Add in joining a gang and participating in gang activities, shooting a rival, defiling public spaces—with paint or urine.[1]

How we foster wise decisionmaking generally and among young people in particular has been the subject of numerous studies. Professionals working in the field of student life struggle to accomplish two goals on campus: foster quality decisionmaking and curb irresponsible behavior. Tough tasks. Given the range of choices confronting college students, it is no small wonder that college presidents have many sleepless nights worrying about the safety of the students in their charge. Danger lurks everywhere on and near campus. No one wants to be that president or dean who calls a parent or guardian with a sentence that begins "I have some terrible news to share with you . . ." or "I am so sorry to report . . ."

For breakaway students, complex decisions arise long before college begins—indeed the choice to go to college itself is only one example of making a remarkable and positive choice. In looking at the breakaway students who have succeeded in college, the question is how these students, consciously or not, made generally wise decisions from childhood onward. Or if they made some bad decisions, how did they recover from them to begin making better ones? For our purposes here, I refer to quality decisionmaking (whether consistent over time or garnered after a time of less quality choices) as *pivoting right*. By this I mean that when confronted with alternatives, a particular child chooses the option that is likely to lead to favorable outcomes for him or her over the short and long term.

Imagine the many choices breakaway children confront from early on. Here are several examples: using drugs or alcohol, skipping school, not completing homework, stealing money or food, not returning home in the evening, finding lovers to fill emotional gaps, having or not having a child. The choice to stay in high school and enroll in college preparatory classes, sign up for and take SAT or ACT tests (and deal with their costs), fill in a FAFSA (Free Application for Federal Student Aid) application with or without parental involvement, apply both to college and for student loans—each is a difficult choice and perhaps outside the norm for a students' families and even their schools.

One of the missing features of resiliency (as well as grit and mindfulness or mindsets) is that they are not centered on quality decisionmaking. One can exhibit resilience by becoming the best and most successful drug dealer in one's community. At least that brings financial well-being and safety and even respect—albeit not for long. One can demonstrate grit by organizing and then running a gang that overtakes a rival gang. Dangerous, yes, but it is a pathway to power that provides some safety for one's family and friends. One can meditate to calm down after a bad choice or one can try to fight the urge to fight with meditation and relaxation. But absent the right conditions, mindfulness may not have the power to overcome group pressure. Growth mindsets, encouraging a belief in self, are value neutral. Developing study habits and other academically oriented skills can help students achieve more in school, but these qualities may not grow or transfer to external events that have nothing to do with academic learning and intellectual growth.

Children and students who are lastic have, for the most part, pivoted right, exercising decisions that lead not only to their survival but also to their thriving more than economically and in their sense of safety.

Now, one can make the argument that individuals who become successful drug dealers or gang leaders are thriving by some definitions, but it is most assuredly not in the way that we, as a nation, want to promote and encourage. One of the reasons we are so eager to encourage college access and degree attainment is that, as noted earlier, those with a degree earn more money over their lifetime, they have better health outcomes, they vote more frequently, they participate and give back more actively in their communities, they can lift their family up from poverty, and their children will be more likely to graduate from college.

While we would like to think there is some inexplicable intuition that enables quality decisionmaking, the reality is that there are many mechanisms that drive choice. Good decisions can be the product of individuals who push students to make good choices—teachers, parents, relatives, friends. Role models can influence choice, even role models such as athletes, actors, and politicians whom one knows about only through social media. Coaches can foster good decisions, as can individuals in after-school programs. Guilt is another driver. So is religion for some. So is fear. So is blind luck.

Reflect on the decisions you have made in your life. Many of us made many bad choices in our youth, and reflecting back, we cannot quite believe we survived relatively unscathed. For breakaway students, the risky choices can be more extreme and more frequent, with life-changing consequences.

For breakaway students' access to and success in college to occur, good decisionmaking needs to start early and often. To be sure, breakaway students' pathway to quality decisionmaking is not always direct. A lot—both positive and negative—can happen along the way. There is a growing chorus of folks who, in complaining about the absence of college success, place the blame for poor decisionmaking on students.[2]

Folks complain about the abundance of choices that students face in college, ranging from course selection and majors to activities and opportunities outside the classroom. Blame may be placed on faculty and staff for not providing adequate advising on courses and careers, omissions that can lead to negative consequences such as prolonged time in school to meet necessary requirements because required courses are not taken, the necessity of retaking a course in which one has not achieved an adequate grade to progress (think anatomy and physiology, which you can pass for credit but not pass for entry into a nursing program), and a lack of career readiness skills. This all costs extra money—on every level. Students need to pay more for their education, employers are dissatisfied with the graduates seeking employment, and faculty and staff are frustrated by the absence of sufficiently good performance in their courses.

However, this criticism misses the real point of pivoting right. There are degrees of "right," and many people make unwise choices and learn from them. So pivoting right is not the same as 100% quality decisionmaking. Far from it. Rather, pivoting right reflects a child's or young adult's effort to pursue a personal pathway that yields positive outcomes in physical and psychic well-being. Pivoting right is in large part about self-preservation.

One important qualification: There is no map of what *pivoting right* means. What it means for one person may not be what it means for another. Decisionmaking is deeply influenced by culture, religion, ethnicity, and tradition. Quality decisionmaking can mean choices on which a child or young adult and his or her parents may not agree.

But we are not talking about some types of decisionmaking that will align children and parents or guardians. For example, a child may not want to be a doctor like his mother; perhaps he wants to be an artist instead. Another child may not want to be a police officer like his father and may instead want to be an economist. A child may want to be a mechanic like his father, but his father may want him to obtain an advanced engineering degree. Following a parent's professional footsteps is not about pivoting right.

Instead, we want children from an early age to be empowered to make their own (age-appropriate) decisions; those decisions need to be informed by facts and circumstances and made through free will, and with self-preservation and well-being as paramount concerns. What we can do is work with breakaway students as they progress through the pre-K–12 pipeline and in after-school programs and community activities to encourage wise choices and create opportunities to correct bad choices when possible. We can help students build an architecture of better choice, in part by making deliberate what may now be done without much thought.[3]

Two concepts are at work. The first involves trying to *nudge*, to use the term referenced in Chapter 4, breakaway students to make wise choices. Structuring available choices in a way that encourages quality decision-making can foster this. For example, completing homework can lead to rewards and positive reinforcement; reading in school can lead to having books one can take home. Nudging in the right direction by parents, teachers, mentors, and professors can feel intrusive, but there is literature supporting such "intrusive" (now less negatively termed *proactive*) advising. And, as we will uncover when we look more closely at reciprocity, nudging can be one means along the pathway to creating a reciprocal relationship.

However, make no mistake about this: Nudges enable quality choices but personal decisionmaking skills are not necessarily enhanced. This is because the default mechanism at the heart of quality nudges is pre-set to ensure success, not failure, of choice. And the students are not setting that default choice! Nudges reinforce at some level an external as opposed to internal locus of control.

The second concept involves the idea that bad choices are all not necessarily outcome determinative, and one can improve or change one's choice architecture over time, with guidance. We create improved choice architecture when breakaway students are in college, often without intentionality. For example, we offer up lectures in evenings so students have an alternative to sitting in their rooms playing video games. We offer student clubs that align with their interests, enabling students to engage and to diminish the amount of time in which they may be idle that can lead to bad choices.

Stated simply, improved choice architecture can be constructed by offering enough alternatives, enough oversight, and enough opportunities to self-correct or be corrected in ways that do not distance the student from his or her support system. It can involve retrenching from bad decisions, with all the concomitant hassles and hurdles.

Take this example: Suppose a female college student has repeated disciplinary issues on campus, such as drinking excessively and while underage, using drugs, or engaging in other problematic behavior. Suppose too that the student is then suspended from her residence by the institution's disciplinary board but has nowhere to live off campus; she has no money to rent an apartment, and her family lives far away and is unaware of her situation. Living at home isn't even vaguely an option. What if a female faculty member agrees to take this student to live with her if certain conditions are met and maintained: if the student comes and goes to campus with the faculty member (even if that is way before classes begin), if the student commits to doing her academic work and sharing it with the faculty member to show completion without the faculty member haranguing her or even helping, and if she agrees to help with cooking and doing the dishes?

Many would suggest that such an "interventionist" approach is impossible or perhaps even inappropriate. It is certainly not easily scalable. There are not enough faculty members to make this happen, and it most assuredly is not within the scope of their employment. Moreover, it seems vastly beyond the role of institutions. The consensus might be that this student was irresponsible and should be punished, not rewarded (assuming living with a faculty member is considered a reward). True enough, based on how we presently think about students and the institutions that serve them.

But ponder what happens if we change our thinking and those within institutions see their obligations differently, even those on campuses with thousands of residential students. In other words, can we help institutions pivot right too? And, for the record, know that the student described here graduated from college after 5 years (there was a lag as the final semester approached, which will be discussed in another context) and is now happily employed and living in an apartment with colleagues near the college.

In terms of taking this idea to scale, ask these questions: Why do we have faculty living in residential halls on some campuses? It's noteworthy that in some instances it is couples with children who live surrounded by students. Reflect on why staff and college faculty invite students who live far from home over for Thanksgiving dinner. Consider why a president periodically invites students over to dinner at his or her home. Ask why coaches invite their student athletes to their homes before, during, and after a season. Ask why coaches will go out during the night to retrieve a student athlete who finds him- or herself in a bad place (literally and figuratively). For the cynical among us, yes, it is to make sure that the student athlete does not get tossed from the team and denied the opportunity to play (and lead to wins). But there is also an effort to turn around decision-making, to enable better choices.

True, these examples are not the same as having a student move into one's apartment or house, but there is a scintilla of recognition that an adult presence and quality rules can and do make a difference in reshaping decisionmaking. Surely it is not an overnight thing (how could it be?). But the presence of faculty and staff—living their lives as they live them with students watching and partaking—makes a difference. And to be clear, while the example given involves a faculty member, community members could and occasionally do take in students. Look at the story of football player Michael Oher; even if the fictionalized version of his "adoption" is one-third true, the value of being "taken in and allowed to engage" is immeasurable. For another example, look at Olympic gymnast Simone Biles, who was adopted by her grandparents.[4]

There are other, perhaps more easily deployable, ways in which we can and should think about enabling more students to pivot right because of an improved choice architecture. Below are four suggestions that can be used throughout the educational landscape. These approaches are not unknown to us but, generally speaking, improving student choice has not been their primary purpose. Nevertheless, there is nothing to prevent strategies that serve one purpose from being redeployed for another purpose—or for dual purposes for that matter. This happens all the time in medicine. A treatment for one illness or diagnosis may have other benefits that initially can be unnoticed or undervalued. For example, suppose an individual has trouble walking because of an arthritic hip. Replacing that hip will, with therapy, eliminate the pain of walking (at least in large part). But there is an added benefit, the prescribed therapy and increased activity, which can reduce weight and improve cardiac output. One intervention, multiple benefits.

CASE STUDIES/HYPOTHETICALS

Pedagogically, we know the benefits of using real or hypothetical problems to facilitate the application of theory and practice. At the highest level, Harvard Business School creates masterful case studies that allow their business students to wrestle with how to solve problems. But even younger children can benefit from problem-based learning. Consider young children reading a story involving bullying and a teacher then asking, "How would you have solved that problem? What would you have done in that situation? Why would one child be bullying another?" Even in commonly told children's stories read to younger children like "Little Red Riding Hood," children can be asked questions such as how they would deal with the big bad wolf.[5]

I want to distinguish case studies from the growing efforts to teach character to students through various approaches, including hypotheticals and problem sets. We can debate what constitutes good character and we can posit that those with character are likely to pivot right. But the goal of lasticity is not to dictate "morality." And pivoting right is about decisionmaking. In contrast, Project Wisdom, which repeatedly references quality decisionmaking, actually provides the decisions *for* the students. Students in essence adopt a credo rather than building one. They opt in to commitments to treat each other fairly, to act responsibility, and the like. There are colleges that actually have students sign contracts whereby they agree to good behavior on campus toward their fellow students. And contracts have been used by student life personnel to bind students to certain tasks when they have violated rules in an effort to get these students back on the right path. These are good values to be sure, but they are not self-generated. Most of the time, the content of these commitments and contracts is drafted by the adult and signed by the student. True, there can be some negotiation in the disciplinary context, if it is done well. But still, these are not student choices—except in the sense that they are choosing to sign.

SOCRATIC METHOD

In addition to case studies, we have much to learn from the Socratic method, commonly used in legal education, although in a modified form rather than as a source of humiliation and intimidation as demonstrated by the infamous Professor Kingsfield in the iconic movie *Paper Chase*, about the 1st year of law school. The main purpose of the approach is to test the strength of student arguments by pressing them further and further through continued, some would say, grueling or threatening, questioning. With each new question, students individually or in a group need to either defend their position or discover the weaknesses in it.[6]

We can look at the Socratic method in a different way and through a different lens: By listening to the quality questions asked by professors, law students learn to ask good questions—the kind of questions they will need to ask clients and that they will have to ask themselves in assessing the strength of their legal arguments. I remember vividly when I held Family Day for the families of law students. Yes, this is usual in a graduate school environment and vastly more popular in other levels across the education pipeline. For many law students, particularly those who were first-generation students, it was an opportunity to share what they were doing in class and show who their "tough," "aggressive," and "demanding" professors were. People half expected me to look and act like an ogre. Every year parents, spouses, girl- and boyfriends, partners, and children asked me some version of the question, Why is my daughter (wife) (mother) (son) (husband) (father) always peppering me with questions? We can't have a conversation any longer. Everything I say is followed by an inquiry akin to, Why did you do that? Did you consider this option? Where did you go then? When you say "green," what shade of green exactly?

What this shows is that the law students had taken the questioning to which they were exposed by their law professors and reversed it—they asked questions of others in their personal circle. However difficult this was for families, it does show how *listening* to questions fosters an increased capacity to *ask* questions, to probe more deeply, to be less satisfied with the surface-level responses commonly given. To be sure, law students were applying this newly acquired skill in a largely inappropriate context, a topic I leave for another day (or another book).

For our purposes here, the point is that I would expect that by listening to quality questions in a classroom (yes, outside the legal context), students could learn to ask questions (something of a lost art to be sure). By asking questions, students are seeing that they can challenge existing norms; they can press against rules; they can probe rationales.

Asking questions is not always easy for students. Some young people have grown up in an environment that discourages challenging the status quo. Questions are answered by adults with responses such as "Because I said so," or "Don't you challenge me," or "This is the way it is." In my own house, early on, the adage was "Children are to be seen but not heard." Across the educational pipeline, we can and should message that, first, there are no stupid questions (a point that needs to be emphasized again and again especially with female students) and, second, we will answer questions and all questions should be encouraged. Questions, then, are a way of fostering the fertile soil in which students are freed up to pivot right. Questions are no guarantee of wise decisionmaking, but they are a "space creator," allowing new possible answers to emerge. They emerge from within the student and are generated based on the content and discussion within a classroom.[7]

FINDING VOICE

Another strategy to consider deploying in classrooms to encourage wise decisionmaking is asking for and encouraging student voice in decision-making within the classroom or school. Some folks pooh-pooh the idea of children or young adults offering their views when adults with experience "know better." But student voice—and it can appear in a wide range of contexts with a wide range of meanings—has power for those who choose to consider its use. Consider how Marlboro College (tiny, to be sure) is run like a town meeting where everyone—from the students to the janitor—gets a vote on issues.[8]

Opening the door for input also offers an intangible power for those who tend to remain silent. For some breakaway students, it is empowering to hear classmates helping to shape the culture in which they are learning. You can almost hear these breakaway students asking these questions (silently to themselves): You can do this without being punished? There are adults who will take my suggestions seriously? There is a way of contributing to a conversation of how I want to be treated? There is a question I can ask that won't generate laughter signaling that I am either dumb or a Goody Two-shoes?

One important point here: There are many reasons to encourage student voice across the educational pathway and considerable literature showing its value. It mimics participatory democracy, it allows for increased buy-in, it adds perspectives that would otherwise be missing, it role models thoughtful inquiry, it creates a culture of trust, and it fosters appreciation for compromise and respect for the views of others. All this is valid.[9]

The point is that student voice can contribute to the capacity of breakaway students to pivot right—in addition to the many other benefits that student voice proffers. Think about asking questions and speaking as creating a breath—a pause. In that pause, other options have room to flourish and be considered. I've often thought we should all have on our desks a button or a computer key that says "pause," warning us of the risks of decisions made too quickly and without reflecting on consequences.

UNDERSTANDING RULEMAKING

The final suggestion for building the capacity to pivot right is to create classrooms in which there is active and continuous learning about rules and rulemaking. When breakaway students grow up in settings in which there are no rules or where the rules are habitually changing or are arbitrary both in substance and application, it is hard—very hard—to accept rules in other settings. Why comply when rules are so unfair? That is why schools and colleges with breakaway students would be wise to spend time in and out of class on rules and their necessity and meaning. Instead, we often just say, "Read the student handbook and ask if you don't understand something and, yes, you are bound by what is in there."

Student voice in creating rules or deciding who broke them can be beneficial. What follows are two exercises that have value and can be integrated into classrooms of students of all stages and ages. While commonly used for younger students, they can be adapted for high school and college use effectively. Start with No Vehicles in the Park, a chestnut of an exercise designed to look at whether rules work and in what situations. The general rule "No vehicles in the park" is introduced to students with the rationale that the hypothetical town was concerned about park safety. Then a variety of situations arise that challenge the rule: Can a baby carriage go into the park? A motorized wheelchair? An ambulance? A garbage truck? The point of the exercise is to test the limits and strengths of rules—and to enable students to reflect on rule application and rule construction. Rules are not etched in stone. They are fluid; they require contextualization; they need interpretation; they are subject to change. Just ponder the obviously more sophisticated arguments at the U.S. Supreme Court that present these same issues: the debate between strict constitutional constructionists (originalists or textualists) and judicial activists (interpretivists). Is the Constitution firmly set in stone or can we adapt its meaning to more contemporary times? Indeed, for decades, women did not even have the right to vote—so there has been constitutional change.[10]

The second exercise involves a game—call it the spaghetti game, although objects other than spaghetti can be used in cases where there is a legitimate worry in communities with food scarcity about using food in a game. (One way to address this is to give each student a box of pasta after the game, if funds are available; this will serve an added purpose, enabling the student to share with their family both the food and perhaps the exercise.)

Students are placed in lines, and the student at the head of the line is given a box of spaghetti. Then all the students are told by the teacher to play the spaghetti game. Students immediately realize that they don't know how to play the game, that games have rules and ways of determining outcomes. The teacher then suggests that students call out rules, and he or she writes them on the board. Then, with the rules all there, the teacher again invites the students to play the spaghetti game. Chaos then obviously ensues. There are too many rules; they are not ordered or prioritized. Every team is doing its own thing, so to speak.

The teacher then has the students select key rules—each student must pass the spaghetti, without breaking it, over his or her left shoulder until the spaghetti gets to the last student in line. The team that gets the spaghetti to the end of the line first, without breaking the strands, wins. As the game starts again, the teacher stops it and says, "Wait, the spaghetti needs to be passed over the right, not left, shoulder." The students in turn respond, "You can't change the rules in the middle of the game." "Why not?" the teacher asks. Then, settling on rules and the need for consistency, the teacher calls yet again for the game to begin. This time, the game plays out, but—and this is important—the teacher assigns a winner based on the color of his or her shirt. Blue wins. The students are indignant. No—you can't pick and choose winners arbitrarily. You can't suddenly decide who's worthy. Those who follow the rules win. Pivoting right in action.

Pivoting right is about empowering thoughtful decisionmaking. It is about students realizing that they can exercise choice—it is theirs to exercise. There is a shifting of the locus of control, not just from an externality to an internality, but also in how one's internal compass can rotate. For breakaway students, that is critical and affords them a greater sense of power over their lives and their decisions. To be sure, it is not a guarantee of quality behavior and quality decisionmaking across all time and place. Decisionmaking is far too complex for perfection given stages of brain development; context; and peer, cultural, and familial pressure.

Consider an image of a young woman who seems to be awaiting disaster (Figure 8.1). A big boulder is headed toward her as if she were merely a pin in the path of a bowling ball. She is not moving, as if being hit is inevitable. Taking away that sense of inevitability and replacing it with an improved sense of control is dramatic. It is life changing. It is the difference between being knocked over and standing up and trying to stop the boulder or step out of its way. It is about decisionmaking.

Figure 8.1. Artwork by Jailene Gonzalez of a woman sitting cross-legged with a rock headed toward her.

The phrase *pivoting right* is intentionally vague in terms of outcomes. It most assuredly is not referencing *right* as in the political Right, the right wing. To return to the image in Figure 8.1, there are many choices available to the seated woman. The phrase being used in the context of lasticity is not *correct decisionmaking* or *moral decisionmaking* or *character-based decisionmaking*. Pivoting is about turning—it is about changing from one position to another. Pivoting is not an end point; it is a process. And so it is with breakaway students: We need to help them turn. We need to recognize that they are unlikely to turn on their own; for breakaway kids, the range of choices has been so narrowed or distorted or tainted or fraught with tension and anger that pivoting is neither easy nor seen as an option. Institutions actually pivot right to help students pivot right.

Reflect on this image as we leave this topic: The breakaway students' pivot (think of a metal apparatus that can move) has a limited range. It is creaky and doesn't go evenly in all directions. Picture pouring some grease or oil on the pivot to loosen it up, to enable it to move more freely, to spin. (That's what the institution does as part of its pivot right.) That's what helps breakaway students to pivot right. We provide the grease or oil. We unstick the stuck pivot.

CHAPTER 9

Lasticity's Reciprocal Heart

Thus far, we have largely focused on the breakaway students themselves—understanding their strengths and deficits, the presence of elasticity and plasticity, and the development of pivoting right. One thread that links the previous chapters covering three of the foundational blocks of lasticity is reciprocity. While *reciprocity* is similar to terms like *trust* and *relationships*, it is at once more complex and more important. Indeed, reciprocity is at the heart of lasticity. Here's why.

Reciprocity between breakaway students and the institutions they attend (and people within them) is central to enabling success. Reciprocity is not manifested by a one-off engagement between a student and people within an institution. It is, in addition to individual instances of engagement between students and their faculty, staff, and coaches, a description of a campus culture.

The origins and multiple meanings of the words *reciprocal* and *reciprocity* animate the intended concept embedded in lasticity. At one level, the terms refer to shared feelings and understandings between two or more people or groups. Mutuality is key, as is an ongoing sharing between parties, something deeply respectful. The use of the term *reciprocity* in math shows the link: Every number (except 1) has a reciprocal. (For those unfamiliar with math concepts, the reciprocal of 9 is one-ninth.)

Reciprocity derives from the Latin *reciprocus*, meaning "moving back and forth." Unlike the term *relationship*, which can be applied (absent some modifying adjective) to engagements that are unequal, flawed, unfair, or even destructive, fairness and equality are embedded in the term *reciprocal*. The *Oxford English Dictionary* definition is worth quoting: "the practice of exchanging things with others for mutual benefit, especially privileges granted by one country or organization to another."[1]

A reciprocal campus culture is not the same as an engaged campus, although engagement is a part of reciprocity. It is not created by teachers or professors "speaking differently" *to* a student ("You are making a great effort; you can improve"), a feature of growth mindsets. It is about speaking and working *with* students in a shared enterprise. A culture of reciprocity is created when institutions (and those within it) see it as part and parcel of their job to facilitate student success by recognizing the students' strengths and weaknesses and acknowledging these attributes affirmatively to the students. And the students give something back to the institution and those within it: their talents, their efforts, their successes, their willingness to take risks and trust.

Usually, when we use the word *reciprocity*, we imagine overt reciprocal relationships; consider reciprocal trade deals between nations. As used here in the context of lasticity, however, the relationship between a student and his or her college may not happen simultaneously, nor is it necessarily equal or mutual in any traditional sense. For the student, overt reciprocity on his or her side may be delayed or could happen without recognition. But this lag in naming or the lack of recognition by students is not unfair or flawed; it is most assuredly not destructive.

Here's why: Reciprocity does involve two (or more) parties but the level of engagement on each side can be quite different. I term this *imbalanced reciprocity* here. While not ideal, this descriptor can be a valuable starting point. Next, for reciprocity to be effective, at least one side needs to have a deep understanding of the other. That requires more than pure knowledge; it requires an appreciation of the implications of that knowledge and then of how the knowledge can be used. This means the institution's recognizing the earlier experiences of breakaway students—the curdled childhood and bent lives. Then, not surprisingly, reciprocity plays out differently between individuals as opposed to between individuals and an institution.

In the higher education sphere, reciprocity must be exhibited by both the institution (college, university) and those who work within the institution (from the faculty to the facilities workers). This is more robust than what many term "student-centeredness," which is very au courant and important; reciprocity requires *actual* relationships between the parties, not just an institutional focus on students and a set of activities or pushes that foster student success. To drive the point home, reciprocity would take the word *on* in the prior sentence and replace it with the word *with*; the words *activities* and *pushes* would be replaced with *relationships*.[2]

Here's an added point: We know that on a campus, you can do 98% of things "right," but one nasty comment or misunderstood encounter can make a breakaway student unsettled or worse. Think about microaggressions that many dismiss as petty and as evidence of oversensitivity. Since we cannot ensure that everyone always treats others in positive ways, we need to create an overarching culture of reciprocity, and if that culture is consistent and continuous, it can help smooth over the inevitable bumps in the educational experience of breakaway (and other) students.

To grasp the meaning of reciprocity as part of a culture, consider this story: At many colleges, new students receive a book when they arrive on campus that is often referenced throughout their 1st year in college. The goal is that all students will have the same reading material and the sessions held around that work will help introduce students to each other, to complicated questions that warrant discussion, and to thematic links between students and the larger campus community and even the outside community—through speakers, conversations, and class sessions. It is an idea that makes real sense, as it fosters sharing.

At Southern Vermont College, we also gave new students a book, selected by the faculty. But we added something to the process: Every book we gave out was signed by hand by virtually every member of the faculty and staff. Indeed, there were book-signing days at the start of each semester when hundreds of books were set out on tables along with baskets of colorful pens. I often provided live remarks on these signing days, sharing with faculty and staff that by signing these books, they were committing themselves to helping our new students succeed. This approach broke down some of the barriers between faculty and staff in terms of their relative stature and importance on campus; they all were being asked to sign.

I remember the son of a math faculty member who was accompanying his mother while she signed the books. At one point he said, "You must be famous, because you're signing a book." The professor downplayed her son's comment, but in a sense he was right—by signing, members of the college's faculty and staff were becoming "known" to their students.

To continue the story, at graduation, we provided every graduate with a different book, this one selected by the commencement speaker. As with the books handed out at orientation, each of these books was signed by every member of the faculty and staff. So with one book on the front end and another on the back, these works became the bookends of an undergraduate education.

What I said to the new students receiving these signed books on their 1st day of college was "I hope that years from now, when you have a family and a successful career, you will pull these books down from the shelf and look at the names of the men and women who helped you become who you are." I repeated that same sentence when they graduated.

The tradition of signing and handing out the books became part of our institutional culture, welcoming students and showcasing the commitment of faculty and staff—as evidenced by their signatures. It is concrete proof of reciprocity.

Deconstructing this scenario, what is clear is that the signed books are a way of sharing with new students that they are being welcomed into a new community with faculty and staff committed to their success. (At some institutions, it is the students, *not* the faculty and staff, who sign commitments; the difference here is absolutely intentional.) The awareness that there is a second book is a way of predicting and directing the future: There will be a second book, students will progress to graduation, and they will not be headed there alone. The faculty and staff "inscribed" in their books are with them.

This approach is ideally suited to smaller institutions where faculty and staff can sign within a reasonable amount of time and at one central location. Nevertheless, larger institutions can create similar events that message similarly, although obviously intimacy is harder to develop on a campus with 10,000 or 50,000 students. In institutions that are subdivided into schools (School of Engineering; School of Business; School of Nursing), the books could be targeted to the subject matter and signed by faculty and staff within that school with appropriate words from the applicable dean. To be sure, if a student changed majors (coming or going) and this would not be infrequent, it makes the back-end aspect of this tradition difficult if not impossible.

Consider huge welcome flags, signed by members of the faculty and staff, across a campus. These flags could be placed in a central location before the start of the academic year and all faculty and staff invited to sign them. Unlike signing 200 books (which is what happened on our campus, as that was the size of the entering student population), they would sign 10 flags (or some similar number). Nothing onerous. Not like signing 3,000 or more books for incoming 1st-year and transfer students. The signatures could be large and written with indelible ink, to survive all sorts of weather. Then there could be a flag-flying ceremony as part of orientation where these welcoming flags were hung—signatures abounding—all over campus. And perhaps the flags could be hung relatively low—so the signatures are visible—low flagpoles as opposed to poles stretching high into the stratosphere. It would be quite a sight. Senior leadership could speak about the welcoming flags at opening events. They could be shared with visitors. They could be shown to trustees and alums. They could appear on the institution's website. And each year, these particular flags would come down (not be destroyed) and the ceremony would repeat itself for the next incoming class. And perhaps at graduation of the class for which each set of flags was signed, "their" flags could reappear—like the second book at Southern Vermont College—serving as a reminder of the individuals who supported students on their journey.

For many, it is hard to conceptualize how an institution can be reciprocal, as it seems a very "human" form of engagement, but that is not so.
Institutional culture—a multifaceted creation—can produce reciprocity,
but not necessarily in obvious ways. Yes, it is enabled by people, but institutions do speak through their policies, their atmosphere, through what
is on their halls and walls, through their methods of outreach, their tone
and tenor, their response to situations involving breakaway students. The
welcome flags are but one example.

Consider the debates over trigger warnings and safe spaces. The University of Chicago, in the name of free speech, sent a letter to incoming
students announcing that the university administration does not believe in
trigger warnings and safe spaces; they believe in dialogue and free speech
and difficult conversations about topics that are controversial or on which
there are deeply felt views. They will not disinvite speakers who are expressing offensive, even hurtful views. Debate and quality engagement are
central to education.[3]

Embedded in this position is the notion that it is okay for students
to be disquieted, that it is acceptable to stir the pot, that probing difficult
topics is something students need to learn to do and with which they
need to deal. The institutional messaging is "We will not shortcut hard
and unpleasant feelings." Basically, students, learn to "deal." This is how
learning happens in academia.

I hope that they do not have many breakaway students there. For the
record, I was there for my 3rd year of law school, and our son spent his
undergraduate years there, and we both received remarkable educations.
But not every student will be well served by their approach.

Other institutions have taken a different tack. Trigger warnings and
safe spaces and cancellations of speeches occur, even if they are curbs on
free speech. No one denies that. But that does not mean the limitations
are unwarranted. Facing what is offensive is one strategy for dealing with
the real world: If you have been raped, face the accused and express your
feelings; if you have had a disagreement with your mother, face her and
express your views; if you are hurt by the words or deeds of a friend, confront the person and share your outrage. That approach, however, is not
only hard and perhaps even unworkable in real life for some students; it
is not always wise. In fact, it can be dangerous—literally and figuratively.

Pause for a moment and reflect on an essay by Professor Erika Price,
written in response to the University of Chicago's position. She uses and
supports trigger warnings for many reasons. She believes they enable students to "confront" harsh truths more easily because students can prepare
themselves and in essence "be ready." She notes that professors are not

ordered to use them; they are permitted to do so. And trigger warnings are in effect acknowledging where a student is coming from in terms of the baggage they carry with them. She goes on to describe how the use of trigger warnings is not a sign of weakness in the student who wants them. She herself was and is, as she asserts with fervor, a survivor of rape and a strong person—simultaneously. Strength—being strong—does not mean that one avoids suffering. Think about soldiers who have experienced war; their showing signs of post-traumatic stress does not mean they are weak.[4]

Price's essay asks educators the following questions (noting that some abused, traumatized students may not have the courage to ask for trigger warnings and instead suffer the consequences): "How can someone call himself or herself an educator and not be sensitive to these incredibly common needs? How can someone be a proponent of intellectual freedom and not want to make their classroom a space where everyone feels free from emotional harm and psychological violence? How does warning a student that a lecture might touch on murder or rape make the university a less open environment?"

Perhaps her strongest argument and one that should touch educators who want to reach their breakaway students is "I want my students to feel emotionally safe so that they can take on cognitive challenges from a position of strength." Brava. She is expressing what I could term *imbalanced reciprocity* in an effort to help students learn to trust and become reciprocal—evidenced by their growing capacity to learn. Why not build a culture in which we use all possible ways to encourage learning by all our students?

I get that students travel across the educational landscape with different amounts of baggage. Some students are fortunate; their baggage fits in a briefcase. Other students arrive in classrooms with steamer trunks filled with baggage. We can try to deny this. We can ignore it. Or we can embrace the baggage—and help the students unpack that luggage, as observed earlier. I am always reminded of the remarkable and sad story Calvin Trillin tells of his college roommate Denny Hansen. As Trillin tells it, Denny walked through life with a backpack filled with expectations he could not fulfill. No wonder he fell from the weight of the expectations. Why can't we lighten that load for breakaway students through institutional understanding of who our students are and what will help them?[5]

At the end of the day, learning itself is a reciprocal process. We have moved away from the antiquated notion that professors are sages delivering content into the passive minds of students sitting in chairs before them. We have come to see, rightly, in my view, that educators need to enter into a reciprocal relationship with their students, engaging with them in an enterprise that is at once threatening and rewarding: learning.

There are many arenas in which we could generate better outcomes were there reciprocity. As an example, consider medicine. The literature shows that health care outcomes are optimized when patients are involved in their care, when they are informed of the choices to be made, when they participate in decisionmaking, when they partner with the medical professionals. But for some health care providers, the idea of partnering with patients is anathema, and these providers' argument (whether or not vocalized) goes something like this: I am educated, I have been trained, I have experience, I know what is best, and I need to get things done and partnering takes time and energy (and is uncompensated, to boot); you are uneducated or unsophisticated and I know better. There's sometimes a godlike feel to how doctors view themselves and their roles.[6] Forget too that this homogenizes patients and their knowledge bases and emotional comfort.

Consider this example: I have a vivid memory (and the concordant visceral reaction) of a cardiologist who entered my husband's tiny room in an intensive care unit. My adult son and I were there. The physician was wearing a white coat with his name and medical specialty embroidered over the left pocket. Then, in a singsongy tone that mimicked that of Mr. Rogers, he stood at the end of the bed and said to us all, "Hello, I am Dr. Davis. I am a heart doctor."

To me, he sounded demeaning. He was infantilizing us with his tone and his effort to "simplify" medical speak by not using the term *cardiologist* and assuming that if he did, we would not understand it. I get the effort; some patients and their families might not have understood the term, and doctor speak can be alienating.

But my husband has a name (as do I and as does our son). One look at the medical chart would have shown that my husband was a professional, something illness does not eradicate. And his son—the holder of the health care proxy—is a professor at a well-known university. That was all in the chart. And me, the wife? I was totally missing in the chart. But this physician had made no effort to know who his patient was (and perhaps who the family were). That's not smart; that doesn't signal preparation and personalization. That bodes badly for trust and outcome success. Already feeling that we were in an out-of-control situation, I responded to the "heart" doctor a tad tartly. "Really! Dr. Davis, you are the cardiologist but best as I can tell, you are not the electrophysiologist, right?" He looked at me as if I had entered some forbidden turf—his turf. Unfortunately, many patients and their families do not speak up, because they are scared and want good care and fear that saying something will prompt the physician to retaliate by providing suboptimal care, lacking in compassion.

Here's my point. My husband got amazing care in the ER and ICU, for which we are deeply grateful. Bravo and brava to the teams. What my husband did not get was a trust-inducing medical introduction from the person responsible for his ailing heart. Instead, he and his family got what felt like a putdown to me (perhaps not to my son and husband).

With a little thought and preparation in a nonemergency situation, it wouldn't have taken much to change the introductory words to "Hello, I am Dr. Davis, the cardiologist in charge of your heart issues here in the ICU." That would have been respectful, open, and clear. None of us were ignoramuses. We may not have been cardiologists, but we know a lot of them and know about the work they do. In short, Dr. Davis underestimated us, making a common error among health care providers when speaking with families.

I think this example can be extrapolated for the educational pipeline, in the context of educators and their breakaway students. Either some educators do not understand their students or they do not take the time to understand them. They do not deploy strategies that will lower anxiety and stress levels. They do not partner with these students and envelop them in a shared enterprise. Perhaps they do not think the students have anything that important or insightful to offer or add to a conversation or discussion—after all, they are students, not professors. Recall the handwritten note shown in Chapter 4 (see Figure 4.1), which is almost worth reprinting here. Some of this is, to be sure, because educators may not know how to engage effectively (like some health care workers who are short on interpersonal skills). And when faced with uncomfortable situations, faculty resort to what they can do based on what they know. They fight for the preservation of what they used to do and what they themselves have experienced.

It is not easy to change culture; it is not simple to develop reciprocal relationships that are authentic. It means throwing out one's old notes and creating new ones. But there is an approach that may help make this change easier and faster and more effective. In the context of health care and efforts to implement improvement, there is an ongoing effort for health care professionals and administrators to check into their own hospitals incognito. Let them see how patients are treated and how doctors perform. Let them sense what being out of control feels like—even if only hypothetically. Let them be subject to grand rounds and new physicians and disruptions throughout the evening and noise and lights at all times of day and night. Let them be stuck for days in a room surrounded by walls painted an unpleasant shade of green. Let them pee into a receptacle under the watchful eye of a nurse (male or female). Let them wear a gown that opens in the back and leaves their backside exposed when they walk down the hall. True, not every individual in health care can do this, but if more than a handful do at each institution and the experiences are shared, there is increased knowledge and awareness.

I have always argued that teachers need to become learners. They need to see how hard it is to open oneself up to new concepts and new fellow students and a teaching style that may not mirror one's own learning style. I am not talking here about professional development workshops (whether good or bad and the subject of yet another book, to be sure). These already start with a positive bent: One is surrounded by people like oneself. They aren't threatening, they aren't graded, and they are often not paid for by the teacher him- or herself. Instead, take an art class if you can't draw. Take a science class if you struggle with math. Take a music class if you can't hold a tune or have a weak auditory memory. Take a poetry class if you have never liked or understood poetry.

In this context, it is well worth reading Roger Martin's stunning *Racing Odysseus*, mentioned earlier. This former college president and professor decides to go back to college. What he experiences as a 1st-year student is startling—to the reader and to Martin. This effort changed him materially, making him a better teacher and leader. True, many of us cannot take a year off as Martin did, or as Barbara Ehrenreich did when she went undercover to learn how hard it was to live on poverty wages. But even short-term experiences are enriching.[7]

On a personal level, been there, done that. I signed up for a drawing class, and I learned to draw from a remarkable teacher when I was on a sabbatical; before I took the class I could draw only stick figures. But I learned vastly more than how to draw. I learned to think differently. I learned to be a different kind of teacher. This teacher was gentle, and she drew (pun intended) talent out from her students through encouragement and a nonstressful setting. I learned how hard it is to learn.

I am tempted to suggest (or to use the phrase made common by naturalist and author Rachel Carson, "If I had influence with the good fairy . . . I should ask her . . .") that all professors and staff enroll in a weekend-long foreign-language course—unless they speak the language being taught or already know multiple languages. See how hard it is to be in an environment when one is so out of place both intellectually and personally. For those with language skills, sign up for an advanced math theory class. I get that this is unlikely to happen for many reasons, not the least of which is that we can't "force" faculty and staff to forgo their weekends in this way. And on large campuses, this would be a massive and expensive undertaking.

But we could encourage faculty and staff to take 2 hours to sit in on a class—even a kindergarten class—somewhere and be a student again. The idea is not to go to a colleague's class at another area college and sit there as a student (or participate as a co-teacher, although that might be good for other reasons). Go to an unfamiliar educational institution and try to learn. It isn't easy, that's for sure.

Returning to the notion of reciprocity, we need to add the other half of the back-and-forth. We've developed here how institutions and those within them can share with students. And how do students share back? They share by evidencing their willingness to trust, their capacity to engage, their openness to new ideas, their joy in learning, their increasingly good questions, their growing comfort with themselves and with others, their increasing capacity to pivot right, and their clear progress along the educational pipeline. That reciprocity occurs only when those with whom they are reciprocating are doing their part. For the students, their sharing may not seem to be that valuable. But for the recipient—their teachers—there is no greater gift than seeing a student flourish.[8]

Also, educators may find the reciprocity revealed in unexpected and indirect ways. A student's capacity to enter into a healthy romantic relationship with a fellow student, a student's growing involvement in an on-campus activity that previously had seemed off limits or too challenging or too threatening, a student's willingness to do research on a project or work in a team or do some independent activity that is then reported on—these are all examples of the success of reciprocity, and while the actual recipient of the sharing may not be the professor directly, it is generated and facilitated by that educator.

For students to be lastic and for institutions to exhibit lasticity, then, culture counts. And a reciprocal culture is at the heart of breakaway student success. Building that culture is our challenge, but it is also our opportunity and it is just sitting there before us—waiting to be embraced.

There is one more piece of lasticity that forms its final building block—belief in self. It is to this topic that we now turn.

CHAPTER 10

Belief in Self Isn't Easy

There is a growing recognition that absent a belief in self, learning and success in school and in the workplace can be in jeopardy. Indeed, there is rich literature on how to build self-esteem, and we most assuredly know what kinds of actions or words can destroy belief in self. And we are poignantly aware that belief in self is, at least for a time, remarkably fragile and can be threatened by the least setback. So building self-esteem is not a linear process—that's for sure.[1]

We know that students who are yelled at, reprimanded, criticized, and repeatedly punished in school or held back a grade lack or lose self-esteem. Students who are humiliated in front of their peers suffer a loss of self-respect. Students who are placed in remedial courses or lower tracks are aware of the message that they are not doing as well as others. We know that students, particularly those who are hypervigilant, can sense which students capture the eyes and ears of the teachers. Kids know when they are liked. Kids sense it when a teacher has a discriminatory bent—even if the teacher believes he or she is totally without bias of any sort.[2]

We also know that a belief in self needs to be genuine. Fake grades to encourage success are self-defeating. Trophies for everything and anything are not taken seriously. Hyperbolic compliments don't work. Kids can see through all that. The word *authentic* has meaning in this context.

One of the by-products of institutional reciprocity, described in Chapter 9, is its ability to create in the breakaway student a sense of self and to put on display, whether publicly or privately, someone else's belief in this student. That recognition can become central to how student belief in self is generated. In some people, belief in self is generated at home and in school. In breakaway students, however, these more common channels are often shut off. Parents may not support a student's quest for a life beyond that which his or her family has known. It feels threatening and disruptive. Some teachers' focus is on what a student does wrong rather than what he or she does right. Indeed, in some schools there is a cultural expectation of failure, something that some of the more recent charter schools and progressive public schools are working to change. Other schools want weaker students to fail so that they leave, allowing the school's scores on standardized tests to rise. One's community often does not build "self," in part because those within it don't have a good sense of self. Towns can have this issue too—they are insecure and thus do not flourish economically, culturally, or educationally. Sadly, I live in one such locality, where the town's belief in itself is sorely lacking. Ironically, those breakaway students with a strong sense of self often manifest it in negative ways—gang membership or bullying or other aggressive fear tactics.

There is no one answer to how to build an authentic sense of self—in breakaway students or others who are struggling to find a sense of well-being. Consider the common example of increasingly successful professional women who struggle with what could be called the "onion syndrome," fearful that as they progress farther and farther up the professional ladder to success, they are at risk of being exposed and their "true selves" (their inadequate selves) being discovered. These women worry that the onion will be totally peeled back and there will be nothing at the center. It's hard to keep moving forward when you sense that each step might be the one that unravels you and leaves you naked.

For breakaway students, building a sense of self is not a short-term project; there is no single, one-time intervention that can enable the self to emerge powerfully and intact. Instead, it is a nonlinear progression in a culture that knows that finding belief in self is a hard-fought battle. There are many actions and steps that faculty, staff, and administration can take to further belief in self. Open-door policies, nonthreatening conversations in dining halls and hallways, positive feedback (and negative feedback given in the context of other items done well), the offering of opportunities (membership in clubs; participation in research or community activities; taking a position as a teaching assistant, community adviser, or mentor). What you need is an institutional culture that has walls and halls that say, You matter, you can succeed, you can do this. And standards are not lowered and compliments are not given for unsatisfactory work. It's worth noting that this description of belief in self is broader than growth mindsets, discussed earlier. Yes, growth mindset focuses on students' belief in their capacity to succeed, but it is largely, as I read the literature, classroom focused and early education centered. As applied in the context of lasticity, belief in self runs wide and deep, informing life choices and decisionmaking and career trajectory and relationship formation and development. To plant a notion to which we will return, belief in self can curb sexual assaults and bullying on high school and college campuses in part because these acts, in addition to demonstrating a pivot "left" as opposed to "right," show a marked lack of belief in and respect for self—one's own self and the self of others.

Make no mistake about this: Lowering the bar does not engender a sense of success in students. In fact, students perform up to the limit that is set and if a bar is set lower, they fall to the lower level. If you want to succeed, you need an environment where success (at least academic success) is a good thing. We almost need a public service campaign that keeps repeating, "Smart is good."

The showcasing of student success is fostered by public sharing (as opposed to the public shaming that we often do). Consider an art exhibit of students' photographs attended by coaches, not just art teachers and other faculty. Imagine a reading of students' creative stories attended by the institution's president. Picture attendance at athletics events by the math professor, the one who looks as though sports were barely on his or her radar screen and certainly not something that was a common activity in his or her youth (although sometimes one can be surprised). Consider evening presentations by faculty in residential halls to discuss how they arrived at their destination. How about faculty and the senior leaders traveling to events with students in tow—to conferences, to donor events, to speaking engagements?

I remember one such event. I was taking two students (and my husband) to Quebec, where there was a conference at which I was leading a discussion. There was a formal opening reception at Quebec's Supreme Court and then opportunities to attend legal education sessions. Neither student had been outside the United States. I remember my assistant asking the students if they had a suit or nice pants and a jacket, and one of the students replied that, yes, he had his matching warm-up suit. Off to shop they went. I remember them crossing the border with us in our car—their looks of astonishment as they entered a different country. (One of them went on to work and live in Europe. If curiosity is piqued, see Chapter 17.) I remember clearly that they drank and ate what was in the minibar and made many phone calls in the evenings, not knowing that it was costly. A wee shock for me at checkout. When I returned to campus, the grants person remarked that those costs were part of the project; traveling with students had financial implications. I remember the students introducing themselves and mingling at the reception, developing a sense of self-confidence. And most important, I remember them attending the session I ran and actually asking questions—unprompted.

A similar experience occurred when I took three women students to Fashion Week in New York City. In addition to the fashion show and backstage adventure and a look at where I used to do my research at the

New York Public Library when I was a professor in the city, I recall their gasps when they saw the famous *Campbell's Soup Cans* by Andy Warhol at the Museum of Modern Art and then proceeded to go painting by painting commenting on which had and had not been in their textbook in art history at the college.

All these endeavors can be characterized as showing breakaway students a new normal—and that is not always easy. There is an aftershock when students realize that the reality of the world as they see it—gaslit and all—is not necessarily commonplace in other settings. That is not instantaneous.

I appreciate two key features of these examples: They require a faculty and leadership willing to engage students in a totally different way, and they require money. Showing up at campus events that are not in one's field takes time. I get it—no matter how we count, there are still only 24 hours in a day. Taking students to conferences and on trips isn't cheap, and it certainly changes the dynamic of "time away from campus," given that people from the campus are with you constantly while away. I get that it takes away from private time with colleagues at different institutions and even with a spouse or partner. But these types of engagement can occur on campuses large and small, undergraduate and graduate; indeed, the idea of traveling with students was suggested to me by a medical school dean who regularly took students with him wherever he went. It was part of how he learned how his institution was performing. For his students, it was a remarkable opportunity to see a different side of medicine and of their dean.[3]

Self-confidence can also grow, perhaps even more rapidly, in situations involving failure—depending on how the institution (and those within it) handle the failure. Indeed, failure is a fertile soil for building confidence. Let me use an example from my own life. I went to college at a time when there were no distribution requirements; anything went. If you wanted to take 25 courses in one discipline, there was nothing to stop you. I decided to create my own distribution requirements; I saw it as a personal challenge and an effort to be well rounded and to fill in gaps I sensed in myself. Well, in some instances, I tried but had to withdraw from a course: music appreciation (I could not hear what everyone else was hearing no matter how many times I listened; still can't). I enrolled three times in art history, but every time the lights went down, I slid down in my seat and fell asleep. That course was an impossibility. That left Biology 101—the basic pre-med bio course.

I remember thinking, How hard could this be? I had taken biology and chemistry in high school. So I enrolled, listened to the lectures, participated in the labs, did the reading, studied for tests. On the first test, I got a 42 (something mentioned earlier on in this book, in Chapter 4.) No joke. I got a 42, and I had studied hard. So I went to the professor (who happened to be the head of the department) and said I had to withdraw from the course; I showed him where he needed to sign on the paperwork. He looked at me and said, "Are you the student who won the English prize?" Yes, I answered, wondering how he would know that. He responded that he didn't think I should withdraw; instead, I needed to learn how to think differently, how to think like scientists think. I needed to study differently.

I agreed to give it a try, and he met with me and shared strategies for studying for the next test. I worked at it; it was like learning a foreign language (something I could do, incidentally, which was perhaps helpful). I was slow at processing. I took the next test and got a 62. The professor called me into his office. "Amazing," he said. "You're learning." I was disappointed and replied that I still had a failing cumulative average and really didn't like the idea of an F on my transcript. In retrospective, I was focused on all the wrong things—grades, grades, and grades.

He suggested I continue working at it, with his help, and not withdraw—yet. I studied hard; I reflected differently on the material. I tried to see trends and themes. I tried to understand why things in biology worked as they did. On the next test, I got a 76. The professor was ecstatic. He arranged a meeting in his office and expressed admiration for the progress I had made. "You are getting it," he remarked. "Look how far you've progressed." Yes, I admitted but observed that my average score was still an F or perhaps a D-. I suggested yet again that I withdraw from the course—even if it meant having the notation WD (withdrawn) on my transcript, given that the time for a no-notation withdrawal had passed.

That's when the professor did something totally unconventional. "The final exam is cumulative," he observed. "If you can get into the 90s," he said, "I'll give you a B in the course; I don't care what the numbers add up to. I'll know that you've learned and you can do this." I'm still not sure why I believed this professor. Yes, I had gone from a 42 to a 62 to a 76. Getting to a 92 did not seem that impossible. Hey, I had gotten this far, and the professor believed I could do it. His point was clear: It's not that you can't do this; it's that you hadn't yet learned how to do it.

I studied. I studied more. I studied differently. I had friends test me on facts. I had other friends listen as I explained biological systems with a newfound precision. I made note cards and flashcards; I studied images of bacteria and birds and bodies. And I got a grade in the low 90s. And true to his word, the professor gave me a B. It was hard earned. And it was the best B I had ever received and better than any that would come later. And my appreciation for scientific methodology grew from that day forward.

If self-esteem hinges on building up a student's capacities (rather than critiquing what students cannot do), why not have students at least initially engage in topics and use skills in which they excel? Instead of directing students to do more of what they cannot do, why not give them extra time to do what they can do and let them have the joy and pleasure of doing something they can see and experience and feel success in?

This works across the educational pipeline. There are young students whose handwriting and fine motor skills are weak. Often we have them practice more and more, as if these exercises and homework will produce improvement. And, yes, the repetition may help some, but if the issue is maturation and development, force-feeding will not help much. These students know they are struggling. They can see that others can write clearly and neatly. Why keep reinforcing what they cannot do? It's that "adversity will be good for you" mentality. Just put your mind to it and do it. Toughen up. This is, at least for me, part of the downside or underbelly of growth mindsets; there is a built-in presumption that with the right effort—well directed by a teacher—everyone can "get it," whatever the "it" is.[4]

What if we identified what these breakaway kids could do well, now? Is it reading? Is it building with blocks? Is it playing music or working out math problems? Is it telling stories or drawing? Is it dancing or shooting hoops? Is it telling jokes? It should be possible to identify student strengths, even nontraditional ones. And when we discover what those skills are, what if we asked these students to exercise these skills more and more and more? Have them read to preschoolers. Have them illustrate stories or build a set for a class play—perhaps even a play performed by older students. Have them make music that can be recorded or a dance that can be videotaped and shared. Have them teach their peers how to rap or do spoken word poetry.

Ponder this possibility (based on an actual pilot project with this very feature): Picture an elementary school with many breakaway kids doing activities that could be posted on the website of a particular published children's book (author willingness assumed, of course). The postings could include student-written book reviews, drawings, music, and videos. The students could even work on ideas for a sequel to the published book (once they understood what a sequel was) and share it with the author. They could create a puppet show. They could meet with students from a different nation via Skype or video to talk about the story and compose a song with instruments of all sorts, showcasing both the diversity and similarities in music. They could engage with younger grades, reading the story to them or sharing the puppet show. And what if the students were asked to design the activities they wanted to do with the book, brainstorming with teachers and the principal and perhaps even the author? The students could choose which of the many possible activities they wanted to pursue, playing off their interests and strengths. Without knowing it, they would actually be preparing for their transition to middle school and beyond: planning, researching, engaging. Here's the point: In this pilot, we would be encouraging success, showcasing success and keying off student strengths, not weaknesses.[5]

As important as it may be to practice what one cannot do, athletes, dancers, and musicians regularly practice what they do well—reinforcing their strengths. Gymnasts practice routines they know and like. Tennis players repeat successful swings so they become a part of their repertoire. Researchers keep plumbing the depths of the library stacks or the Internet to find information for their work.

Some teachers expressly set aside time each day (or week) for students to work on things of the students' own choosing—things at which they excel. How powerful, how empowering, how important for building capacity. This is often, and not without intention, called Genius Hour. It is actually a notion used by Google to energize their workforce (other companies do it too); each employee is allowed to work on a project of his or her own choosing for a certain number of hours a week.[6]

In developing a sense of self, two more established strategies can work—and both tie into reciprocity. First, teachers need to listen carefully to what their students are doing and saying and feeling. Teachers need to read body language. They can offer assistance: "Can I help you?" They can ask, "Are you doing okay?" And when the student says, "I'm fine," teachers have to gauge whether that response is genuine. "I'm fine" can mean I'm miserable.

Second, teachers need to develop group projects that call for different skill sets for the project to work effectively. That way, students with many different strengths can work together and see each other's skills and notice that some kids do some things better than others (yes, there are always kids who can do everything well and students who struggle with everything).

In this context, think about what has become known as the marshmallow game. The idea here is to give students spaghetti (yes, again; see Chapter 8) and a marshmallow and some tape. The goal is to see which group can build the tallest freestanding tower with an uneaten marshmallow on the top. (Of course, it makes sense among younger kids to make sure to have extra marshmallows for them to eat.) Watch how different groups approach the task. Look at how many different structures are created. Consider the possibility that there are many ways to get to success. See how students engage with each other—the students with the best construction (fine motor) skills can work with those with untamed imagination. Some can write the approach. Others can draw the design. Some can videotape the process or photograph the final project.[7]

It is hard to succeed in any arena in life if one is lacking belief in self. Sadly, by the time many breakaway kids get to school and later college, success has been drummed out of their heads and inadequacy has been drummed into their heads to make them feel that they are not made of the right stuff. Through teachers or family members or peers, they sense that they are not going to be able to do what they need to do to succeed. Indeed, many first-generation students who head off to college have this fear, even if they have been selected to attend an "elite" college. They think: Maybe this acceptance letter came by mistake. Maybe I cannot do this. Maybe I would be better if I stayed home and went to a local college. Maybe they will see beneath the surface and realize I really cannot do this. Maybe I made the wrong decision by choosing to attend this college far from home.[8]

Role models can help—particularly when these are older students who have "been there" and can speak to the need to take a risk, to step off the diving board. Those older peer mentors can verify that the feelings these younger students are experiencing are real but they are passing. If one can ride out the storm of newness and arrive at the other end, one can reflect back with pride. It helps enormously if one has regular contact with peer mentors. Think about *The Pact*, a book that describes how three friends pushed themselves and each other to make it through college and then medical and dental school. The bumps along the way were real but all three ultimately succeeded—in large part because when one of them lacked self-belief and strayed off the path, threatening the pact, the other two were there to provide scaffolding.[9]

As educators we have much to learn about how to build self-esteem. I remember a common strategy employed by law professors (myself included) to help students improve their grades on a go-forward basis. We'd show the students with low grades an A paper and ask if they could identify the differences between their test and the A test. What should not have come as a shock, but it did, was that this approach did not work: The students with the low grade could not pick up the differences—at least not in a meaningful way. In part, that was because if they could, they would have done what the A test exhibited. And many of the students with low grades thought—seriously thought—they had done what the student with the A test had done. (Forgot too that law school courses usually have only one exam at the end of the semester, one shot to get it right or wrong and no opportunities for improvement. Yes, a deeply flawed approach but a topic for another day.)

So instead of reading an A paper—which is humiliating, by the way, even if the A student's name is redacted—I started something different. I offered to meet with any student with a grade of C- or below. When I met with such a student, I would ask the student to explain verbally what he or she was trying to say in response to the posed hypothetical. Most often what such students thought they said and what they actually did say did not match. They knew the material vastly better than had been exhibited on the exam and better than I had imagined when reading what they wrote. I reminded them that the only tool I had to measure what they knew was what appeared in writing on the paper. If they knew the material but did not express that they knew it, the grade could not reflect that knowledge. Here's what I did: After talking through one of the questions, I suggested that students rewrite the answer and I would grade it again and we could meet again to measure progress. (The new grade did not change anything on a student's transcript—another flaw in legal education.) Not many students took me up on this; it was a time-consuming process, and some figured out how to get better at law school exams just by practicing and developing a better sense of what professors were looking for in the answers.

But I remember one student who started with a D in the first semester of a yearlong contracts course. His other grades also were low. I tried the process described above, and he worked with me, and at the end of the second semester, his grade for the second part of the course was a C+. A real improvement. But the student was not satisfied. He took another of my courses after we continued to work together and he got a B (totally different subject matter, although thinking "legally" is transportable and can cross subject matter, to be sure). His overall grades were improving. He got my message: It's not that you can't do it; it's that you haven't learned how to do this task, and it is teachable and learnable (as I had learned from Biology 101 decades before).

I then suggested that I thought he had "got it," and I respected all the hard work he had committed to. He said, without a pause, "I'm not done yet. I won't stop until I get an A in one of your classes." With more work and more time, he did just that. And the part that still makes me smile is that in his 3rd (final) year of law school, he took one more course with me—his fourth. He got an A-. He stormed into my office, mad as all get-out, wondering what he had missed. An A- was not good enough. I tried to remind the student of where we had started. He did then remember but insisted that I explain why this paper was not good enough for an A and how he could have improved. Saying there were very few straight A's awarded was not a sufficient response.

Some part of belief in self is, of course, internal. But here's the key point in the context of lasticity: Institutions and those within them can create an environment in which students can come to believe in themselves and understand their enormous, though different, strengths.

Lasticity's building blocks depend not just on pouring qualities into a student. Not at all. Rather, lasticity requires that institutions know their students and help them through that understanding to grow and flourish. That requires reciprocity and a deep commitment to helping students believe in themselves.

Some students are just lastic. Others can develop lasticity. However acquired, lasticity is an umbrella "entity" into which some of our best existing student support efforts can fall. The term explains in a fulsome and systematic way how we can help breakaway students across their long educational and personal journeys. And the existence of the larger conceptual umbrella can inform us in how to improve our educational system and narrow the achievement gaps in meaningful and timely ways.

How lasticity works in the real world—with all its building blocks—is the topic to which we now turn. We can breathe life into the concept and test out its veracity and durability. We can see if it can withstand the pressures of the real world and the real students we are now serving. That is no small challenge.

Chapter 11

Animating Lasticity
on a College Campus

Lasticity's foundational conditions—elasticity, plasticity, pivoting right, reciprocity, and belief in self—now need to be animated. But before addressing how to activate or meet these conditions for the benefit of breakaway students, here's a mini-reminder on the basics of lasticity. Lasticity is at once an outcome, a process, a goal, a trait, a characteristic, a construct, and an architecture to facilitate and foster breakaway student success. But those descriptors do not do justice to lasticity's meaning, because it is also a catalyst for culture change. Lasticity is broader than grit, resiliency, or growth mindsets, although these skills/attributes are certainly under the lasticity umbrella and help lasticity to take root. It is about self-worth but it is broader than that. It is about trust but it is more than that. Lasticity is fluid in the sense that its presence can change over time, although some aspects of it can become more durable. It can move people and institutions (and those within those institutions) from where they are to a new place—so lasticity has transportive qualities. Lasticity is also not an all-or-nothing proposition; since it is composed of conditions, the fulfillment of these conditions or the absence of their fulfillment leads to outcomes that are positive or negative or something in between. It is something that has primary applicability for individuals who have experienced toxic stress or trauma, but aspects of lasticity can most assuredly improve outcomes for other children, adults, and educational institutions.

Even understanding the basic concept of lasticity, we are left with myriad of as-yet-unanswered questions. Consider these, among others: How do we actually apply lasticity in the trenches? What turns it on and activates it, remembering there are no "lasticity switches" on our walls or in our person? How can its continuity be ensured? Can it be taught? Can it be replicated and scaled? How do we know if lasticity is even present? How can we measure the presence of lasticity, and how can we assess the effect and effectiveness of lasticity?

In a sense, the effort to wrap one's mind around lasticity reminds me of the problem of two people who speak different languages trying to communicate with each other. Speaking more loudly in one of the languages, a strategy that is often used, does not improve the level of understanding. Nor does speaking slowly. The problem is not that the person on the receiving end is deaf or mentally challenged. He or she doesn't speak a language and needs help learning the meaning of words.

One strategy for the communication barriers described here is to use visual imagery—hand signals, drawings. Many a young person traveling abroad uses a form of charades to communicate. And that approach is useful, too, in the context of lasticity where we can create a concept mobile that shows both the meaning and dynamic intersecting and interacting aspects of this term. Concept mobiles, useful educational tools more generally, visually depict in shapes, words, lines, squiggles, and connectors how a particular chosen concept operates in all its dimensions. It is a mobile that can then guide decisionmaking and strategy on a go-forward basis. To be sure, concept mobiles range in complexity but even very basic ones can be valuable learning tools, not only for visual learners but also to facilitate conceptualization. They can also inform cultural change. Concept mobiles free us from narrow definitional confines and allow us to engage with concepts in two or three dimensions.[1] Consider the concept mobile of lasticity shown in Figure 11.1.

Stated most simply, as informed and represented by the concept mobile in Figure 11.1, lasticity forces us to ask different questions, to form different relationships, to alter our cultural norms, to reflect more comprehensively on the students we teach, to abandon formerly tried and true approaches for new strategies and forms of engagement. As you reflect on the lasticity mobile, focus on the fluidity of lasticity, the myriad ways the pieces in the mobile, which represent the elements of lasticity, can engage with each other; lasticity is anything but linear. And note too that the pieces move and shift and represent growth in that they are nonstatic and ever moving, even with a wee breeze.

Constructing a culture of lasticity is also not a one-size-fits-all process. The size of the school, its location, its student population, its leadership, its teachers, and its physical plant all contribute to the many ways a culture can be developed. This is important because each institution has its own ethos that it seeks to foster and preserve. For institutions with abundant resources, the approach might be different from that of resource-starved institutions. The new cultural memes can differ.

Let me share something we did—which is not something that others will necessarily want to replicate but which showcases the ways lasticity

Figure 11.1. Lasticity concept mobile.

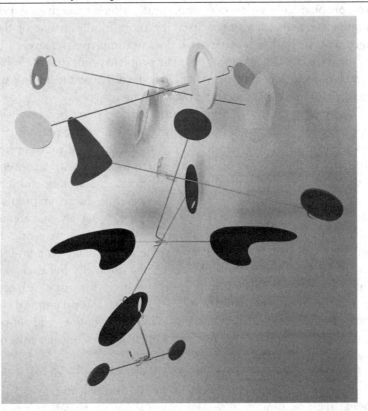

can find its place within colleges and universities. We created a piece of art that, while designed by the amazing artist Mary Corey March, was actually installed from start to finish by the faculty, staff, students, administrators, alums, and trustees. Indeed, students were involved from the get-go. The artist and students installed about 80 pegs with sayings on them that related to identity. They were informed by the artist's visits to campus and talks with campus constituencies. So these conversation points were institution, not artist, generated. These pegs said things like "I have been loved," "I am the first in my family to go to college," "I am religious," "I have been raped," "I have lost someone I loved," "I have lots of friends," "I prefer being alone," "I adore sports," "I like to draw and paint," "I often feel left out," "I usually feel a part of a group," "I have served in the military," "I have experienced illness personally," "I have lost a parent," "I have been afraid," and "I want to be a leader" (see Figure 11.2).

Figure 11.2. Detail of posts of installation art by Mary Corey March around which yarn is wound by participants.

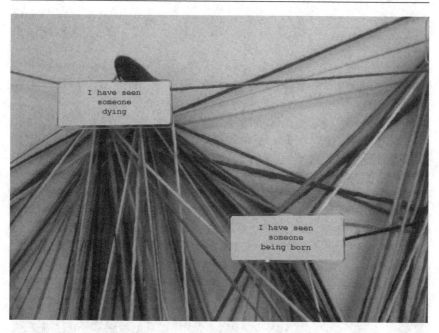

Then there were 280 different-colored balls of yarn, and each person who participated wound yarn, color by color, around the pegs that had meaning for that person. The participants wove across the pegs alone—privately. Over the course of several weeks, an astonishing tapestry was built that showcased the individuals in our community, both their remarkable diversity and their shared characteristics. What emerged was a piece of art that reflected the amazing, larger community of which we were all a part (Figure 11.3).[2]

But there was an unusual type of disclosure and reciprocity occurring through the construction of this tapestry that is central to lasticity; those who wove the yarn were disclosing personal information about themselves. And those who saw the weaving were acknowledging that information—often revelatory information. To be sure, for the audience (the institution), it was not person-specific knowledge, because one could not untangle who wrapped his or her yarn where on the tapestry. The colors were not assigned. But the work's participants knew, and the institution as a whole accepted their deep feelings; there was reciprocity.

In other words, we demonstrated lasticity. It took a risk to wind one's identity and reflect on who one is. Then it took courage to share that

Figure 11.3. Example of completed installation art by Mary Corey March with tapestry woven by institutional participants (2012).

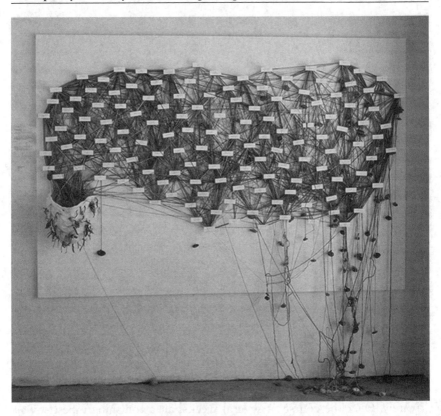

identity with others. Then it took courage to be part of a permanent piece of art reflecting your identity and the identity of the college community in which you play a part. And there were pegs that were wrapped more extensively than others, showing visually that individuals were not alone in our community. And the most frequently wrapped pegs were for "I have loved someone" and "Someone I loved died." Says a lot about the college and those within it. It informed how many of us reflected on the institution and the many challenges and capacities of our students, staff, and faculty, among others.

In short, the installation enabled the participants to exhibit lasticity's five building blocks: elasticity, plasticity, pivoting right, reciprocity, and belief in self. While the photograph of the artwork shown in Figure 11.3 gives one a sense, it hardly does justice to the process described and the piece of installation art that emerged. That is because the piece itself was a process—mimicking the process of learning and the process of growing and the process of developing lasticity.

And once was not enough for this art concept at the college! We had the same artist return to create another work, which is different in design but again involved our students and staff, for a new admissions building that was opening. The repeated use of yarn was intentional—to link this new building, which was located on the lower campus, to the upper campus, where the first tapestry hangs. It was to create a sense of community despite physical distance.

The new piece was installed in a corner where two 3-foot walls met. On the left wall were round pegs with sayings grounded in what new students, particularly first-generation students, might be thinking as they visited a campus. These were inspired by what the artist learned from talking to our students and to our admissions staff. The pegs had items like "I am excited," "I am not sure college is right for me," "This is the first college I have visited," "I like rural environments," "It took 4 hours to get here," "It took 30 minutes to get here," "I know what I want to major in," "I have no idea what I want to study," "I want to play on a DIII athletic team," "I don't like sports," "I wonder where my roommate will be from," "I think I'll be homesick," and "I am ready to leave home" (Figure 11.4).

Again, you get the idea. We tried to tap into what breakaway students (and other students) might be feeling as they approached the college process and visited a campus. It was making silently held feelings visible and, in another positive, it gave prospective students—whether they arrived alone or with friends and family—the chance to be engaged. Literally. It was and remains a tension-cutting device.

Then on the other adjacent wall (where the corner was formed) there were statements of what the students' goals are: "I want to help others," "I want to be a nurse," "I want to go into business," "I want to be an athlete," "I want to earn enough money to support my family," "I want to major in biology," "I want to major in everything," "I want to live in a city," "I want to get married," "I want to be single for years," "I want to find a way to participate in politics," "I like helping children," "I want to find a mentor," "I want to graduate," "I don't want bad grades."

Then, as with the first piece of art, new prospective students took a ball of yarn and wrapped it around the pegs on the left side of the wall. They then took their yarn around stone cairns at the base of the corner, stones that resembled the abundant stonework at the college, and then wrapped the yarn around the posts with their goals and dreams. The goal was to show progression from applicant to graduate. The remaining

Figure 11.4. Installation art by Mary Corey March at Southern Vermont College (2014).

ball of yarn was tossed upward into a large net, as if one were launching one's college career.

Here's the point: College admissions tours and visits tend to be cookie-cutter events for those who are privileged to visit more than one institution (meaning, fit is easier to identify for some than others). Student guides—carefully selected and trained—take students on campus tours that are often superficial. A tour is difficult to do with 20 people, let alone 40. In the admissions office, there can be group sessions where an admissions officer explains the process of applying and key features of the school. Pretty pat, if you ask me. Where are the real people? The professors, the coaches, the students who have not been carefully vetted and wear uniforms?

In an illustration of this question, a high school senior named Simon Kuh (visiting apparently elite colleges), in addressing the weaknesses of campus visits, remarked, "As much as colleges want to find the students best suited to them, I want to find the perfect college for me. Every prospective student deserves an info session that delivers more than basic facts and a tour that provides a true feel for campus life. I want to see the real you, colleges, just as you want to see the real me."[3]

To return to the installation art, after admissions season (April), when students graduated, they could return to the admissions office and unwind the yarn in the artwork and ready it for the next group of prospective students. This act is the visual and actual representation of moving on and reflecting on where one has been and where one is going and leaving fertile soil for those who follow in one's tracks. Indeed, and significantly, this unraveling stood intentionally in contrast to the tapestry up at the college's main building, a work that is a permanent installation. In terms of the second installation, the dismantling had several levels of meaning for graduates. It says, I have made it. My ball of yarn is launched. I can share my success with prospective students and ready the campus for them—I know how they feel. I was there.

So this second piece demonstrated lasticity but also, importantly, signaled institutional culture. There was overt recognition that admissions visits are stressful for most students and their families. For breakaway students, such visits are fraught with difficulty—they might be there without a parent. Perhaps they are there with a sibling or a grandmother. They are anxious, and they have traveled some distance. They are in a room with other students who are also applying, and that feels like "competition" and forces up such questions as, Do I look like them? Do I like the way they look? and How do I look? Students fantasize about who will get in and who will be rejected, about which students they might see come fall if they were accepted and decided to enroll. The installation art here is designed to give prospective students a way to engage—within themselves and with others. It separates them from their families, not in distance, but in their thoughts. It encourages sharing and self-reflection.

But it also enables the institution to speak: The institution enabled the artwork to happen; it acknowledges the feeling new students may have and accepts them. The art itself is revelatory, and the institution embraces those revelations as a collective. That enables each student to see him- or herself as part of the whole, having shared in a safe way some difficult thoughts and upcoming choices and experiences.

In a strange way, the installation art at the college resembles the concept mobile described above (see Figure 11.1). The mobile and the installation art show how a group of ideas or feelings or experiences get expressed and how they connect us to each other while preserving and recognizing who we are and from whence we came. Lasticity—visually and viscerally.

Two further approaches for encouraging and fostering lasticity are the use of new symbols (which is a double-edged sword, as we will see) and collectively written publications. The idea of using symbols to send a message is by no means new in American culture. Engagement rings are a symbolic gift, representing love and a promised future. Corporations employ symbols to showcase their values and often their roots, sending a message (often without conscious customer awareness) about their brand. (We will return to this in Chapter 12.) And symbols can work on many levels—there can be symbols within symbols, and they can appeal to one's culture or gender or ethnicity.[4]

Reflect on the symbol of the Olympics—the intertwined rings that symbolize five different continents coming together to celebrate a shared enterprise. With the five different colors of the Olympic rings and the white background, at least one color of every nation's flag is represented.[5] Symbols are a valuable pathway for animating and sustaining lasticity, in part because they are understandable and move us away from one-off actions or activities. Folks in athletics already use this approach. They have trophies and banners and plaques. They have T-shirts and other memorabilia. They encourage cheering and community engagement. They create pride. Are coaches developing at least aspects of lasticity? The answer is some are and some aren't. Some encourage and foster not only athletic skills but also personal growth. Sadly, others tear students down as a precursor to building them up. (We can leave for another time the National Collegiate Athletic Association's approach to coaches who have been known to abuse players and yet are free to move from institution to institution.)

Symbols are a tangible way of giving students, faculty, and staff (and alums and trustees too) evidence of a lastic culture. The giving can be figurative, literal, or both. The cookies referenced earlier in the book are an example (see Chapter 4). Symbol gifts, literally and figuratively. Two other items, also mentioned earlier, are yet further examples: the Kimochis (see Chapter 5) and the books that were given out at the start and end of school (see Chapter 9).

A powerful orientation activity took place at Clemson University in August 2015 that involved forming the outline of an enormous tiger paw (the institution's emblem) and filling its shape with entering students. Here's how it worked: New students filled in the gigantic paw shape set out by older students (band members) on the football field, and it was all beautifully recorded on video. When Clemson students saw that video, I suspect, it helped them feel that they were part of a community. They saw the paw image being formed and filled, just as the institution planned to help them be formed and filled personally and intellectually. This is an activity suited for large campuses with thousands of incoming students.[6]

One year, when we were growing too fast at Southern Vermont College, leading to crowded classrooms and a lack of parking, among other consequences, I gave every member of the faculty and staff a bamboo shoot (I paid for them myself, importantly). Bamboo is the fastest-growing tree and also the strongest. I shared those facts and then I attached a note to each shoot: "Come Grow with Us." Another year, worried about the high level of change the board and I perceived was needed, I bought many books on change and change management and placed them throughout the campus. Then I gave each professor and staff member a "decision maker," the executive toy that spins and lands on a stop that says: "yes," "no," "maybe," "never," or "forget it." And I wrote everyone a note saying, "We'll be making lots of changes, and that means lots of decisions. Help me make those decisions."

And on my desk was a sign that read, "Work with Me, People."

In short, symbols speak volumes through tiny sounds.

We can also change pedagogy in ways that demonstrate a deep belief in student capacity and institutional commitment to larger social issues. We usually ask students to deliver finished work—a report, an exam, research outcomes, solutions to math problems—to a teacher or professor. It is work the educator has asked for, usually on a deadline, which is then worked on and delivered back to the educator—showing completion. Then the educator evaluates the quality of what he or she receives. Rarely do students design the tests or paper topics on their own. To be sure, there are some professors who approve research paper topics and some educators who let students write creatively, even without a prompt. There are even professors who let students write their own exam questions, which students then need to answer.

But the more usual approach is for teachers to ask students to perform a quite specific task: Identify one of Milton's epic similes and analyze its meaning. Or examine the reasons for World War I and assess whether in retrospect this war had achieved the outcomes desired by the countries fighting it.

I believe we can rethink writing and research and its traditional assignment flow (teacher–student–teacher) and, instead, create an environment where students and teachers are working together and writing together and producing a shared product. Reflect on two examples.

A group of students at Bennington College and I worked on a problem in higher education as a class project: how to get more breakaway students to attend college, most particularly historically black colleges and universities (HBCUs). HBCUs are institutions that can serve these students well, but many prospective students are not being directed toward them. After our reading and research and interviews and intense dialogue, here was the result: a four-part blog series that has been published in *MSI Unplugged* (an online publication of the Penn Center for MSIs [minority-serving institutions]) with the students' names and bios prominently featured in the byline (along with mine). The students engaged with a professor and created—together—a product that reflects in a lasting way their efforts to improve the world in which we live. Collaboration, an absence of entrenched hierarchy of students and faculty, the valuing of youthful voices, guided research and exploration with room for mistakes, risk taking—these are some of the factors that enabled the students to grow and flourish in that class. In addition to learning about HBCUs and higher education, they learned about teamwork and collaboration. They critiqued my work and I critiqued theirs and they critiqued each other's. Not bad workplace skills—in the context of a liberal arts institution.[7]

These examples of animating lasticity may strike some as resoundingly impossible on a large campus with thousands of students. That is true—at least for some of the examples. The Clemson paw is a notable exception. The installation tapestry described above, with its 280 balls of yarn (see Figure 11.3), would not lead to the participation of even a small percentage of faculty, staff, students, alums, donors, or trustees on a state university campus. A president's paying for and providing symbols across an institution for all faculty, staff, and coaches would be prohibitively expensive, even if it were limited to those engaged in undergraduate education. Kimochis are not manufactured in the tens of thousands, leaving aside expense for a moment. The student–faculty undergraduate coauthorship suggestions might be workable, but many institutions would never be able to muster sufficient faculty for the needed small classes to give this approach universality.

There are, however, other ways that lasticity can be animated, replicated, and scaled on large campuses, and it is to those issues that we now turn our attention.

Chapter 12

Lasticity Goes Big

Lasticity's reach matters. If it can be deployed in only small liberal arts colleges or smaller educational systems along the pre-K–12 educational pipeline, then our efforts to reach and enable the success of millions of breakaway kids will be thwarted. As so aptly supported by data in the collection of essays titled *Our Compelling Interests: The Value of Diversity for Democracy and a Prosperous Society*, breakaway kids are not going away; they are increasing in number. But, as *Our Compelling Interests* rightly cautions, "We recognize the tension between what is professed and what is experienced. In principle, a society can profess a belief in the value of diversity and in practice limit the benefits of its application (whether through political attacks, legal battles, or social worries) to a small community of participants. . . . For this nation, and our world, diversity must be valued, defined and leveraged."[1]

This chapter seeks to demonstrate, as have some earlier examples, such as the Clemson paw described in Chapter 11 or the signed welcome flags discussed in Chapter 9, how lasticity can be introduced in and leveraged for the benefit of larger academic institutions. To that end, and with an approach that is anathema to many in academia, I want to begin by looking at how corporate America establishes culture and how various successful companies have created amazing working environments for their employees and equally good customer service for those who purchase and use their products and services.

I am aware that this is a risky approach and corporate analogies don't suit many academics; I know that both intellectually and from personal experience. Many decades ago, the then dean of the law school where I taught foresaw the shaky foundation on which legal education rested and the vulnerability of law schools. He was extremely prescient; his statements preceded reality by a couple of decades. In anticipation of the challenges to law schools, he invited in a team of corporate marketing specialists who talk to faculty and staff about customer service, namely, how we treated our law students. Attendance was mandatory (at least as mandatory as things can be in a law school). It happens that I had just attended a legal conference where representatives of the Walt Disney Company came and shared how they had developed their culture and customer service ethos. The audience was mostly lawyers, and the effort was directed at how to improve law firms and ways in which they serviced clients in a competitive environment. It cost many thousands of dollars to get the Disney folks to present (no shock there), and I was enthralled. These people had a formula, and it worked; it was well reasoned and was quite startling in its profound understanding of human nature and consumption.

So I was eager to hear the law school consultants, unlike my colleagues. And to be fair, the group started out their presentation with this (or a very similar) first sentence: "Hello, we are here, at the invitation of your dean, to share how customer service at this law school can be improved."

Well, just that sentence set people off—how dare we speak about "customer service" in the context of students? What are we, "hired service providers"? Folks did a combination of things: Some walked out, some snickered under their breath to the person sitting next to them (disruptive for sure), and in typical law school tradition, some chimed up and asked pointed (some might say impolite) questions such as "Why exactly does customer service in the corporate world have anything to do with academia and what is your experience as consultants in the academic environment?" Things went downhill from there. The presentation was a fiasco, and the "customer ethos" conversation ended before it had begun.

It's true that times have changed and folks within and outside academic see the "business" nature of education, a point brought home by the fiscal vulnerability of some higher education institutions and the growing costs to and accompanying debt of students enrolled in college. But the effort to translate corporate principles into academia has rightly not always been met with glee or even success. An influx of academic leaders drawn from the corporate and political worlds who have simply misunderstood academic culture has not helped. Think about Mount St. Mary's and their president's observation that "his" institution, to improve retention and graduation rates, needed to simply drown the early failing 1st-year students like bunnies or put a Glock to their heads. Perhaps it was British humor gone awry but out that president went—a tad too slowly for some of us.[2]

However, here's what is valuable to consider: Large corporations—with thousands of employees and many thousands of customers—have been able to establish or even change their cultures. They have become successful because their culture attracts and retains both employees and customers. They go about this in different ways, depending on the company's particular bent or product or attitude. I am sure certain names of companies that have accomplished this easily pop into the heads of readers. Much ink has been spilled over the approaches of some of them: Google, Southwest Airlines, Zappos, REI.[3]

There being no single recipe for success means that different strategies have worked, and here are some: free food; free classes, including yoga; free trips and retreats to glorious places; group excursions and community-building activities like building race cars and then racing them. (The Coca-Cola Company has done that; I know because I was there to witness it.) Some have shared work clothing; some work on shared community service projects; all understand the goals, aims, and purposes of their employer; and the central corporate values are repeated again and again. Many tell their own story—their own company's story from its birth. Many of these companies that meet with cultural success make cultural fit central to hiring decisions, and some even offer a financial incentive for a new employee to quit if they do not sense a quality fit within the first few weeks.

There is one aspect shared by most of these approaches: They cost money, and not a small amount. To be sure, in a corporate context, the return on investment is good. If you can get quality employees who stay, that helps the bottom line because losing employees and hiring new ones is expensive, and retaining customers is key to making a profit.

In the academic context, particularly in today's fiscal environment, expenditures of this sort are a serious no-go. For starters, except at the most elite institutions, there is simply not enough money to allow such items, which may appear frivolous or unnecessary at best. And at wealthy institutions, they may not be a priority—although the benefit packages for some employees at elite colleges are very sweet indeed. Further, academics aren't necessarily enamored with what appeals to corporate types—building motorcycles and racing cars may not do it for the neurobiologist (although we might be surprised, for sure).

What follows are possible ways to make campuses more lastic, without breaking the bank or bending academic culture too far. One caveat: I am keenly aware that identifying some options for developing lasticity across large institutions may limit and impede rather than encourage others to use their own imagination and institutional strengths to build lasticity. However, I think the risk is worth it because seeing and considering concrete examples helps anchor lasticity and fosters its potential adoption. Add to that that there are instances of lasticity occurring on campuses across the nation but they have not been identified as such. Those are worth identifying—out loud. And there may be things we are doing on our campuses that if slightly changed could promote lasticity overtly. Finally, there may be things that we are doing or that exist on campus (whether on the part of individuals or through symbols and traditions and existing norms) that undercut lasticity; these are worth identifying and addressing too. (Think images in stained-glass windows of slaves and buildings named after slave owners.)[4]

Let's start with hiring; as corporate America and Jack Welch have noted ad nauseam, it's who's on the bus that matters. We assume that most campus hiring committees are, even if not explicitly, looking for a "fit" when they suggest particular hires, whether for faculty or staff. We surely know or can sense that the culture at the State University of New York, Purchase, is not the same as the culture at the University of Nevada, Las Vegas. The culture at the Massachusetts Institute of Technology is not the same as the culture at the University of North Carolina. These aren't value judgments about which culture is better; it is to say that a prospective faculty or staff member might feel more comfortable and fit in better at one institution than at another. Corporate hiring is very explicit about fit in some instances. One impressive and successful CEO I knew told me that he met every *potential* hire personally (in a large company) because he wanted to get a sense of fit and wanted the person to see him and how he operated. After a visit to Southern Vermont College, he suggested that I do the same; even in a small institution, however, it turned out to be impossible for me to meet every job candidate, and in most instances I wanted to empower those making the choices rather than asserting my own and assuming—rightly I think—that they were keenly aware of our Southern Vermont campus culture.[5]

But in addition to being more overt in articulating what would be a good fit within our particular academic institutional culture, why don't we do a better job of orienting new faculty and staff—on the topic of values and norms and goals? I am struck by what we don't do to orient new people to campuses (faculty and staff, not students, although comparisons with student orientation may be beneficial). We teach folks how to gain access to technology generally and how (and which) course management systems are used. We show people to their offices and provide some basic supplies. We walk with them to key offices to meet key personnel. We may hold an info session with all new employees (segregated by faculty and staff) at the start of a semester. And, then, basically, we hand over swipe cards, make necessary IDs and parking permits, get signatures on copious paperwork, and say, "Bonne chance." We hope their department chairs and deans will finish off or perhaps continue the orientation.

What a lost opportunity! Surely we could do better, even in group orientation sessions for new faculty and staff. Do we give newly hired individuals anything that has meaning to the institution? A bumper sticker? A T-shirt? A keychain with the institution's name emblazoned on it? What is on their desks when they arrive? Is there a small card with the institution's mission or its key values written on it? Do we give them a voucher for the student dining halls or campus cafés? Do we invite new hires to the president's house (or the dean's) for a reception? Do we share with them some of the institution's remarkable history? Do we tell stories about the institution—those that are funny and those that are endearing and those with significance? Do we share how the institution got its name or its nickname or its mascot? Do we point out key buildings or art or space on a campus that has particular meaning?

In sum, I think we sell our institutions short; for the most part we don't tell our story to those we hire. And by not doing so, we neglect to create cultural buy-in that then can be shared with current and prospective students. We can't ask folks to be reciprocal if they don't get what their side of the equation is all about. If we want students to feel comfortable in a new setting, it seems to me, we need to make sure that our employees—our faculty and staff—are comfortable and welcomed and "in the groove," to use a dated term. (Why don't we display messages in campus transportation systems as happens with public buses on city streets?) In reflecting on this, I can't recall a single institution where I was a faculty member or leader where a quality orientation for faculty or staff occurred, with one notable exception: when I served as a visiting faculty member at Bennington College (an institution that I actually knew quite well from having been president of Southern Vermont College, which is in the same town, and knowing and conversing regularly with Bennington's former, long-serving president Elizabeth Coleman.) They went out of their way to make sure I "got" their institution, their culture, their students. And they worked to ensure I didn't forget, either; I got reminders of events; I got free meals in the dining halls; I had ways to ask questions and got rapid responses. Pretty impressive.

Next, what if we thought about a valuable commodity, such as time, and how we could use it more effectively to message our culture, our reciprocity, our ethos, our belief in self, our level of interest and engagement, our understanding of our students and their needs? When I was at Smith, I was struck by Mountain Day, when, unannounced, the bells would ring and students could take the day off to meander around the beautiful Northampton hills. Okay, the idea didn't quite work. Folks figured out when it would be and left campus ahead of time to visit family or friends at other colleges. Some folks stayed in their rooms and studied (yes, that was me). Some students did enjoy the foliage, but where were the faculty and staff? At the University of Chicago, in February, as I recall, there was simply a day when all classes stopped. We jokingly (and it is not funny) called it Suicide Prevention Day (given the amount of work in class and the darkness, cold, and wind of winter in Chicago). What exactly did faculty and staff do on that day?[6]

What if instead of repeating these efforts, we tweaked them and had a day—a surprise day—when all faculty, staff, and students would engage in a shared enterprise? Imagine a community service project in which people would build a Habitat for Humanity home in town. Or consider farming out teams of faculty, staff, and students to visit nursing homes, assisted living centers, homeless shelters, and food pantries—all together, across disciplines, across "rank." I had even considered a "ski day" where we transported everyone (and I mean everyone—skiers or not) to a local ski area.

Or instead of having everyone head off campus, what if there were a set of unexpected activities on campus that day? Unusual and fun activities that created pride and community and a sense of commitment among the campus constituencies? How about bringing in tap dancing (inviting Michelle Dorrance, for instance)? Bowling teams with prizes? Group readings of a book whereby students, faculty, and staff each read a paragraph and it continued for hours?

What if in the week prior to exams, there was a midnight breakfast in all the dining halls and faculty and staff cooked and served? Imagine the reaction of students when a Nobel Prize winner handed out cinnamon buns and the head football and basketball coaches flipped pancakes and the English literature professor cooked bacon. Consider how this type of event would change the engagement between faculty, staff, and students. Seeing your organic chemistry professor wearing a kitchen apron instead of a lab coat or your Latin professor clearing tables sends messages— about lasticity—caring, reciprocity, role modeling, belief in self, engagement, candor, transparency.

One final idea: contests or challenges. The federal government has used contests to solve problems that plague government and our nation. Okay—I get that this hasn't worked visibly enough or optimally to solve all that ails us, but look at the website Challenge.gov. Here's how it works: In a competition format, individuals and groups submit proposals to address or solve a pre-identified problem or issue or concern. Winners are selected and receive financial rewards and, most important, their solutions are implemented and advanced.[7]

What if large, and small, campuses did this for problems both large and small that seem difficult, if not intractable, on campus? Theft of student property such as computers or bicycles. Weak transportation systems on and off campus. Poor communication of information across campus (why not use information tents on dining hall tables and streaming across screens on campus?). Absence of understanding of an institution's history and story and alums. Dealing with suboptimal or controversial art and images of old White men and stained-glass windows with images of slave traders or religious events with sacrifices of animals and humans. The list is endless.

Why not get teams of students or teams of students with faculty and staff to solve these problems? Many are problems on which an institution is already spending time and money and for which it is hiring consultants. It actually would be cost saving to create a challenge across campus with a sizable enough reward that would make a difference in the winner's life (or winners' lives). An amount of $10,000 or $15,000 would do it. And by the by, for participating students, what a way to showcase skills that are transportable to the workplace: teamwork, creativity, problem solving, prioritization, respect. Imagine the pride one would feel if one's ideas were adopted to improve the lives of others on campus. Imagine if the teams were cross-disciplinary as well as cross-status. This would be good for one's résumé too, as participation exhibits important workplace skillsets.

To be sure, all these suggestions need to be grounded and their underlying values identified. Lasticity necessitates—demands, even—a reciprocal, engaged, caring, respectful culture. It begs us to welcome others into the fold and enable them to use their talents and bring their best selves to the table. It takes people from where they are and moves them to places they might not have imagined—and they are not traveling alone; they are traveling with fellow students, faculty, staff, coaches, and administrators. They are making the path, to paraphrase Antonio Machado from Chapter 5.

I get that there will not be 100% buy-in on any campus—large or small. I get that for some faculty, staff, and coaches, autonomy trumps and there is no way on God's green earth that they will serve bacon or flip pancakes or hammer nails with students. Nor will they use any sudden unexpected and welcome free time to engage with others; they will pursue their own interests and their own research projects and their own agendas. I understand all that. And we reward that currently on campuses in how we decide issues of tenure and raises and rewards and movement up the academic ladder.

But I actually think that Malcolm Gladwell has it right: There is a tipping point.[8] There is a moment in time when things do shift, when efforts are rewarded, when changes happen. Call it optimistic. Call it hopeful. Call it audacious. That's fine. But I think on this we can all agree: We can and need to do better in serving our breakaway students. We don't just want them to succeed; as noted at the start of this chapter, we *need* for them to succeed.

There are hurdles in implementing lasticity to be sure. Note the story in Chapter 9. High hurdles. And it is to these hurdles that we now turn.

CHAPTER 13

Lasticity's Hurdles and How to Surmount Them

Implementing the multidimensional aspects of lasticity is no small task. The challenges are of different kinds, some more difficult to surmount than others. In a sense, there are macro and micro challenges, to play off economic language. We need to overcome both macro and micro impediments, but they do not necessarily operate at the same speed; nor are the same skill sets and approaches implicated.

MACRO CHALLENGES

To get a concrete sense of the complexity of implementing lasticity—remembering that it cuts across individuals, institutions along the educational pipeline, and cultural norms—the 2016 Summer Olympics in an odd way gives us some insights. Willingly suspend belief for a minute and suppose that the challenges take a human form and are represented by an athlete who had to compete in five distinct specific events (paralleling the five building blocks of lasticity): the 100-meter dash, the 26-mile marathon, the hurdles, the pole jump, and the long jump. These events are obviously not usually combined, even for decathletes and triathletes.

Each of these events uses different muscle groups and represents a different mental orientation and strategy to garner success. Each requires training and a coach; success rarely if ever comes without a support team. The dash uses twitch muscles, and the race is almost over before it begins. Bursts of speed and intense focus are needed; even the turn of a head can cost precious half seconds. In contrast, the marathon requires endurance and decisionmaking every step of the way in terms of speed, positioning, and an awareness of one's competition. Hurdling involves getting over 42-inch barriers along a course, with the athletes trying to curb the disruption between hurdles to save time. Speed, balance in the face of asymmetric movement, and multitasking are key skills. The pole vault, with its bendable composite pole, requires athletes to harness horizontal speed into vertical lift, body awareness in space, and flexibility; it takes an appreciation for the risk or thrill of flying over a pre-set and ever rising bar. The long jump demands that athletes self-propel, using speed, power, and agility. It is easy to commit a foul, to step over some predefined boundary. Can one see elasticity, plasticity, pivoting right, reciprocity, and self-belief embedded in these skills? They are also the skills needed to enable sustainable change.

Start with the realization, to repeat earlier observations in this book, that change is difficult, even for those who want it. Those old slippers feel mighty comfortable if one is about to turn them in for new ones. The closer change gets, the bigger and riskier it feels. For educators, lasticity's implementation involves numerous changes in and outside the classroom, in and outside their institution, in and out of other institutions with which they have not previously engaged. Unions may not be too pleased with the added or changed responsibilities of those within educational institutions, including in the expanded recognition that many people's titles currently do not label them as educators—but lasticity acknowledges that they are performing (or should be performing) that critically important role.

There is a rich literature in how to make change—in business, in our personal lives, in medicine, in education. There is no one easy pathway to change. Change is not linear. For every step or two forward, we hit an unexpected issue or challenge and may even slide back a step. Or we may struggle to see progress and get frustrated, given the seeming gap between where we need to go and where we are.

There is no magic to making change happen. Desired change is easier than mandated change. Helping people appreciate the need for, the value of, and the personal benefits of change are helpful. So is transparency. For me, there is this realization: Doing nothing is making a decision; nothingness is not cost free. So as hard as change is, the price of no change may be even bigger. We use that argument in support of education: If you think education is important, reflect on the cost of ignorance. Same idea.

I also think that the phrase *the faster the better* can work effectively in the context of change—if we follow certain parameters. We should not adopt Nike's "Just Do It" slogan. I think there is value in planning for change, talking about change, reflecting on change—not forever and not for years, as is now all too common in academia. We do way better if we are as prepared as we can be for what change will be, recognizing that many aspects of change are ones for which there is no preparation. Here's why: We want change that has stickiness; for that to happen, there has to be considerable buy-in. That may take some micro steps, before macro change can occur. For those within institutions whose lives have involved frequent change in their years growing up, the challenges of change can be hard; having found stability, one finds it hard to uproot.

A second major impediment to implementing lasticity is the relatively newfound demand (and desire) for empirical data before changes are made. For many decades, we made changes and measured later, if at all. Now, at least within the realm of education, there is a push for data-informed decisionmaking, and I appreciate the importance of data and the desire to see that monies are well spent on initiatives that make sense. No one wants to flush good money down the drain.

But gathering data is neither simple nor inexpensive. And it takes time. Social scientists, with economists leading the way, want to quantify everything and regress for variables and have predictable results with assurances of reliability. They are searching for proof of Pareto efficiency. And in the absence of all these checks, we are sort of flying by the seats of our pants.

However, the construction, execution, and analysis of quality empiricism assume that we have the time to measure. It assumes we can afford to measure. And it assumes that the risk of bad change is so great that we do not want to make errors, particularly if there are systematic implications. Best to model out changes before creating catastrophic results. And of course, there are the change naysayers who use the absence of empiricism as the excuse for nonsupport of the new initiative (as if no one can see through the guise). Pilot projects are a place from which to start and are well worth our time and attention.

For example, we know the value of getting new drugs to market quickly in cases when what we are doing in dealing with a certain fatal disease is not working and we need to try something else so more people will not die. To be sure, we need to be cautious about endangering people more than their disease already is. But in the absence of alternatives, what is the real harm in trying something new and thinking out of the box—created with thoughtful and quality practices and preexisting knowledge—to move the needle?

I think we are in that place in education, a place where we need to move that needle, where failures are so significant that we need to try something different. Our existing efforts on closing the equity gap are not moving fast enough, and a generation of kids is being lost in the process. We can't afford this, because in a decade or 2 or 3, these are the very people who will be making up our workforce, innovating across the disciplines, contributing to our communities, and having children. I am worried that we cannot wait to see if lasticity works in all its dimensions; we already know that aspects of it are data informed; we have promising practices; we have academic thinking on students' development and success in a wide range of disciplines, among them psychology, psychiatry, neuroscience, behavioral economics, education, sociology, medicine, and law. We have knowledge from the STEM disciplines and from technological advances.

So our reluctance to make change because we do not know enough or because our accreditors will not have the verification that they want for making change does not seem either wise or justifiable. Sorry. Instead, I think we need to make change and measure and evaluate as we go. Yes, there are risks, but lasticity is not shaped out of entirely new cloth. It brings together lots of existing data and research and seeks to use that information to steer different outcomes. Seems to me that we don't have much to lose and huge amounts to gain.

The final macrolevel change is the predisposition and cultural bias in the United States against partnering and collaborating in the educational sphere. This plays out in a wide range of ways. Start with this realization: The academy (and many of those within it) favors autonomy. It is a prized value and is reflected in our approach to our institutions. We place ourselves in an ivory tower. We create an academic bubble, frequently disconnected from the communities where we are situated and from local K–12 schools just a stone's throw from us. It continues to startle me that where I live in Vermont, the four colleges in one geographic region—within 15 miles of each other—barely interact. Faculty stay where they are; students stay where they are. Add to that the schools from early childhood through 12th grade that do not engage with each other either. Perhaps competition is one reason; perhaps they are all competing for the same students. Perhaps some institutions worry that if they align with a less well-known institution, their own reputation will falter, as if lower status were a catchable disease. Perhaps we are strangely unwilling to see how others do what we do—worrying perhaps that we might come up short in the comparison. In different words, more elite institutions think they have nothing to learn or gain from their less elite collegiate neighbors. Sad.

Many years ago, I heard Vartan Gregorian commenting on the absence of engagement among the traditional Ivy League schools (when he was provost at the University of Pennsylvania, as I recall). He recounted a story that stays with me still—and to be candid, I am not sure we have progressed that far over the past couple of decades on the same issues. The situation involved the purchase of electron microscopes, which were very expensive at the time. Each of the schools wanted one. A vendor agreed to cut the cost substantially if all the Ivy institutions made a joint purchase; the price would drop from $1 million per microscope to $750,000. None of the schools were willing to partner, despite the savings. Perhaps the discount wasn't big enough in the context of a wealthy institution. Perhaps the hoopla for each institution would have been curtailed by a shared purchase; no one institution could have claimed to be the first to get the new tool. But given that there would have been total savings of more than $1 million, I am hard pressed—even now—to see what justifies such institutional behavior. Perhaps the explanation lies in this catch: The electron microscopes would be delivered to one locale—meaning the other institutions could not claim they "received" one (at least not in a traditional sense of having it delivered as opposed to retrieving it).

That mentality persists. We can debate its causes; we can try to break down silos. We can try to showcase the economic savings from shared purchasing. This much is clear: If we have trouble with joint purchasing or shared IT support, it is no wonder that many find threatening such ideas as shared faculty development, shared faculty members, merged departments, or the designation of certain departments as located in only some collegiate locations (astronomy or meteorology, with their need for specialized equipment, are good examples). We can share books through interlibrary loan. On occasion, we can have joint presentations, but even that is rare. What institution that can afford to host Beyoncé wants to say that several other schools are sharing in this event?

Unlocking our capacity to share, unraveling the benefits of leveraging resources, and diminishing the value of autonomy and self-congratulation seem difficult cultural hurdles to overcome—certainly in the short term. Like the reluctance to change and the demand for data as a precursor to making any adjustments, diminishing our love affair with autonomy seems unlikely. Indeed, the economic recession would have seemed to be an impetus for substantial, measurable, and hugely augmented partnering and collaboration. The hue and cry over college costs would seem to be another impetus. Nevertheless, despite these clear avenues for improvement, we remain firmly entrenched in our silos—with rare exceptions that were often implemented with considerable friction.

I worry that this love of autonomy is felt by and almost injected into students, and that will not put them in an optimal position in the workplace (at least some workplaces). Health care professionals work together; lawyers work together; businesses even find ways to work with other businesses, formally or informally.

Perhaps, just perhaps, the academic affection for autonomy is partial-ly a problem of nomenclature and packaging. Instead of saying we want change or we need to bust silos or we must have forced partnerships to leverage resources more ably, what if we spoke differently about what current educational improvements would require? For example, instead of mergers or partnerships among institutions, what if we spoke about col-laborations and knowledge exchanges? What if instead of silo *busting* we referenced silo *ventilation*—not tearing down the structures but opening the windows? What if instead of change, we spoke about improvement and innovation and enhancement of institutions? What if we spoke about adaptations and adjustments and being ahead of the curve (who wants to be behind the curve)? And what if we realized that in the absence of more working together, our livelihood and economic productivity over the lon-ger hall would be threatened? We have already seen some smaller colleges going the way of the dodo bird.

Here's why I think this approach offers more power than we might know. Think for a moment about fashion (and don't trivialize it, please; it's a big global business). We seem to be able to accept and adopt to fashion changes rather easily. Changes in colors that are "in"; changes in lengths of women's skirts and dresses; changes in casual wear, from omnipresent jeans even among older adults. Add in the omnipresence of sneakers, among adults and as a fashion statement. Somehow, these al-most annual changes seem to be liberating in a sense, freeing one from past norms and offering new ones. There is also a culture of change in the fashion industry, an expectation that change is always happening, as in hairstyles and hair color for both women and men.

There are two other perspectives from which to look at the develop-ment and deployment of lasticity. First, lasticity isn't totally new in the following sense: It draws from existing work (on grit, on resiliency, on growth mindsets, on strategies for first-generation student success, on re-search on trauma and toxic stress, on behavioral economics). What is new is how the pieces are put together and how the approach is enunciated and made cohesive and systematic. Look again at lasticity's five building blocks: elasticity, plasticity, pivoting right, reciprocity, and belief in self. Yes, there are new approaches within each block and the linkage of the five blocks is new. But many of the concepts are drawn from existing information, data, studies, and experiences in the trenches. That should make the implementation less threatening.

Second, the implementation of lasticity is not an all-or-nothing prop-osition. It is not like being a little pregnant. Not at all. Lasticity has many pieces (represented by its five foundational elements), and while lasticity is optimized and fully realized when all five of its building blocks are animated, there are definitely aspects of lasticity that can (and currently do) have an impact—even if there is not systematic and systemic implementation.

Think about it this way: Suppose one decides to redecorate one's apartment or house. One could do it all at once—empty out what is there and move in new things. On the other hand, one could pick a room or two to redecorate, live with the changes, and then make other changes if needed, if desired, and if there is willingness to do so. Ironically, at least with home repairs, once you change one room, the rest of the rooms take on a shabbiness that hadn't been noticed before the improvements elsewhere took place.

In a sense, lasticity is unlike purchasing a car. If you want a new car, you need to buy the whole thing—it's not like you can take the engine now and wait for the body and headlights. It's not as if the car can drive incrementally—only forward but not backward. One side mirror isn't good. Lasticity, in contrast, can operate in pieces, not in full gear, to be sure, but operating nonetheless. And it can produce positive results even if only partially animated.

Moreover, even if the impediments to lasticity's implementation seem insurmountable, there are ways to increase its prevalence that are less threatening and fit more into the category of systemic improvements—that happen to lead to a more lastic culture. In other words, some adjustments to what we do now across the educational pipeline (micro changes) could be beneficial and serve more than one master—improving how a particular process works to ease the burden on breakaway students and administrators *and* open pathways to the broader implementation of lasticity. What follows are several examples of micro changes.

MICRO CHANGES

Start with the problem of teacher turnover. We know that teachers leave schools, particularly schools with breakaway students. The turnover data are enough to turn your stomach; approximately 30% of teachers leave over a period of 5 years, with the largest departures in the schools where the students are most in need. (This is an improvement over now less reliable but frequently cited data that pegged teacher turnover at 50% over a 5-year period.)[1]

Teach for America, viewed by many as a pride and joy of the nation, has what I would characterize as stunning teacher turnover and weak retention. After 5 years, barely 15% of participants are still teaching in the low-income school where they started. More than half leave the needy schools where they were placed after the end of their 2-year commitment. We may bring the best and the brightest into schools in low-income neighborhoods, but the teachers do not stay. Well, some 40% percent stay beyond their commitment period, but not for that long.[2]

We can observe the level of turnover and its causes. We can lament its occurrence. We know there is a significant cost, and not only in dollars. And even if it is true that the less effective teachers tend to be the ones who leave, we know that teacher departures are disruptive on many levels, causing diminished continuity within the institution, decreasing levels of experience of the teacher workforce, time lost that had been expended on teacher development, and decline in esprit de corps.

The real price, however, is paid by students, particularly students with weak attachments, a common problem for breakaway students, as noted repeatedly. Indeed, the data show that student achievement is affected by teacher departure, with the greatest impact felt by low-income minority students. And such impact is sizable. By way of example, to cite a study by Matthew Ronfeldt and his colleagues, "Students in grade levels with 100 percent turnover [every teacher left] were especially affected, with lower test scores by anywhere from 6 percent to 10 percent of a standard deviation based on the content area." Ouch.[3]

Lasticity sits upon one major building block that is undercut by teacher change: reciprocity, as that quality itself is premised on trust relationships that are authentically built. I would bet (not that I am a betting person) that change in teacher longevity at low-income schools is not improving in the relative near term and perhaps not even longer term. We are unlikely to improve the schools fast enough or enhance pay enough to move the teacher retention needle sufficiently. And for schools that use looping, which keeps a teacher with a group for more than 1 year and has many benefits, departures have an even larger impact because student expectations are dashed; the teacher they relied on being with them in the year ahead (or perhaps the next 2 years) disappears. Interestingly, that is not one of the named "cons" in the looping literature.[4]

What, then, can be done to promote lasticity despite this very real hurdle? My answer rests on my experience and thinking with respect to children connected with the military, kids whose experiences may at first blush seem vastly different. But hear me out. These kids often change schools between six and nine times from kindergarten to Grade 12. Just pause and reflect on the impact of that. So while their teachers are changing for these students, the students (and parents) are changing too. This produces, as one might expect, considerable disruption; it affects some military students vastly more than others, depending on the schools from and to which they move.[5]

Adding to the already difficult situation of moving between schools, for military-connected children these changes also can occur at odd times of the year, meaning children often struggle to adjust to classes that are already ongoing and well established; they lose opportunities to participate in athletics as they miss tryouts; they also miss opportunities to participate in clubs for which there is preplanning, such as choir or drama. Add to this that these children may be moving from a public school to a Department of Defense Education Activity (DoDEA) school. DoDEA schools are run by the Department of Defense in regions of the world, including the United States, where public schools are inadequate or there are none. Sometimes they are moving from a DoDEA school to a public school where there are few military-connected children and there is both an absence of military culture and a lack of sensitivity to it. Moreover, these military-connected students are leaving behind friendships they have developed and are arriving at a place where they have few or no friends and instead depend on siblings. (I leave for another day whether we can curb the number of moves made by deploying service members and their families in a different and less disruptive fashion, with limits on frequency.)

The data are decidedly mixed on the impact these changes have on military-connected children. Not all experience these events as traumatic or stressful, and others may process the trauma and stress remarkably effectively. As one study observed, "Multiple transitions have been shown to equip military children with more adaptability, accelerated maturity, deeper appreciation for cultural differences, and strong social skills in comparison to their civilian peers."[6]

How is it possible that at least some military-connected kids are able to navigate extremely difficult situations, and repeatedly? The extant literature suggests that two pieces are critical to improving the transition: increased cultural knowledge of military life by the receiving public school *and* supportive relationships with adults (whether within or outside a school). Recognizing the difficulties of transitions, some schools have a special student newcomer club, peer guides, and events for new parents.

I think that there are several other contributory pieces that go unmentioned. These military-connected children are moving with one or both parents, at least one of whom is in the military. So, as stressful as the situation is, the entire family is "in it together," so to speak. And since moves are frequent, families can compare and contrast transitions; they can anticipate hurdles; and with new technology, they can remain connected with the many places where they had been stationed and with friends they made there, including abroad. They can even have moving traditions. The military, both individuals within it and as a culture, understands these changes, provides support (both economic and psychological), and often works with independent organizations to ease the burdens families new to a region face. Depending on where you are moving, those stressors can be better or worse.

What I see as the ameliorating factor here, one that contributes to military-connected children's capacity to manage more effectively, is culture. These children and families live within a culture where moving is common; they themselves move, and they have witnessed others move as well. Within military culture, they are acutely aware of two things: the absence of understanding between those in and outside the military and the presence of traditions. While students may change schools, they are also connected to bases where people often wear the same uniforms, where the flag is raised and lowered with identical music and traditions, where people engage with each other in an embedded, acknowledged structure and hierarchy.

All this is not to say that moving is easy and that all military-connected kids adjust equally, or well, for that matter, and the age and stage of the child does matter. But there is an educational message embedded here that I suspect can ameliorate teacher turnover for nonmilitary children and could, as a side benefit, further assist military children: the creation of traditions across schools—wherever they are located.

A strong, symbol-based culture in a school with high teacher turnover should be instituted. For example, every year, there is field trip to the local museum in Grade 4; each year, the 1st-graders make clay tiles that are hung in the hallway. Fifth graders read to kindergarteners every Monday at 10 A.M. There is a schoolwide celebration of music from different cultures every other Thursday, with 2nd-graders playing different instruments. Every graduating class gives a speech to the whole student body. The point is that whether teachers come or go, these "traditions" continue.

This idea could be ratcheted up even further through the installation of thematic learning across the entire school, obviously a major change but one with enormous potential. Picture a school where all subjects in a given year were taught—to the extent possible—through the chosen theme. Each grade level would have a theme that would continue year after year after year. Regardless of teacher turnover, children would engage in thematic learning, and because the themes and accompanying traditions would be so appealing, students would look forward to being in certain grades where the theme had particular appeal to them. Because of the complexity of employing a theme across multiple disciplines, there is added structure within each grade and there is teamwork among faculty. Co-teaching is possible.[7]

So, for example, consider a K–5 school where the 1st-grade theme was Native American culture, the 2nd-grade theme was birds, and the 3rd-grade theme was medieval times. First-graders learned to read through books about Native Americans; they studied different Native American cultures and differences between different tribes; they studied how Native Americans grew food and made medicine; they listened to and played Native American music. They built a teepee. They visited a local museum and viewed Native American artifacts. They studied how Native Americans were treated by "White" people and the impact of that approach. They learned about Native American symbolism and art, including totem poles and beading and pottery.

You get the point. With thematic learning, there is continuity, there is institutional expectation, there is regularity. There is creativity to be sure; there is student collaboration. There is teacher collaboration, and even if one teacher "drops out," the theme remains. There is tradition. Having watched our son attend an elementary school with thematic learning and having actively participated within that school, I can attest to it being an extraordinary way to learn. Even a weaker teacher could be supported (buoyed) by the theme. As an educational benefit, children learned to think and learn across the disciplines, gaining an appreciation for depth and knowledge acquisition. As an aside, schools that serve military-connected children could benefit from thematic learning too. And I get that the Common Core, had it been implemented and tested with consistency, might have contributed to the consistency goal as well.

A similar idea could be tried within colleges, albeit in different ways, to create institutional tradition and stability. Suppose that a college decided that every 2 years the institution would focus on one of the four basic classical elements of matter: earth, air, fire, and water. (There are other versions of what the basic elements comprise; other elements could be added.) Or an institution could pick a major social or political issue that cuts across disciplines: heath care, poverty, education, crime, democratic processes, immigration, fraud.

Individuals, groups, classes, and residential halls would research, address, and solve the social, political, cultural, and scientific issues arising under the umbrella of each element or theme. Professors along with students could write papers that would inform legislatures; groups of students, alone or with faculty and staff, could do public advocacy work; students, along with professors, could do scientific research; the institution could organize symposia. There could be debates. There could be a campuswide effort both in and out of class that focused on the elements or themes. The issues addressed are limited only by our imagination, given the complexity of our society and the magnitude of the political, social, environmental, and cultural issues we face.

In sum, while the hurdles of implementing lasticity are hard to overcome, there are shorter-term strategies that hold promise even in the absence of systemic change. These micro suggestions share certain variables: they emphasize relationships, they are symbol and tradition rich, and they enable creativity that listens and is responsive to student voice. We now turn to yet another hurdle to creating lasticity where there is promise for meaningful improvements rather than intractable obstacles over which we cannot leap—regardless of our intellectual and emotional capacities. Money (or the lack thereof) is our next topic.

CHAPTER 14

Money and Its Meaning

As a topic, money is complex, to say the least, and how we think about and handle it in our individual lives is deeply affected by (among other variables) our gender, culture, religion, ethnicity, and family experiences. Our understanding (or lack of understanding) of money affects our long- and short-term choices and decisions, some of which can have large impacts and others of which may barely create a ripple. Our handling of money affects how we raise our children, how we engage with others in intimate relationships, and how we reflect on and make decisions about our future. And regardless of socioeconomic status, money is an omnipresent topic—whether we have a lot of it or only a little. Money is a language we all speak—day in and day out—although we may not have a strong awareness of how we developed our money language and how others view money in ways that differ from our own. We may not recognize how money speaks to some of our most deeply held values as people and as a society.[1]

Given the omnipresence of money, it should not be a surprise that it affects lasticity and its implementation. For many breakaway students, money stands in the way of lasticity, although perhaps not in the ways one would anticipate. The amount of money needed to pay for higher education seems unimaginable to some breakaway students and their families. The amount needed for 4-plus years—even though there are scholarships—can be frightening. It is more than some parents anticipate earning in a lifetime. Whether those thoughts represent reality is in some sense irrelevant; fear isn't necessarily based on rational thought or information.

Add to this that for many breakaway students, there are cultural impediments to borrowing money, causing a disinclination that may be based in religion or family beliefs. The old adage "neither a borrower nor a lender be" can hover over some breakaway students as they reflect on college. Moreover, some breakaway students help support their family financially, and there is a concern—a real concern—that if they head to college, there will not be enough money for food and rent and utilities. For

147

those breakaway students who decide to go to college, there is guilt over money, and also there are students who continue working to send money home.

Such impediments to lasticity can be overcome, but for this to happen, we need extremely sensitive and savvy school counselors and financial aid officers who can anticipate and address these concerns with breakaway students and their families. In short, these professionals need to understand money's language and be able to speak it to help breakaway students find pathways to higher education and solutions for their financial and family obligations.

Problems related to money, however, do not end there. For many breakaway students, the federal financial aid system stands in their way—for reasons that may also affect other prospective students. For starters, the ticket to enter the system, the FAFSA (Free Application for Federal Student Aid), remains too complex and there is a lack of understanding of the benefits that flow from completing the form. (Without it, one cannot access federal financial aid!) As a consequence, despite considerable efforts to encourage completion of the FAFSA (which can be used in a variety of educational contexts, not just 4-year colleges), students do not finish filling out this necessary form. If one doesn't complete the FAFSA, the financial train never leaves the station. (Whether we even need a form as a practical matter is a different issue—why not make financial aid automatic, based on tax returns?) The final result is that these breakaway students leave available dollars on the table—over $2.6 billion in 2016. That's a *b* as in *billion*.

The FAFSA completion rates are inconsistent across the nation, and there is considerably lower uptake in some states than in others. For example, uptake is higher in Massachusetts (62% of eligible students completed the form) than in Montana (48%). Uptake is lower in Vermont (51% of eligible students did not complete the form) than in West Virginia (42% of eligible students did not complete the form).[2]

Why, one might ask, if there were a financial benefit, would folks leave it sitting on the table? Lack of knowledge is one reason. Lack of an adequate number of school counselors in America's public high schools is another. Lack of a college-going culture in some states and some high schools is yet another. There are many reasons; for an analogy we can look to the lack of uptake on the earned income tax credit. Two possible explanations for the lack of uptake: complexity and a lack of understanding of the tangible dollar benefits. If you can't detect the actual dollar benefit and how that offsets tuition and room and board, it is difficult to navigate the process, because the end point appears so uncertain or so far into the future for folks who are not ahead of the college curve.

It is for these reasons that simplification of the entire financial aid process would make real sense—think KISS ("keep it simple and straightforward"—not "stupid," as in the original phrase used by the navy). Indeed, an analysis counted 56 different repayment options available to students. Seriously. Even if the count is off by 10% or 20%, how ridiculous is a system that has so many options that even experts struggle to navigate the possible and optimal approaches? Is there any logical reason why we need so many repayment options related to federal student loans? Seems to me we just kept adding on new options without eliminating older ones. Indeed, why not pick the best approaches and make it the default selection from which graduates could opt out if they wanted to do so?[3]

We also know from studies in choice theory that too many choices are paralyzing, and so we do way better to offer limited (and better) choices—unless of course we are either explicitly or tacitly trying to create confusion and want to encourage poor financial decisionmaking because that is profitable for lenders (not to be too cynical). A similar issue occurs in health care, where an abundance of choices makes it harder, not easier, for consumers to ferret out the best insurance and pharmaceutical solutions.[4]

We may not agree on how to simplify the federal student aid program, and we can vigorously debate the best ways to do so. But surely we can agree that the system is not serving our students optimally and changes are doable—in the relative near term if we have the collective will to make that happen. Consider the following possible ways to simplify and improve the system as exemplars.

First, federal law requires that entering college students who receive federal student aid be provided an interview or information session; there are mandated exit interviews as well. This is a costly and time-consuming process with unproven benefits. I cannot think of two less teachable moments than these for breakaway college students. On the front end, students are trying to navigate their way around campus and acclimatize themselves to the new environment—even finding the dining hall can be a challenge, let alone dealing with a roommate. On the exit side, students are focused on graduation and on transitioning out from college into the workforce or graduate school. They are dealing with the familial tensions of their impending graduation, which is a joyful occasion but also a symbolic step forward into a future that will be vastly different from that of their family members.

Try this idea: Change the system completely. Don't wait for students to arrive on campus to carry out the entry interview, and move the back-end interview to a time that is closer to when loan repayment begins (usually 6 months after graduation unless there are further deferments). Embed learning about federal student aid at other moments in time, pre-, during, and postcollege.

Second, create a new, simple financial product for parents, guardians, family members, and friends who want to borrow to assist students in progressing through higher education, as a replacement of the flawed Parent PLUS Loan. The current Parent PLUS Loan product is too expensive (including interest rates) and too keyed to credit worthiness. The individuals who most need this product are those who are more vulnerable. And the definition of *parent* is much too narrow, given the contours of American families today. Further, the amount that can be borrowed needs to be capped so that parents are not encouraged and enabled to overborrow, with the monies going to noneducational needs. And let us reconsider how such obligations are treated by the federal bankruptcy laws; might they be dischargeable if certain conditions are met? And, no, this does not necessarily create a moral hazard pursuant to which people borrow just to get the bankruptcy benefit. Please, who wakes up in the morning saying, "Yippee, I get to file bankruptcy today and admit that I failed at the American dream for myself and my children and my children's children"?

While we're at it, let's look at other possible ways to finance higher education—to benefit students as well as the educational institutions that serve them. The great minds of finance could put their talents behind thinking through the implications of social impact bonds and income share agreements—with or without any government monies on the table. For the record, if we can help institutions, particularly those that serve first-generation low-income students and that do not have gargantuan endowments, then tuition and room-and-board costs can become stabilized and the added support programs paid for without passing along costs.

There is one more major doable change in the context of financing higher education—dramatically improve how students can obtain available nongovernmental scholarships and grants. These are potential sources of money, but the process of getting scholarships is cumbersome at every level: identifying possible scholarships; completing the required documents, including essays; meeting deadlines that vary from organization to organization; and handling notifications that arrive at different points in time, often after aid packages are proffered by colleges. None of this enables breakaway students to gain access to money, and there is no reason for the complexity other than the desire of grantors to maintain their own approaches to awarding scholarships and preserving independence. Autonomy rearing its ugly head again.[5]

This whole process could be simplified if there were a standard application for all scholarships that then enabled a database to create a set of matches between students and scholarships. Think of an online system akin to a combination of the Common Application (Common App, or Universal App) and the medical student matching system for residencies. Then, the deadline for seeking scholarships and the date of notification of awarding (or denying) a scholarship could be standardized. These dates could enable coordination with other deadlines and decisions in the college application process. Why not facilitate the awarding of scholarships and the elimination of hassles and of the middle people who often charge a fee to help students get scholarships? Access to scholarships should be cost free, and we need knowledgeable individuals to help breakaway students obtain these monies—sending them to a guidebook or a website is not enough. Moreover, some scholarships are small—some are worth just several hundred dollars and some are only 1-year awards. Students are obliged to consider whether the time needed to apply is worth it. With a database and the ability to stack scholarships, applying would make vastly more sense. Indeed, that is why with the Common App, colleges saw more applicants. It became easier to apply.

However, I think something else is happening in the context of breakaway students and their families in the way the whole financial/scholarship process is handled: We ignore that, for many students and their families, public disclosure of financial information, including available assets, is invasive and troubling. For some, identifying one's poverty on paper is tough sledding. Why would folks admit their financial struggles to complete strangers at a college, where they do not know how those strangers will handle the information they see? For some, financial disclosure feels like being naked, and why go naked with folks whom you have no reason to trust? This issue may be less acute in the context of the Internal Revenue Service and earned income tax credit because we know the government regularly collects information on individuals.

Many decades ago, I helped court personnel and others who worked with or encountered consumers who were seeking bankruptcy relief with their understanding of the individual debtors with whom they were dealing. Lawyers, creditors, law students, and trustees all benefited from a better awareness of how it feels to be a debtor. Bankruptcy requires that individuals disclose massive amounts of personal financial information, and, in an era that predated electronic filing of documents that bypassed human interaction, debtors encountered flesh-and-blood people who recorded their case filing. Debtors were then questioned about this information in a hearing, a public setting.

In addition, completed bankruptcy filing documents are publicly accessible; evidence of a debtor's downfall and his or her denuded assets are there for all to see. Yes, I would show students the actual bankruptcy filings of individuals they would know from the world of sports or the arts. Lorraine Bracco (from the TV show *The Sopranos*) was one person whose file I used frequently. Extremely personal information is revealed in her file and those of other debtors about job loss, health situations, divorce, and addictions.

For court personnel, there was a problem in that the filing of these documents was perfunctory, and mistakes made by debtors were a source of aggravation and wasted time. As I engaged in this work, I would ask court personnel and others to join me in a series of exercises. I asked them to write down on an index card how much money they owed. After they completed that task (which was quick), I asked, "How many of you owe money?" Most would reveal that they did, but there was always a handful of people who said, "I don't owe anything. I pay all my bills on time" (putting them in direct contrast to the public they served at the courthouse). For those who said they owed nothing, I would announce boldly, "I can name three creditors to whom you owe money." "No way," they'd respond. I'd continue, "Do you own a home or rent? If yes, you owe a landlord or a bank pursuant to a contract. Do you have utilities for which you are obligated or a cellphone or cable? Do you have a credit card that you use?" If the answer was yes (which it always was), I'd point out that they did owe money (for example, to the credit card company). The difference between those court personnel and debtors was not the existence of debt and obligations to others; it was that the court personnel paid their debts generally on time and perhaps in full, while debtors often did not.

So there was less of a difference between court personnel and debtors than one might think. Both owed money. What distinguished them was a difference in degree, not in kind. Shock—debtors are not that different from the rest of us.

Following this exercise, I would ask attendees to return to their original index cards and write down to whom they owed money, with dollar amounts next to the top three creditors. This took a tad longer than expected. I would then ask anyone who was willing to reveal what was on that index card to do so to the person seated to his or her left or right—a person who might be a co-worker or supervisor or someone that person supervised. Suddenly, there were attendees who were reluctant to share. I then asked how many attendees were willing to share that information with me up on the dais. Many looked skeptical. Then I asked how many were willing to get up from their seat and read what was on their card to the assembled group.

A hush usually fell over the room as I said, "This is what consumer debtors do. They entrust you with their most private information, and they have no ability to deny you access. They do not know you or trust you. And there isn't such a chasm between you and them."

Since the idea of free college has been and no doubt will continue to be in the news and the subject of proposals emerging from the legislative or executive branches of government, it is worth observing that the efficacy of this idea lies in the details. Free for whom? Free in what portion of costs? Tuition? Room? Board? Books? Travel? Personal items like soap and tampons and razors? Short of *free* in the fullest sense, students of low socioeconomic status (SES) will still need to think about money, the costs of an education, and methods of repayment. "Free" college is not a complete answer. And there are hidden (or perhaps not so hidden) ways in which pricing of housing and food has a potential adverse and discriminatory impact on low-income students at some institutions (both public and private). New housing tends to be more expensive; full meal plans are more costly. To save money, low-income students may find themselves (by choice or because of how they are packaged by the institution's financial aid office) in lower-priced housing and with meal plans that have fewer meals. Nice—we create campus segregated housing and we have less food for those in the lowest SES quartile. Hard to believe that in this day and age we have not thought through the consequences of room-and-board pricing on student behavior and living patterns. Where is the disparate-impact analysis?[6]

My point in detailing the example of money and the story of court personnel dealing with consumer debtors is that it is tough to understand what it feels like to walk in someone else's shoes. But if one can, that vastly improves the engagement; it ramps up the empathy engine and enables insights into changes that could improve a process—not just mechanically but in terms of the human engagement as well.

If the examples just described don't drive home the point, here's another situation that demonstrates the difficulty of walking in someone else's shoes: Faculty at most institutions are required to keep office hours. However, often the lament is heard that no students come to visit or the students who do are those who need the least attention. (Other student inaction, in uptaking support services, is noted earlier in this book.) Probably true. The problem, however, is that showing up in a professor's office can be threatening for many breakaway students. Actually, the fear extends even to students attending elite colleges, as mentioned in the book *Practice for Life: Making Decisions in College*. Most students do not know what to expect. They are worried about being demeaned. They are not accustomed to adults who are in positions of authority extending themselves to them. They would not be sure of the protocol—what to say, what to ask, what to wear, what to do, what to bring. For some, going to a professor's office feels eerily similar to being sent to the principal's office, and even if the meeting is initiated by the student, that is not a welcome feeling.[7]

One could try to solve this in many ways—mandating at least one visit by every student to a professor's office (at least in institutions with small enough classes to make that a realistic possibility). More than a tad intrusive. Resident assistants and advisers could talk about the value of visiting a professor and how it not only could help with course material but also might lead to a mentorship opportunity or a relationship that would enable the professor to write a recommendation for a job or graduate school. Another approach would be to encourage students to come to office hours in groups—study groups or just with an assortment of other students. That could cut the tension level. I used to say that since no one seemed to want to visit me in my office, I would come early to class and stay afterward and answer questions and respond to concerns then. It helped, but it was not a panacea. And to be sure, not all professors are that good at engaging one on one or even three on one with students.

To address this situation, Arizona State took to humor, creating an advertisement that resembled a television ad for a drug. This drug was called Faculty Office Hours, or FOH. FOH can help you, the ad asserts, by allowing you to see your professor as a person. The contraindications are minimal, such as seeing that a professor is human and has a family.[8]

Whether this will be an effective tool is hard to tell, but it does highlight the institution's recognition of the issues that its students confront and the institution's willingness to help students see the value of visiting with faculty and, through humor, cutting down on the level of tension that could be felt.

I am not suggesting that money is a humorous topic or that figuring out college finances is a matter for jokes. Nevertheless, there is a need to ease the stress that accompanies the reality of money for many breakaway students and their families. We are called upon to see the problem, understand it, and then address it in a sensitive way. This is not about student fragility or coddling or self-absorption. No, it is about coming to understand that many of the students of today and tomorrow—breakaway students—need those within institutions to comprehend who they are and the challenges they face and why what seems so easy to some is so difficult for others. Pretend that students are repeatedly saying to those of you who work across the educational pipeline, "Walk in my shoes for a day. You'll understand more then." There's nothing weak in that request, and those who take students up on their suggestion will be struck, I believe, by students' strength, of which we remain largely unaware.

If lasticity is recognized and implemented, at least in part, we will have accomplished something sizable. We will have done more than educate a generation; we will have changed culture. Lasticity's power—its reach—is the topic to which we now turn.

CHAPTER 15

Lasticity's Growing Urgency

Thus far, we've explored the foundational elements of lasticity and the features that can animate its implementation. We have wrestled with the not inconsiderable number and range of hurdles standing in the way of adoption of this concept/process/attribute across the pre-K–20 educational pipeline.

What we have not addressed explicitly is the urgency of this effort. That urgency stems from two distinct sources. First, the absence of a lastic school pipeline has extensive implications for children's future in the near and longer term. Our failure to act with all deliberate speed has consequences that will be felt for many decades to come. I am not exaggerating.

Second, we have a host of commentators, educators, and politicians commenting on our educational system and the students who populate it. There's plenty of room for thoughtful debate and discussion. However, the ways in which students are addressed, the assumptions about their behavior, and the focus of our attention have profound impacts on how we treat students now and into the future. This also influences our priorities. In a world filling with a growing nastiness in rhetoric and in actions, we are damaging our students in ways that will have decades-long implications. We need to clean up our act now, before negative descriptors and misplaced attentiveness to certain issues become reified.

Let's be clear: Despite all the attention paid to college completion, getting postsecondary degrees, certificates, or badges is not the end game. It is not the piece of paper that matters. Getting a quality education is what matters. And that education has a reach beyond the mastery of subject matter content. A quality education fosters personal growth, curiosity, creativity, and problem-solving capacities. We want individuals postgraduation who are workforce ready and who recognize the need, and have the capacity and desire, to contribute meaningfully to their communities, our economy, and our democracy. The appearance of such books as *Our Compelling Interests*, referred to earlier (see Chapter 12), attest to this need.

Getting more and more breakaway students to gain access to and proceed through postsecondary education is what lasticity, as developed here, can help accomplish. To be clear, it is not the only approach that is needed. Nor is it necessarily the best one. We, as a society, have a number of other adverse situations that are sorely in need of being addressed and that, if ameliorated, would benefit children and their educational success: poverty, homelessness, food scarcity, lack of access to health care and medicine, a dearth of mental health programs.

The effort to create lasticity does not start at colleges and universities, nor is it their responsibility alone to produce a workforce-ready citizenry. To get more breakaway kids to progress through the educational pipeline and contribute down the road to their families and communities, we need to start way earlier than post–high school graduation. We need to start in infancy. Actually, we need to start before then. And we need to have started yesterday.[1]

The provision of maternal health care contributes to the wellness of a new baby. Use of alcohol and drugs and smoking (cigarettes or anything else) can lead to premature birth and low weight in newborns. Those who can afford and obtain prenatal care are better off. How exactly can we ensure that all pregnant women, most especially those who are very young, partake of the care they need? We need quality care. Trust, not money, is often the issue.[2]

We also know that infants (whether preemies or not) need maternal touching, including being held. It is hard to do this in neonatal units. But not all parents bond immediately, even with normal-term babies; some parents simply do not connect with their infant children in ways that build comfort and a sense of safety. Many parents need to return to work immediately—it's not as if America has the best family leave policies on the planet; other developed nations have long surpassed us in providing paid leave for both parents, and in those countries it is not viewed as a sign of slacking off for folks to use it.[3]

We also know that the degree of richness in speech that an infant hears affects his or her language acquisition, and children who are not exposed to language at an early age suffer considerably; they are behind before they even start. The staggering differential between low- and high-income children at 18 months in the number of words they hear is frightening, but what is even more so is that it suggests the battle on the achievement gap needs to start early or kids are lost by preschool, and everything else is playing catch-up.[4]

We know too that children in elementary school start showing language and math gaps that have a lasting impact. Low reading and math scores among low-income children mean those kids are held back in the work they do and the books they read and the pathways presented to them. The self-perception of whether they are "smart" is etched in early by teachers and peers. As noted previously, it is remarkably easy for kids to see/sense "who is smart" and "whom the teacher likes." If we eliminate sports and art and music, in which some children excel elsewhere before they do so at school, then the problem is exacerbated. Some say that by 3rd grade, kids know whether they are college-bound material. Then there's the summer slide, whereby higher-SES students improve their intellectual life through expensive activities over the summer months, while lower-SES students fall behind, not even staying level in terms of capacities. Ouch.[5]

The phrase *opportunity knocks* takes on new meaning in this context. If children are not exposed to opportunity, it is hard for them to know it is there. Children who participate in summer enrichment programs, travel with their parents, listen to dinner conversations about current events, and overhear political debates have opportunities before them daily, without even knowing it or realizing that what they are experiencing is not universal. For children who do not eat together with their families because both parents are working to support them, whose families cannot afford vacations or high-cost after-school programs, and who are not exposed to continual conversations at home, it is far too easy and common for them to fall behind their economically elevated peers. Remember, none of this has anything to do with a child's abilities and surely is not the child's doing. But the impact of poverty is felt early and often. Add toxic stress and trauma on top of that.[6]

Then move forward and consider the diminished quality of the education low-income children receive relative to their higher-income peers. As Robert Putnam points out, as education progresses in today's world, there is a growing division between rich and poor. Richer families move to areas with better school systems or pay for private education. Poorer students are left with schools that struggle financially and have discipline problems and a potential lack of parental support. True, there are exceptions and there are growing numbers of smaller public schools and charter schools and quality free or low-cost after-school programs, but the basic premise remains: The quality of education our poorest children receives pales in comparison with that enjoyed by our richest children.[7]

Further, if we look at teacher quality, it is fair to say that the best teachers migrate to the best schools. Yes, there are wonderful dedicated and quality teachers in low-income schools, but if one were looking at teacher assessment, the better teachers (however we measure better, which is in and of itself a challenge) tend to teach in the better public and private schools.

We also know from researchers at Harvard that one good teacher in 4th grade can influence high school graduation rates. One is tempted to then say, Let's hire good 4th-grade teachers and all will be well. Of course it is not that easy. First, how to we measure good teachers? Second, how do we get good 4th-grade teachers into all schools? Third, high school graduation is not our ultimate goal—postsecondary graduation or receipt of a certificate isn't either. A productive life, ideally not intergenerationally tied to support programs, is our longer-range goal.[8]

But the problems continue. Children are advised about which courses to take or not take. Sometimes, there is a total absence of advice. And stratification occurs in middle school (if not before in more subtle ways) and thereafter. High school course selection affects college trajectory. Some high schools do not offer gifted programs, or if they do, they are underenrolled in by low-income students because of entry criteria. Indeed, this underenrollment is not limited to students from low-income households. Many schools have internal tracking mechanisms and discourage certain students from taking honors classes. The students who want to take these classes often need to submit essays to be granted permission. Picture that: A student wants to take a harder course, and impediments are placed in his or her way. Have we gone a tad off course here? If a student wants to try an honor's course, why aren't we applauding?

There is work that explores teacher biases based on race. Because of informational asymmetries, neither students nor their parents know the impact of the choices they are making based on teacher and institutional bias—even when that bias is hidden or unrecognized. So within high school, some students see themselves as college material while others do not—based on teacher reaction, course placement, parental observation, and self-perception.[9]

Add into this mix the role of school counselors and National Association for College Admissions Counseling data that point out the problems that occur in the whole counseling process. We have noted many of these issues in earlier chapters. Many counselors do not spend most of their time on college counseling, and there is immense complexity in completing financial aid forms and college applications, making quality completion difficult for counselors, who themselves may not be fully up to date and are working with families without experience or resources. Then, there is the college selection process itself, which is fraught with problems, from identifying a school that is the right fit, often without a visit, and then taking the needed tests (SAT, ACT, or AP), commonly without the benefit of tutoring. And even if we get all that right—and there is every indication that we do not—issues of financial aid packages come into play. Low-income parents need help navigating financial aid comparisons. They need to ask the right questions. They need access to the right information.[10]

There is also this reality: Even for kids who are accepted to college from low-income families, many do not land on those campuses where they were accepted and made a deposit. This is caused by what is termed "summer melt," which occurs in the summer between high school grad-uation and attendance in college. In other words, the high school records that a student is headed to college because that student received an accep-tance letter and said he or she was enrolling. But the student never gets to college, perhaps because of financial constraints. Perhaps because of a change of mind. Perhaps because the student became scared. The high school has "completed" its work upon the student's graduation (student into and deposited at a college), but in truth, that is the beginning, not the end, of the process. The need to address summer melt, a critically import-ant issue for low-income students and breakaway students, looms large.[11]

As if this were not sufficiently challenging, the rate of stopping out and dropping out during college is considerable for low-income and breakaway students. Nontraditional students (returning students, veter-ans, adults) face other challenges, including lack of navigational skills in a school environment, lack of recent academic readiness, and a sense of possible failure. For all students, life interferes; there can be family illness or dysfunction that necessitates leaving school or distracts from school success. In some cases, the lack of academic readiness presents challenges, leading to poor grades and low self-esteem. In other instances, the col-lege fit is not a good one; the school is too large or too small or does not have the needed major or is too close or too far from home. In still other instances, there are no mentors or peer role models to ease the transition and overcome the inevitable bumps in the road. Low-income students and breakaway students often enter college as if they were going into a foreign land where they do not know the language and have few translators.[12]

Stated most simply, there are high hurdles all along the educational landscape, and the running between the hurdles does not have the evenness demonstrated so ably by Olympic track and field competitors. While we have interventions that can be instituted all along the way, they are hard to coordinate and to replicate and scale. While I laud all the individual and collective efforts to improve the educational pipeline, I worry that there is not enough time to make the changes needed to get a sufficient number of low-income and breakaway kids to and through postsecondary education.

Lasticity may be a made-up word (at present!), but its five building blocks have power, and there are data supporting their application. We need to move fast. Here are several suggestions, lest we lose a generation or two while we plot and plan for wide-scale implementation, assuming (a big assumption) there is desired uptake.

Why assume that the burden of lasticity's implementation rests with the educational institutions? What if we brought in others to help with this process? For example, what if obstetricians had videos or classes in their waiting rooms about how new parents (or second- or third-time parents) could help their children—prenatally and in early childhood? What if pediatricians held reading groups once a month for their low-income families? What if churches and after-school programs had many free support programs with resources that families could take home? How about free books? What if preschool and elementary school principals visited parents in local community centers, with childcare provided, to talk about their needs and wants and desires for their children and how those items can be met? What if we had mechanisms for learning which wee kids had high adverse childhood experience (ACE) scores? To be sure—and don't fly out of your seats here—some of these efforts are happening, which is commendable on every level, but these initiatives are not consistent and systemic and systematic. And they are not well publicized nationally, nor are they seen as part and parcel of the overall national strategic effort to foster the success of breakaway students across the educational pipelines.

Consider this example: A study published in the *Journal of the American Medical Association* demonstrated that programs that educate parents of prekindergarten children on how to assist their kids in developing social skills while the schools also worked with their children led to improved educational attainment and fewer psychological problems. How about replicating efforts like this?[13]

I appreciate all the resources that get poured into colleges (and prep schools); I understand the benefits of gargantuan endowments. I also am aware of the increased focus on helping low-income, first-generation, minority kids success in college. The number of organizations in this space is growing—some might say flourishing. But after decades in higher education, and despite its importance, we find that our efforts there are, sadly, too little, too late. We need to put our time, money, attention, and creativity into the effort of thinking about ages 0–7. Really.

I recollect the story of a Florida elementary school principal who obtained funding to send home plastic-covered table runners to put on the kitchen tables of families who had students enrolled in his school. These runners had buckets of information—on upcoming events, on what was occurring in the classrooms in the school, and about things parents could do with their kids after school, as well as questions that could be used to activate thoughtful dinner conversations. The runners had phone numbers, and they were bilingual—just flip the runner, so to speak. Monthly, the runners were replaced by new ones. This principal saw remarkable improvement in parental engagement on every level. It was a program that was replicable and scalable. And then suddenly funding just disappeared, and with it the runners. One effort—a valuable flash in the pan—gone.

Within the conversation on testing—a hot topic on every measure—we can ask if there is a way to test for lasticity. And the simple answer at present is no. To be sure, there are many things for which we test—academic subjects, personality traits, traumatic upbringing, grit, and resiliency. We could develop a lasticity scale and then measure whether students were becoming—with appropriate interventions—more lastic. The same holds true with the schools our students attend.

However, as a starting measure, I'd like to suggest a different approach, given that vetting verifiable testing for lasticity is a long way off and will take years of data input and calibration, assuming there are quality measurement tools in place. Since lasticity has its origins in students who succeed rather than those who fail, we could—as this book does throughout—identify the key personal and institutional behaviors and activities that make up lasticity's building blocks and make them part of institutional culture.

Rather than a lasticity test (and whether we need one or more such tests is a topic for another day), we could create another type of instrument: a checklist. A quality checklist could alert institutions all along the educational pipeline on key issues, strategies, behaviors, and events that they could be paying attention to and conducting—things that could shift toward a more lastic institutional culture in the near and longer term. And the checklists could be tailored to each age range and have sets of options that could be deployed with the names of the individuals responsible for overseeing progress. Faculty and staff could assist in the preparation of the checklists and could adapt existing checklists to serve their institutional culture more effectively.

There is increasing appreciation of checklists and the thought that needs to go into their construction. Starting in medicine with the groundbreaking work of Peter Pronovos, we saw empirically how checklists could curb medical errors. This led to expanded use of checklists in other aspects of medicine. Then, we progressed to the development of a wide range of checklists in different disciplines outside medicine, including education. Atul Gawande wrote an entire book on the value of checklists and observed that some of their key attributes are simplicity, prioritization, and teamwork. Indeed, as we reflect back on lasticity and its messages, these three qualities are key in that arena too—meaning that checklists are a suitable means of pushing for lasticity's adoption, and sooner rather than later.[14]

Checklists in the sphere of education run the risk of being treated in a perfunctory manner and becoming mechanistic. Just check the box, so to speak. They can cap creativity, and they can be too directive. They can ask, Did students read X? Did they understand Y? Did they spell Z correctly? Did they use proper grammar? Was their paper neat, with a staple at the top?

Well-designed checklists with respect to lasticity, however, could be bold and expansive and empowering. Consider, in constructing such a checklist, the acronym developed by Dennis Sparks with respect to checklists, CREATE: Core tasks of teaching, Results for students, Every day, All teachers, Team-based learning, Evidence-based decisionmaking. Imagine a checklist (part of a list) for all institutions across the pre-K–20 pipeline (Table 15.1).[15]

The call for urgent change also relates to the current rhetoric that is used to describe our students, including but not exclusively limited to breakaway students. We have allowed "rhetorical capture"; lots of ink is spilled on elite institutions when millions upon millions of students do not attend these institutions. While we can claim that some of the student bashing is an effort to get headlines and otherwise attract media attention,

Table 15.1. Checklist

Activity/Event	Tried	Not Yet Tried	To Be Tried	Ignore
Meeting students before start of school	√			
Greeting students personally on 1st day of classes	√			
Teacher training across disciplines	√			
Teacher training with faculty across different age levels		√	√	
Student input on rules in classrooms and residential halls			√	
Syllabus deconstruction and samples				√

there is a pernicious quality to the terms used, and negative attributes tend to have stickiness. We can ill afford to damage our students even further. And we can ill afford to focus on those institutions that have the most money, the highest prestige, and the fewest low-income, first-generation students.

In the preface to his coauthored *Generation on a Tightrope*, certain statements made by well-known academician Arthur Levine make my blood boil: "Today's college students have extraordinarily close ties with their parents and are in 24/7 contact with a tribe of friends, family, and acquaintances. . . . In contrast to their predecessors, today's college students are more immature, dependent, coddled, and entitled."[16]

Really? Of whom is he speaking? The students who attend elite colleges and universities who are from high-wealth families? Even for those students (as opposed to low-income students), his observations are misguided and offensive. Should I assume—and this is without personal knowledge—that Dr. Levine grew up with great independence, with a lack of entitlement, and with maturity fostered through not being coddled? I am only half kidding. Dr. Levine is not alone in his assessment of current students.

In another instance, I was rendered speechless by a book, referred to above, that claims to explain how liberal arts colleges prepare students for life. Titled *Practice for Life: Making Decisions in College*, the book focuses on seven elite colleges and the students who attend them over a period of years. The book tries to draw conclusions about how students (I assume the authors mean all students, to increase the book's relevance and audience) view time, connections, home, advice, and engagement. While I buy into the value of a liberal education for many students and find it consistent with and complementary to workforce readiness, this book represents the views of a only tiny portion of America's students.

Consider certain observations in *Practice for Life*—ones that are grotesquely out of place in the context of the many breakaway students populating our institutions. The authors note that college provides opportunities for restarts, as if this were the first time students had this opportunity. For breakaway kids, restarts are part and parcel of everyday existence. At another point, the authors observe, "Virtually all of the students in our study planned to go directly from high school to college. . . . Assumptions about going to college were, for the most part, assumptions about going to a highly selective, prestigious college."[17] This student population, then, is totally disconnected from the 7-plus million students who are not attending elite colleges and for whom thinking about college has not been a reality since childhood. There is an assumption that many college students study abroad, perhaps at elite colleges, but that is most assuredly not true for most low-income students. In describing the college search process, the authors note that most parents were involved in helping their children navigate through it, with the exception being many parents of first-generation students and international students. The book continues to describe students who had close personal relationships with their high school guidance counselors (who knew them well) and were not willing to reach out to college faculty their 1st year in the same way. In a sense, these students had been spoiled by extraordinary attention from their high school mentors.

Yeek. Breakaway student Jailene Gonzalez, whose artwork appears elsewhere in this book (see Figures 4.2 and 8.1), created an image (Figure 15.1) that stands in sharp contrast to the preceding descriptions of today's students. In her artwork, note the faces. Note the boulders or impediments. Note the struggle. See the small green pathway to success. Observe the red hand.

Figure 15.1. Artwork by Jailene Gonzalez of faces, a red hand, a green path, and rocks as impediments.

Here's what's really wrong: Folks read a book like *Practice for Life* and assume that what they are reading is applicable to all students. We need—urgently, in my view—to move away from reifying privilege and from spending all our time and attention on institutions and students who need our help the least. That is not to say that breakaway students at elite institutions have an easy time of it. They don't. But in a world of limited resources and priorities, where should we be spending our time and directing our attention?

Ponder microaggressions, a topic that gets scant attention in *Practice for Life*. I wrote a piece on microaggressions and how hurtful they are to students. I spoke about how they have a cumulative effect. As I expressed in my piece, "The best current example of the importance of recognizing, acknowledging and responding to subtle-discrimination [*sic*] (microaggressions) is the scholarship conducted by Professor Destin and his team with respect to how to make low-income students feel more 'at home' on campuses—a critical issue if they are to progress to and through college. The scholars refer to 'chilly' and 'warm' institutional messaging, the difference being the degree to which students feel welcomed on campus."[18]

I received several "chilly" messages in response to this piece on microaggressions; others who support efforts to curb this behavior have received similar comments. A sampling of replies (direct quotes) to my piece (with names deleted) is revelatory: "Here's some major aggression for you: Thought Gestapo, go **** yourselves. Enough of this PC madness already!" "What is this drivel? Get a thicker skin."

What do students feel and experience, then, in response to their experiences of microaggressions? Now, whether or not one believes that there even are microaggressions, hostile responses like those just cited seem over the top to me and hurtful. But perhaps there is an added layer to all this: Some adults are not comfortable with today's students and their behavior, but rather than trying to understand the students, they seek cover by criticizing them or treating behavior like microaggressions as if they did not exist.

Consider the behavior of the former president of the University of Missouri who, when confronted by protesters in a parade on campus, out of fear refused to exit his car, which was surrounded by security guards. What, exactly, did this president think would happen if he got out to talk to students? They would hurt him physically?

Many moons ago, I remember running onto a college baseball diamond to break up a fight between a coach from another college's team, an umpire, and a parent of one of our players. To be sure, the situation should not have escalated, but that was and is water under the dam. In retrospect, my rush to the field was probably not the wisest move. I could have been hit by any number of people—with fists, bats, or baseballs. Nevertheless, I thought I could help resolve the situation and lower the tension, and my well-being seemed to pale in comparison with the impending danger of a rush to the field by players from both teams, as well as fans.

To those who want safe spaces and trigger warnings and who experience microaggressions, a common response on and off campus is "Lighten up. Get a sense of humor. Stop asking for such political correctness. This isn't anything to get all hot and bothered by, anyway." Campus personnel have commented on how hard it is to find a comedian who can perform without being offensive. I know about offensive comedians. I grew up in the era of Lenny Bruce and George Carlin and Lewis Black, among others. And I found them funny. Crass, too. Disrespectful, too.

But that was a different time, and what is funny in one era may not be funny in another. Quiet humor among friends is not the same as live humor in a gathering with hundreds of people. Humor within the confines of a cultural group joking with each other does not mean those jokes can be made by others outside the group. Some terms are acceptable in some circumstances and totally off limits in others. Same with Jewish humor. Teasing within one's subgroup is not the same as teasing that is done by outsiders.

Here's why expanding the focus beyond the elites and cleaning up language matters: The offensive, inaccurate terms tend to get reified. They become part of the way people are described, even if they are totally inaccurate. In light of this, I did a wee experiment (true, it does not meet social science standards) in which I did an Internet search for the terms *coddled* and *fragile* in the context of contemporary college students. The results were frightening. Hundreds upon hundreds of references were made—unapologetically.

However, the majority of children and young adults today are neither coddled nor fragile. If anything, they are the opposite: They have been forced into independence way too early and they are tough, having survived more life experiences in their 10 or 20 years than most of those who criticize them (other than members of the military). (I got a lot of flak for that observation too.) Now, it is true that there are some coddled and fragile kids. Yes, their parents and schools protect them to their detriment, and these students are what I term "trophy kids"; they get a trophy for everything. Books are written about them.

The bigger and better question is, Why do we create national norms based on the few as opposed to the many? Why use terms that apply to the few to refer to the many?

I am still reeling from events involving Yale students at Silliman (a residential college at Yale) and Nicolas and Erika Christakis, the house masters of the college referred to in Chapter 3. Forget the tone of Erika's Halloween email to students in which she encouraged offensive costumes. Forget Nicolas's body language when he confronted students (evidenced repeatedly in widely seen videos of a student confrontation with him in the Silliman quadrangle as he stood firm) and his total inability to apologize and deescalate the situation (all the more shocking, since he is both a renowned sociologist and a physician).[19]

Here's what really got to me: Erika and Nicolas Christakis stopped teaching. The events occurred in the late fall, and both husband and wife said they would not be teaching at Yale in the spring. Really. They wanted to pick up their marbles and go home. (To be fair, I have always assumed this was their choice and not Yale's.) They had lost the battle with the residents of the college they oversaw and now they were not going to teach. They are educators; shouldn't they have used these moments to educate the next generation? Shouldn't they have had the courage to teach students who lived in Silliman or in another of Yale's colleges? By all accounts, both were excellent teachers. Who's depriving whom and why?

The Christakises' decision to take their toys and go home is what reinforces the ability of outsiders (and perhaps insiders) to complain, "Look at these kids. They are so coddled. They can't even speak civilly and they are hypersensitive. Who would want to teach these privileged snoots?" Seems to me that the roles are reversed: It is the Christakises who are oversensitive, who are retreating and failing to carry out their responsibilities. What this whole episode shows me is two grown adults who can't handle the concerns of breakaway kids. They plain missed the culture at Yale, and the differences in culture between Yale and their predecessor academic base, Harvard. Their behavior could lead to a lesson that is easily adopted by other faculty: These kids are unteachable or do not deserve to be taught by us.

The examples described in this chapter, including the book *Practice for Life* critiqued here, suggest to me the urgency of improving education and how we treat each other. The examples also suggest that lasticity is not a concept on paper that can wait for decades for implementation. We need it now—for our individual and collective benefit.

With that urgency in mind, we now turn to how a new word, in this case, *lasticity*, can and should enter our lexicon both informally and formally.

CHAPTER 16

Lasticity's Entrance
into the Lexicon

Lasticity is a made-up word (for the most part) designed to improve the lives of the very real and plentiful breakaway students in our educational system. My hope is that, through this book and the explanations and exemplars given, this new word has developed a nonhypothetical raison d'être, that its five component building blocks have value as we think about enabling breakaway student success. *Lasticity* is a word that fills a deep descriptive void in the English language.

As has been noted throughout the book, there is no umbrella word that encompasses the process and characteristics and behaviors that will enable breakaway student success and how institutions and those within them need to be an integral part of the process of enabling that success.

In the interest of full disclosure here, for decades I have been drawn to make-believe words, particularly those for which one can divine their meaning by repeating them aloud. Indeed, some words are better spoken than read. They sound real even if they are not. Case in point: Lewis Carroll's powerful poem "Jabberwocky."[1] Here is its opening stanza:

'Twas brillig, and the slithy toves
Did gyre and gimble in the wabe:
All mimsy were the borogoves,
And the mome raths outgrabe.

Yes, it is filled with make-believe words. But when one hears the poem or even when one reads it, but less so, those make-believe words gather meaning. We understand the words even though we know they are not real words. Indeed, there are whole bodies of literary criticism that reflect on the true meaning of Carroll's poem and the exact words used—real criticism of make-believe words.

Two other examples from my own life: There is a make-believe word that I have used (and still use) with our sheepdogs when I want them to leave an area that is dangerous on our or other people's property (remembering that the job of sheepdogs is to herd sheep). The word is *bah-bah-zee* (emphasis is on the first two syllables). It means "Don't go there" and often needs to be repeated. And, for whatever reason, it seems to be understood, at least by my four-legged creatures.

Then we have Ishkahbibble Mahzie—the name of the imaginary person who lived with us when our son was two. Ishkahbibble, as he (yes, he) was called for short, was of course invisible and never came when called, but one could accidentally sit on him at the dinner table, and we did refer to him by name when we spoke to our son about him or spoke to this imaginary friend directly. There was humor in the name, and it was sort of an inside parent (and perhaps child) joke that we all knew Ishkahbibble was a fiction, but we treated him as if he were real. His name expressed that very quality.

And so it is with *lasticity*. I hope that as this book has progressed, the word *lasticity* has come to have meaning. As explored in the copious literature on the subject, words can enter dictionaries, becoming part of the lexicon as the language changes. Frequency of use is key; if the word is coined by a person who is a media personality or a politician or has fame in the arts or music, that helps considerably. Hmm, that's not much help here—unless I can get David Brooks or Hank Paulson or Oprah to start using the word, and to use it frequently, and take ownership of it, so to speak.

Allan Metcalf, a forensic linguist, uses the acronym FUDGE as a guide to determining which words are truly worthy of entering the lexicon, and, yes, he admits to fudging a bit in applying this process.[2]

In FUDGE, the *F* refers to *frequency*—the more the new word is used the better. Time to capture a website name with the word *lasticity*. (Done.) Yes, I have given speeches using the word, with increasing frequency beginning in 2016. The *U* relates to *unobtrusiveness*, namely, that the word should feel natural and normal within our language and sound system. *Lasticity* would seem to meet this test, as it sounds like something that actually should be a word, as noted in Chapter 2. And it is composed of real words—*elastic, plastic, last*. The *D* refers to *diversity* and the abundance of ways the new word can be used. We have a whole book and a concept mobile and illustrations demonstrating just that—revealing the absence of a simple, one-dimensional meaning attached to the noun *lasticity* and its adjective form, *lastic*. The *G* relates to the need for the word to be available for *general* use and not for a subgroup of specialists. For example, words that appeal to only paleontologists would not meet the test. *Lasticity* is a broad term and not limited to educators, although it is used in that context here in this book. Its application is also not limited to people; it can refer to institutions too. Institutions need lasticity, as do people. Since the word can be applied outside the realm of education, broad as that area is, that adds to potential usage. Businesses could be lastic and demonstrate lasticity. So could governments. So could categories of professionals, such as physicians. Personally, and to offer a friendly amendment to Metcalf's acronym, I think the *G* could also stand for *gap* filling, putting something in the language that is sorely needed but not there. Lasticity goes well beyond grit and resiliency, growth mindsets, and mindfulness. Finally, the *E* represents *endurance*—meaning the concept has durability and the concept for which it stands has value. Certainly a term that can improve education across the infancy-to-adult pipeline for breakaway students has endurance, particularly as institutions start to implement its foundational pieces. And if the data needle on student success moves, all the more "durable" the term becomes. Add to this the well-established changing demographics of our nation, making the effort to foster breakaway student success not just a theoretical construct but also an urgent national imperative. In sum, then, I think *lasticity* satisfies the FUDGE test. So what would a dictionary definition look like? Try the definition shown in the box, although lexicologists clearly are better at this particular task than I am.

LASTICITY

las/tic/i/ty
la-ˈsti-sə-tē

Origins: Combination of the American English word *elastic*, derived from the Latin root *elasticus* and Greek root *elastos*, meaning "ductile and flexible," as well as the American English *plastic* from the Latin *plasticus* and Greek *platikos*, meaning "to be molded or formed." Related also to the noun and verb *last* (as in *endure*), derived from the Old English *læstan*, "to continue, endure," and describing the wooden model of a human foot used by shoemakers.

Noun: The description of a set of conditions that exist under an umbrella concept that, if met, provide a process (of which reciprocity is a key element) that can be deployed and redeployed to assist individuals who have experienced toxic stress or trauma or other impediments in their lives to flourish in childhood and thereafter in education and in life.

Similar words: adaptation, adaptability, adaptable; adapt, elasticity, plasticity

Synonyms: None

Antonyms: deficient, deformed, incapable of improvement

Sentence use: We need to promote *lasticity* across the educational pipeline so more students can earn postsecondary degrees.

Another example: *Lasticity* exhibited by educational institutions and those within them can foster student success across the pre-K–20 educational landscape.

Adjective: lastic: the descriptor of the combination of foundational elements that involve other people and organizations, enabling a person to overcome obstacles and use his or her experiences (both positive and negative) to succeed in education or in life.

Sentence use: Janice is *lastic*, and that accounts for her graduating from college on time and entering the workforce.

Another example: Would that more students could be *lastic* so the educational divide could be narrowed considerably.

This formalized definition, with its connection to existing words and with a basis in words from centuries ago, gives some texture to the new term *lasticity*. It involves flexibility and being reshaped (molded) and indicates the presence of endurance. But in an odd way, like the wooden model of a foot just referenced, it creates a unique footprint—the footprint of the person who can now move forward, sharing his or her strengths and drawing on his or her negative experiences in unexpected and unanticipated ways. Not to be too trite here, lasticity (if fully animated with its five conditions met) does facilitate the creation of the footprints of breakaway students—ideally millions of them.[3]

Lasticity is also a clarion call for a culture change, one that will encourage all of us—educators in the broadest sense—to provide shoulders that others can learn on. And make no mistake about this: It takes many shoulders out there that our students can lean on in order for them to learn. I hope you will join me in becoming a shoulder to learn on.

CHAPTER 17

Promises Made and Kept

Lasticity describes a pathway pursuant to which breakaway students and the institutions serving them can garner success. While supported by theory and data, it is grounded in real-world experiences across the educational landscape. It is premised on reciprocal relationships and is animated by real people and the institutions that employ them.

This last narrative, a true story and a bookend to the true story shared at the beginning of this book in Chapter 1, captures lasticity in all its complexity and demonstrates its five foundational building blocks—elasticity, plasticity, pivoting right, reciprocity, and belief in self. Some background adds meaning to this final story. And there is more, an update on this graduate now, as he and I continue to remain in touch.

Nick Harrington was a star basketball player from New York City, and my first year as president of Southern Vermont College was his first year back on campus after a hiatus caused by poor grades and becoming ineligible for collegiate athletics. He had spent the year working in Vermont to earn money and working out to keep in shape. Nick had (and still has) an easy charm, covering up a life that was by no means easy.

Nick became my project. I was determined to see him graduate, propelled by a conversation I had had with his mother in the college gym while she was watching her son play.

Seated next to Ms. Harrington at a game, I remarked that I wished she could be at more of Nick's games. She replied, somewhat tartly but also sadly, "And how would I make that happen? Just suppose I could get off work. And how exactly would I get here to Vermont? And even assuming I got to Albany by train and Nick could come to pick me up (by borrowing a car) and get me to campus, where would I spend the night and how would I get to and from a hotel to campus and where would I eat? Not possible." I sat there stunned, having, to my chagrin, received this response, and I was again struck by the hurdles of breakaway students and their families. That moment, when I was so cavalier as to say in essence, "You really should support your son by coming to more games," still haunts me. Still.

No one in Nick's family had traveled abroad. This will be relevant as the story unfolds. No one in the family had a passport. But even if they had, they could not have afforded a trip to, say, Europe. They could not have paid for such a trip, nor could they have taken the time off work and then returned to their job. Nick had made that clear to me.

In some ways, this entire book seeks to respond to the issues raised by Ms. Harrington those many years ago. Lasticity is an approach, a concept, a process to make the seemingly impossible possible. It is a concept that is empowering; it is a concept that gives us hope. It is a concept that changes us and how we respond to the students we serve.

Here is Nick's story and mine, originally published in 2010 on the Southern Vermont College president's blog.

THE PROMISES WE MAKE; THE PROMISES WE KEEP

We all make promises, promises to ourselves, promises to others; oft-times, we do not keep these promises. This is a story about promises made and kept.

The first part of this story is well known on the SVC [Southern Vermont College] campus. SVC student Nick Harrington was offered a contract to play professional basketball in Europe in Spring 2008. At the time he was offered the contract, he was one course short of graduating with his bachelor's degree in business from SVC.

Nick and I made promises to each other: he promised to finish his undergraduate education while playing basketball in Germany, and I promised Nick that he could celebrate the signing of his professional contract in our home. We both kept our promises. Nick's contract was inked on our dining room to many cheering members of the SVC community, and he proudly marched in Commencement in May 2009—after completing his one remaining course with SVC professor Bob Consalvo.

Now fast forward.

After his year in Germany, Nick began playing professional basketball at a higher level in Luxembourg, for the Grengewald Hostert. He came to my office with this new proposition: "If my contract to play in Luxembourg is renewed, will you come see me play abroad?" I said yes. This past summer, Nick's contract was renewed. Earlier this month, I made good on that promise.

Last week I flew via a rather small plane to Luxembourg where Nick and his team were playing in an exhibition tournament at Am Sand, his home court. I arrived with 15 extra-large tee-shirts that said "Southern Vermont College" and three containers of maple syrup—one for Nick, one for his professional coach, and one for his team president.

At the arena, I immediately saw Nick and his teammates on the court practicing for their first of two games and looking as graceful and poised as I remembered him from his SVC playing days. I could not just stand there; so, I found my way onto the court, and Nick greeted me with a big hug.

Shortly after the first game, Nick came up to the team president's suite and said to me: "Wait 'til you see this." One by one, Nick's Luxembourg teammates came up to meet me, each of whom was proudly wearing an SVC tee shirt. When they were all gathered, one of them remarked to the assembled crowd, "Now, Nick will feel at home here." (See Figure 17.1.)

Figure 17.1. Karen Gross, Nick Harrington, and Grengewald Hostert team.

Nick's entire team practiced with those SVC tee shirts for the second game and wore them on the bench when they were not on the court. The Grengewald Hostert team won that game handily, with Nick playing with remarkable intensity and strength (the dunks were spectacular). I wondered to myself whether these SVC tee shirts were good luck.

At the awards ceremony following the game, Nick and his team-mates presented me with a signed team basketball, and his team president gave me a Grengewald Hostert team uniform, all items now proudly displayed in the SVC Athletic Hall of Fame. And, the Grenge-wald players advised me that from that moment forward, they would warm up in SVC tee shirts—symbols, they decided, of good luck for the upcoming season.

It was wonderful seeing Nick play basketball again—what a joy to see him excelling on the court. But what was even more wonderful was seeing Nick thrive in a new environment. Nick is working at a job he loves; he is making friends. He is always smiling, always gracious, always welcoming, and always cheering on his Grengewald Hostert teammates. He is making himself at home in a foreign nation and mak-ing us proud each and every day.

We both made promises; we both kept our promises; we are both better for it.

Lasticity at work. However, the story does not end there. Nick and I have continued our relationship. First, I handed him his diploma (he re-turned to the United States to be able to cross the stage, although he tech-nically received the degree the prior December, as promised). His mother and father were there, and his family had come to our home before the ceremony. I had a tradition that all graduates and their families visited our home before the graduation ceremony so I could congratulate them personally and share their successes with them in an intimate setting. Lit-erally hundreds of people came into our home for pregraduation brunch on those days, and these events remain some of my fondest memories of my time as college president.

I remember Nick's mother coming in holding a box of tissues—a whole box. I looked at the box and asked if she was okay (as in "Do you have a cold?"), to which she responded, "This is a big day for our family and I plan on using every single one of those tissues throughout the day, as I will be crying so much." Again, she was teaching me. I still have a picture of Nick in his graduation garb with his parents, his coach, and me, all celebrating that day.

Fast forward: Nick continued his basketball success in Europe, until he was injured in 2014. Following surgery, he has been rehabbing in the United States and has started to work full time as a concierge at a hotel in

New York City. He's looking to buy a car. It's not clear if his hoops days are over. I harbor fantasies that he will coach, so hundreds of kids can be mentored—Nick's quite a role model. He still lives at home in New York. In addition to exchanging emails with Nick, I stay up to date on his activities through his prior basketball coach. Here's a selection of emails Nick and I have exchanged since my trip to Luxembourg. They are slightly edited (to correct errors and typos and to protect privacy); they are dated and appear in chronological order from oldest to newest.

Nick Harrington to Karen Gross (June 16, 2014)

Hey mom how are u doing?

Karen Gross to Nick Harrington (June 16, 2014)

I am fine—recovering from a wee fall. A couple broken bones and torn bicep . . . but more importantly, how are you? How is the knee? When are you back in US? Weren't the Spurs amazing????? Miss you . . . nice to be your second mom.

Nick Harrington to Karen Gross (June 16, 2014)

I am happy u are recovering . . . happy it was nothing too bad. I am doing well—been going to rehab and stuff and the knee is way better. No longer on crutches and I can bend my knee and walk. I still have the brace on . . . I am also doing a side business or should I say I am an independent business owner? So I am working on that now, trying to do something to help other people and help them to change their lives and get out of their comfort zones. Miss and love you and u will always be my second mom.

Nick Harrington to Karen Gross (August 31, 2016)

Good morning Mom. I am doing well, working in the city now as a Concierge in Manhattan and taking classes with my Union. . . . And that's awesome you are writing a book and i am happy you included me in it. I am excited to read it. The knee is gettin' better. I miss you a lot; i am so happy to be in contact with you still. Me and my parents were talking about you last night. Hope you and your husband and son are doing well. Would love to come see you. Let me know when u are in Vermont and I'll drive up and see you. It has been way too long since i have seen you. Always thinking of you.

Karen Gross to Nick Harrington (August 31, 2016)

Aw . . . I also come to NYC periodically. So, we can meet there too.
Our son is fine—now a professor. . . . My husband has had a lot of
health issues—so that is tough on many levels. I wrote a children's
book too—will give you a copy to give your mom when I see you—
visit the website: www.ladylucysquest.com. Adult book is called
Breakaway Learners, out in early 2017. Glad you are doing well.
And, yes, I will always be your second Mom. Always.

Shoulders to learn on. Yes, indeed. Lasticity. Yes, indeed.

Notes

Chapter 1

1. "Lorraine Maxwell, Cornell University—Schools Falling Apart" (blog post), by David Hopper, September 20, 2016, *Academic Minute*, academicminute.org/2016/09/lorraine-maxwell-cornell-university-schools-falling-apart/; "Why Leaders Need to Be Great Storytellers," by Christine Comaford, September 10, 2016, *Forbes*, www.forbes.com/sites/christinecomaford/2016/09/10/have-something-to-say-heres-how-to-ensure-people-hear-you/2/#7dee02a043f1; "How Storytelling Affects the Brain," by Eric Garland, March 29, 2016, www.ericgarland.co/2016/03/29/storytelling-brain/.

2. For the value of storytelling, a theme that runs through this book, see "Why Leaders Need to Be Great Storytellers," by Christine Comaford, September 10, 2016, *Forbes*, www.forbes.com/sites/christinecomaford/2016/09/10/have-something-to-say-heres-how-to-ensure-people-hear-you/2/#7dee02a043f1.

3. For a sampling of scholarship and general books and articles on these topics, see *Our Kids: The American Dream in Crisis*, by Robert D. Putnam (New York, NY: Simon and Schuster, 2015); *The Student Loan Mess: How Good Intentions Created a Trillion-Dollar Problem*, by Joel Best and Eric Best (Berkeley and Los Angeles, CA: University of California Press, 2014); "Poverty and Merit," by Paul Fain, January 12, 2016, *Inside Higher Ed*, www.insidehighered.com/news/2016/01/12/high-achieving-low-income-students-remain-rare-most-selective-colleges; "On Wealth Gap, Old Song, New Words," by Karen Gross, May 28, 2015, *Inside Higher Ed*, www.insidehighered.com/views/2015/05/28/possible-solutions-higher-ed-wealth-gap-old-problem-essay; "College Tuition and Fees Increase 63 Percent Since January 2006," August 30, 2016, *TED: The Economics Daily*, www.bls.gov/opub/ted/2016/college-tuition-and-fees-increase-63-percent-since-january-2006.htm; *Early Warning! Why Reading by the End of Third Grade Matters*, by the Annie E. Casey Foundation, 2010, www.ccf.ny.gov/files/9013/8262/2751/AECFRepor-ReadingGrade3.pdf; "The Alarming Effect of Racial Mismatch on Teacher Expectations," by Seth Gershenson, August 18, 2015, Brookings, www.brookings.edu/blog/brown-center-chalkboard/2015/08/18/the-alarming-effect-of-racial-mismatch-on-teacher-expectations/; *Cheated: The UNC Scandal, the Education of Athletes,*

and the Future of Big-Time College Sports, by Jay M. Smith and Mary Willingham (Lincoln, NE: Potomac Books, 2015).

4. *America Needs Talent: Attracting, Educating, and Deploying the 21st-Century Workforce*, by Jamie Merisotis (New York, NY: RosettaBooks, 2015); "Nontraditional Students Like Me Face Enormous Challenges," by An Garagiola-Bernier, September 14, 2016, *Community College Daily*, www.ccdaily.com/Pages/Campus-Issues/Nontraditional-students-like-me-face-enormous-challenges.aspx.

5. *Bowling Alone: The Collapse and Revival of American Community*, by Robert D. Putnam (New York, NY: Simon and Schuster, 2007); *Our Kids: The American Dream in Crisis*, by Robert D. Putnam (New York, NY: Simon and Schuster, 2015).

6. "A Wider Lens on the 'Match' Between Students and Colleges," by Beckie Supiano, August 22, 2016, *The Chronicle of Higher Education*, chronicle.com/article/A-Wider-Lens-on-the/237519; "Research: Teacher-Retention Rates Higher Than Previously Thought" (blog post), by Stephen Sawchuk, May 1, 2015, *Teacher Beat*, blogs.edweek.org/edweek/teacherbeat/2015/05/research_teacher-retentions_ra.html; "'Our Compelling Interests," by Scott Jaschik, October 4, 2016, *Inside Higher Ed*, www.insidehighered.com/news/2016/10/04/new-book-scholars-make-case-value-diversity-higher-education-and-society-generally; "The Business Decision Segregating College Students by Income and Race," by John Marcus, September 26, 2016, *The Hechinger Report*, hechingerreport.org/business-decision-segregating-college-students-income-race/; "This Chart Debunks Some Common Myths About University Students," by Joe Myers, July 12, 2016, World Economic Forum, www.weforum.org/agenda/2016/07/this-chart-debunks-some-common-myths-about-university-students/.

7. "A Solution as Obvious as It Is Rare: Making High School Graduates Ready for College," by Jon Marcus, August 18, 2016, *The Hechinger Report*, hechinger-report.org/solution-obvious-rare-making-high-school-graduates-ready-college/; "Making Modern Toughness," by David Brooks, August 30, 2016, *The New York Times*, www.nytimes.com/2016/08/30/opinion/making-modern-toughness.html; "Teachers Seize On 'Growth Mindset,' but Crave More Training," by Evie Brad, September 20, 2016, *Education Week*, www.edweek.org/ew/articles/2016/09/21/teachers-seize-on-growth-mindset-but-crave.html; "Remedial Education: The Cost of Catching Up," by Laura Jimenez, Scott Sargrad, Jessica Morales, and Maggie Thompson, September 28, 2016, Center for American Progress, www.americanprogress.org/issues/education/report/2016/09/28/144000/remedial-education/.

Chapter 2

1. The full quote is "I like a word that embodies its meaning within its sound, dances and somersaults within its sound. 'Shimmer' is an example. Other wonderful words: *cringe, tinkle, grimace, farrago, thump, squirt, mumble, wisp*. The

sound unlocks an imagined scene, the sound puts me in the action, tells me what to be suspicious of and what to believe in. It's not just *onomatopoeia*—maybe you need to know English to know what these words mean, but they could all be acted out by amateurs and the speaker of Portuguese or Turkish would understand. They are 'sound glimpses,' perhaps into a room that has no fourth wall" (Roa Lynn, quoted in *Favorite Words of Famous People*, by Lewis Burke Frumkes [Portland, OR: Marion Street Press, 2011]); see also "Sound Symbolism (Words)," About.com, updated January 1, 2016, grammar.about.com/od/rs/g/soundsymbolismterm.htm; "The Ugliest Words; Marilyn Monroe's Dog; and Wacko Races," by David Crystal, Kate Mosse, John Dugdale, and Alison Flood, *The Guardian*, July 17, 2009, https://www.theguardian.com/books/2009/jul/18/ugliest-words-michael-jackson-biographies.

2. "Making Modern Toughness," by David Brooks, August 30, 2016, *The New York Times* (op-ed), www.nytimes.com/2016/08/30/opinion/making-modern-toughness.html; *How Children Succeed: Grit, Curiosity, and the Hidden Power of Character*, by Paul Tough (New York, NY: Mariner Books, 2012); *Helping Children Succeed: What Works and Why*, by Paul Tough (Boston, MA: Houghton Mifflin Harcourt, 2016); *Grit: The Power of Passion and Perseverance*, by Angela Duckworth (New York, NY: Scribner, 2016); "Mindset Scholar Angela Duckworth in the *New York Times*: 'Don't Grade Schools on Grit,'" by Lisa Quay, March 29, 2016, Mindset Scholars Network, mindsetscholarsnetwork.org/mindset-scholar-angela-duckworth-in-the-new-york-times-dont-grade-schools-on-grit/.

3. "Raising Resilient Children: Fostering Strength, Hope, and Optimism in Your Child," by Robert B. Brooks and Sam Goldstein (New York, NY: McGraw Hill, 2001); "The Resilience Dividend: Being Strong in a World Where Things Go Wrong," by Judith Rodin (New York, NY: PublicAffairs, 2014); "Building Resilience in Children and Teens: Giving Kids Roots and Wings," by Kenneth R. Ginsburg (with Martha M. Jablow) (Elk Grove Village, IL: American Academy of Pediatrics, 2014).

4. "Teachers Seize on 'Growth Mindset,' but Crave More Training," by Evie Brad, September 20, 2016, *Education Week*, www.edweek.org/ew/articles/2016/09/21/teachers-seize-on-growth-mindset-but-crave.html; "Building Self-Esteem: Children 1–8 Years," last updated or revised November 21, 2012, Raising Children Network, raisingchildren.net.au/articles/self-esteem_different_ages.html; *Practice for Life: Making Decisions in College*, by Lee Cuba, Nancy Jennings, Suzanne Lovett, and Joseph Swingle (Cambridge, MA: Harvard University Press, 2016).

5. "Continuum of Engagement: From Compliant to Flow" (blog post), by Barbara Bray and Kathleen McClaskey, March 6, 2016, *Personalize Learning: Transform Learning for All Learners*, www.personalizelearning.com/2016/03/continuum-of-engagement.html.

6. *Pedagogy of the Oppressed*, by Paolo Freire, translated by Maya Bergman Ramos (30th anniversary edition) (New York: Continuum, 2000).

Chapter 3

1. "A Solution as Obvious as It Is Rare: Making High School Graduates Ready for College," by Jon Marcus, August 18, 2016, *The Hechinger Report*, hechinger-report.org/solution-obvious-rare-making-high-school-graduates-ready-college/.

2. "Mandatory for Minority Students," by Scott Jaschik, August 5, 2016, *Inside Higher Ed*, www.insidehighered.com/news/2016/08/05/anger-concordia-st-paul-over-mandatory-orientation-minority-students.

3. "Course Sections for Black Students Only," by Andrew Kreighbaum, August 8, 2016, *Inside Higher Ed*, www.insidehighered.com/news/2016/08/08/community-college-pilots-course-sections-african-american-students.

4. "Leaked Faculty Letters Expose Racial Fault Lines at Smith's Social-Work School," by Steve Kolowich, August 18, 2016, *The Chronicle of Higher Education*, chronicle.com/article/Leaked-Faculty-Letters-Expose/237491.

5. "This Chart Debunks Some Common Myths About University Students," by Joe Myers, July 12, 2016, World Economic Forum, www.weforum.org/agenda/2016/07/this-chart-debunks-some-common-myths-about-university-students/.

6. "The Mindset List," 2016, Beloit College, www.beloit.edu/mindset/; "Nontraditional Students Like Me Face Enormous Challenges," by An Garagiola-Bernier, September 14, 2016, *Community College Daily*, www.ccdaily.com/Pages/Campus-Issues/Nontraditional-students-like-me-face-enormous-challenges.aspx.

7. "Swapping Places: Three School Leaders Switch Jobs for a Day—and Learn Valuable Lessons," by Mary Francis Bisselle, Trudy Hall, and Karen Gross, Fall 2015, *Independent School*, www.nais.org/Magazines-Newsletters/ISMagazine/Pages/Swapping-Places.aspx.

8. "Defining the Relationship," by Rob Jenkins, August 8, 2016, *The Chronicle of Higher Education*, chronicle.com/article/Defining-the-Relationship/237388.

9. "Snowflake Totalitarians at Yale" (blog post), by Scott Greer, November 11, 2015, *Minding the Campus*, www.mindingthecampus.org/2015/11/snowflake-totalitarians-at-yale/; "The Perils of Writing a Provocative Email at Yale," by Conor Friedersdorf, May 26, 2016, *The Atlantic*, www.theatlantic.com/politics/archive/2016/05/the-peril-of-writing-a-provocative-email-at-yale/484418/; "A Dialogue on Race and Speech at Yale," by Conor Friedersdorf, March 24, 2016, *The Atlantic*, www.theatlantic.com/politics/archive/2016/03/yale-silliman-race/475152/.

10. "Toxic Stress," 2016, Center on the Developing Child, Harvard University, developingchild.harvard.edu/science/key-concepts/toxic-stress/; "Teaching Traumatized Kids," by James Redford and Karen Pritzker, July 7, 2016, *The Atlantic*, www.theatlantic.com/education/archive/2016/07/teaching-traumatized-kids/490214/;

"Students Traumatized by Loss and Violence Get a Fighting Chance to Learn," by Sonali Kohli, August 19, 2016, *Los Angeles Times*, www.latimes.com/projects/ la-me-edu-share-care/; "How Childhood Trauma Could Be Mistaken for ADHD," by Rebecca Ruiz, July 7, 2014, *The Atlantic*, www.theatlantic.com/health/ archive/2014/07/how-childhood-trauma-could-be-mistaken-for-adhd/373328/; "Is PTSD Being Misdiagnosed as ADHD?" by David Hosier, April 13, 2015, Childhood Trauma Recovery, childhoodtraumarecovery.com/2015/04/13/is-ptsd-being-misdiagnosed-as-adhd/; "Pediatricians Take On Toxic Stress," by Carol Gerwin, May 30, 2013, Center on the Developing Child, Harvard University, developingchild.harvard.edu/science/key-concepts/toxic-stress/tackling-toxic-stress/ pediatricians-take-on-toxic-stress/; "Brain Architecture," 2016, Center on the Developing Child, Harvard University, developingchild.harvard.edu/science/key-concepts/brain-architecture/; "InBrief: The Impact of Early Adversity on Children's Development," 2016, Center on the Developing Child, Harvard University, developingchild.harvard.edu/resources/inbrief-the-impact-of-early-adversity-on-childrens-development/; *Excessive Stress Disrupts the Architecture of the Developing Brain*, by the National Scientific Council on the Developing Child, 2005, updated 2014, Center on the Developing Child, Harvard University, developingchild. harvard.edu/resources/wp3/.

11. *Our Kids: The American Dream in Crisis*, by Robert D. Putnam (New York, NY: Simon and Schuster, 2015).

12. "Take the ACE Quiz—and Learn What It Does and Doesn't Mean," by Laura Starecheski, March 2, 2015, *Shots*, www.npr.org/sections/health-shots/2015/03/02/387007941/take-the-ace-quiz-and-learn-what-it-does-and-doesnt-mean; "Got Your ACE Score?" (blog post) (n.d.), *Aces Too High*, acestoohigh.com/got-your-ace-score/.

13. "Adverse Childhood Experiences (ACEs)," April 1, 2016, Injury Prevention and Control: Division of Violence Prevention, CDC, www.cdc.gov/ violenceprevention/acestudy/.

14. "Is PTSD Being Misdiagnosed as ADHD?" by David Hosier, April 13, 2015, Childhood Trauma Recovery, childhoodtraumarecovery.com/2015/04/13/ is-ptsd-being-misdiagnosed-as-adhd/.

15. *Toxic Stress: Effects, Prevention, and Treatment*, by Hillary A. Franke, 2014, *Children*, *1*(3), 390–402, doi:10.3390/children1030390.

16. *The Glass Castle: A Memoir*, by Jeannette Walls (New York, NY: Scribner, 2005); "Top Definition: Gaslighting," Urban Dictionary, www.urbandictionary. com/define.php?term=Gaslighting.

17. "Epistemic Trust, Psychopathology, and the Great Psychotherapy Debate," by Peter Fonagy, Patrick Luyten, Chloe Campbell, and Liz Allison, December 2014, The Society for the Advancement of Psychotherapy, societyforpsychotherapy.org/ epistemic-trust-psychopathology-and-the-great-psychotherapy-debate/; *The Impact*

of Trauma and Toxic Stress on Infant and Toddler Development (n.d.), eclkc.ohs. acf.hhs.gov/hslc/tta-system/ehsnrc/docs/000886-impact-trauma-toxic-stress.pdf.

18. *Culture Eats Strategy for Lunch: The Secret of Extraordinary Results, Igniting the Passion Within*, by Curt Coffman and Kathie Sorensen Coffman (Denver, CO: Laing Addison Press, 2013).

19. "Bennington Museum Puts Body Art on Display," by Derek Carson, August 7, 2015, *Bennington Banner*, www.benningtonbanner.com/localnews/ci_28605018/bennington-museum-puts-body-art-display; "Tattoo Psychology: Art or Self Destruction? Modern-Day Social Branding?" by Reef Karim, November 9, 2012, *The Huffington Post*, www.huffingtonpost.com/reef-karim-do/psychology-of-tattoos_b_2017530.html; Cindy Dampier, "Artist's Mastectomy Tattoos Reveal the Beauty of Survival," *Chicago Tribune*, September 30, 2016, www.chicagotribune.com/lifestyles/ct-sun-david-allen-mastectomy-tattoos-20160929-story.html.

20. "Proudly Bearing Elders' Scars, Their Skin Says 'Never Forget,'" by Jodi Rudoren, September 30, 2012, *The New York Times*, www.nytimes.com/2012/10/01/world/middleeast/with-tattoos-young-israelis-bear-holocaust-scars-of-relatives.html; "Grandchildren of Holocaust Survivors Get Inked Up in Remembrance," October 1, 2014, CBS DC, washington.cbslocal.com/2012/10/01/grandchildren-of-holocaust-survivors-get-inked-up-in-remembrance/; "Wearing Their Grandparents' Tattoos: A New Generation Remembers the Holocaust," by Daniel C. Brouwer and Linda Diane Horwitz, *Communication Currents*, December 2015, www.natcom.org/CommCurrentsArticle.aspx?id=6740.

Chapter 4

1. "Hey, University of Chicago: I Am an Academic. I Am a Survivor. I Use Trigger Warnings in My Classes. Here's Why," by Erika D. Price, August 25 (no year), Medium, medium.com/@erikadprice/hey-university-of-chicago-i-am-an-academic-1beda06d692e#.vtp28hl9l.

2. "Teaching Traumatized Kids," by James Redford and Karen Pritzker, July 7, 2016, *The Atlantic*, www.theatlantic.com/education/archive/2016/07/teaching-traumatized-kids/490214/.

3. "Implicit Bias May Help Explain High Preschool Expulsion Rates for Black Children," by Bill Hathaway, September 27, 2016, *Yale News*, news.yale.edu/2016/09/27/implicit-bias-may-help-explain-high-preschool-expulsion-rates-black-children.

4. "Send the Right Message: Abolish Red Pens for Correcting Papers," by Karen Gross, January 28, 2016, *The Huffington Post*, www.huffingtonpost.com/karen-gross/send-the-right-message-ab_b_9100560.html.

5. "The Next Equity Challenge?" by Estela Mara Bensimon, August 26, 2016, *Inside Higher Ed*, www.insidehighered.com/views/2016/08/26/work-faculty-members-classroom-next-equity-challenge-essay; "How to Keep Children from

Skipping School," by Robert Balfanz and Leslie Cornfeld, June 9, [2016], *The Washington Post*, www.washingtonpost.com/opinions/how-to-keep-children-from-skipping-school/2016/06/09/0cb8cc90-2dc3-11e6-9de3-6e6e7a14000c_story.html; *Literature Review: A Trauma-Sensitive Approach for Children Aged 0–8 Years*, by Women's Health Goulburn North East, 2012, www.whealth.com.au/documents/work/trauma/LiteratureReview.pdf; "What Colleges Can Do Right Now to Help Low-Income Students Succeed," by Sara Goldrick-Rab, August 28, 2016, *The Chronicle of Higher Education*, www.chronicle.com/article/What-Colleges-Can-Do-Right-Now/237589.

6. "Have You Used Trigger Warnings in the Classroom?" (blog post), by Andy Thomason, August 26, 2016, *The Chronicle of Higher Education*, www.chronicle.com/blogs/ticker/have-you-used-trigger-warnings-in-the-classroom/113779.

7. "College President: 'This Is Not a Day Care. This Is a University!'" by Susan Svrluga, November 30, 2015, *The Washington Post*, www.washingtonpost.com/news/grade-point/wp/2015/11/30/college-president-rejects-safe-spaces-writing-this-is-not-a-day-care-this-is-a-university/; "The Coddling of the Conservative Mind," by Jim Sleeper, January 13, 2016, *Salon*, www.salon.com/2016/01/13/the_coddling_of_the_conservative_mind/; "The Coddling of the American Mind," by Andrew B. Myers, September 2015, *The Atlantic*, www.theatlantic.com/magazine/archive/2015/09/the-coddling-of-the-american-mind/399356/.

8. "How Colleges Can Help Students Who Are First in Their Families to Attend College," by Mikhail Zinshteyn, March 8, 2016, Education Writers Association, www.ewa.org/blog-higher-ed-beat/how-colleges-can-help-students-who-are-first-their-families-attend-college; "The Challenge of the First-Generation Student," by jeffrfrost@gmail.com, May 18, 2015, Monroe County Education Foundation, www.monroecountyedfound.com/?p=1170.

9. *The Tipping Point: How Little Things Can Make a Big Difference*, by Malcolm Gladwell (New York, NY: Little, Brown, 2013).

10. *Ready, Willing, and Able: A Developmental Approach to College Access and Success*, by Mandy Savitz-Romer and Suzanne Bouffard (Cambridge, MA: Harvard Education Press, 2012).

11. *Nudge: Improving Decisions About Health, Wealth, and Happiness*, by Richard H. Thaler and Cass R. Sunstein (New Haven, CT: Yale University Press, 2008); "A Brief Social-Belonging Intervention Improves Academic and Health Outcomes of Minority Students," by Gregory M. Walton and Geoffrey L. Cohen, 2011, *Science, 331*(6023), 1447–1451, doi:10.1126/science.1198364; "Nudging Students to Succeed: A New Approach to Retention and Graduation," by Antonio Henley, Cathy Jones, and Cecilia Le, March 29, 2016, *MSIs Unplugged*, msis-unplugged.com/2016/03/29/nudging-students-to-succeed-a-new-approach-to-retention-and-graduation/; "How to Help First-Generation Students Succeed," by Mikhail Zinshteyn, March 13, 2016, *The Atlantic*, www.theatlantic.com/education/

archive/2016/03/how-to-help-first-generation-students-succeed/473502/; "UVA Professor Leads First Lady's Campaign Aimed at Increasing College Completion," by Audrey Breen, July 19, 2016, *UVA Today*, news.virginia.edu/content/uva-professor-leads-first-ladys-campaign-aimed-increasing-college-completion; "Helping the Poor in Education: The Power of a Simple Nudge," by Susan Dynarski, January 17, 2015, *The New York Times*, www.nytimes.com/2015/01/18/upshot/helping-the-poor-in-higher-education-the-power-of-a-simple-nudge.html.

12. "Conquering the Freshman Fear of Failure," David L. Kirp, August 20, 2016, *The New York Times*, www.nytimes.com/2016/08/21/opinion/sunday/conquering-the-freshman-fear-of-failure.html.

Chapter 5

1. "Kintsugi: The Art of Broken Pieces" (blog post), by Christopher Jobson, May 8, 2014, *Colossal*, www.thisiscolossal.com/2014/05/kintsugi-the-art-of-broken-pieces/.

2. "What It Really Takes to Be an Artist: MacArthur Genius Teresita Fernández's Magnificent Commencement Address," by Maria Popova (n.d.), Brain Pickings, www.brainpickings.org/2014/12/29/teresita-fernandez-commencement-address/.

3. "What Is the Definition of Hypervigilance?" by Matthew Tull, updated May 4, 2016, Verywell, www.verywell.com/hypervigilance-2797363.

4. "Overcoming Long Odds," by Paul Bradley, June 9, 2016, *Community College Week*, ccweek.com/article-5209-overcoming-long-odds.html; "Who Can Help First Gen Students: Not Just First Gen Administrators!" by Karen Gross, May 19, 2015, LinkedIn, www.linkedin.com/pulse/who-can-help-first-gen-students-just-administrators-karen-gross; "Supporting First-Gen College Students," by Ioanna Opidee, February 25, 2015, *UB: University Business*, www.universitybusiness.com/article/supporting-first-gen-college-students.

5. *Afterwar: Healing the Moral Wounds of Our Soldiers*, by Nancy Sherman (New York, NY: Oxford University Press, 2015).

6. "Students Traumatized by Loss and Violence Get a Fighting Chance to Learn," by Sonali Kohli, August 19, 2016, *Los Angeles Times*, www.latimes.com/projects/la-me-edu-share-care/.

7. "In 'Poster Boy,' Parsing a Cyber-bullying Victim's Digital Clues," by Jeremy D. Goodwin, July 25, 2016, *The Boston Globe*, www.bostonglobe.com/arts/theater-art/2016/07/24/poster-boy-parsing-cyber-bullying-victim-digital-clues/IjEw05aYpWpyIfkPK82RsJ/story.html.

8. "Four-Star Recruit Says He Decommitted from Michigan After Thank You Card Mistake," *USA Today: High School Sports*, by Mark Snyder, August 23, 2016, usatodayhss.com/2016/four-star-recruit-says-he-decommitted-from-michigan-after-thank-you-card-mistake.

9. *Lady Lucy's Quest*, by Karen Gross (ShiresPress, 2016), www.ladylucysquest.com.

10. "Vermont in Basement for Higher-Ed Funding," by Tim Johnson," April 24, 2014, *Burlington Free Press*, www.burlingtonfreepress.com/story/news/local/2014/04/23/vermont-maintains-low-ranking-higher-ed-funding/8062207/; *SHEF: FY 2015; State Higher Education Finance*, by State Higher Education Executive Officers Association, 2016, SHEEO, sheeo.org/sites/default/files/project-files/SHEEO_FY15_Report_051816.pdf.

11. "What Are Kimochis?" 2016, Kimochis, www.kimochis.com/about/what-are-kimochis/; "Military Families," 2016, Kimochis, www.kimochis.com/about/resources-for-military-families/.

12. "I'm First! Scholarship" (n.d.), I'm First, www.imfirst.org/scholarship/; "Team Strive" (n.d.), Strive for College, striveforcollege.org/our-staff/.

13. "Compassionate Schools: The Heart of Learning and Teaching," updated July 30, 2015, State of Washington Office of Superintendent of Public Instruction, www.k12.wa.us/compassionateschools/; "Compassionate Schools Project," 2016, Compassionate Schools Project, www.compassionschools.org/program/.

14. For strategies to help traumatized children, see "Students Traumatized by Loss and Violence Get a Fighting Chance to Learn," by Sonali Kohli, August 19, 2016, *Los Angeles Times*, www.latimes.com/projects/la-me-edu-share-care/; *Development and Implementation of Standards for Social and Emotional Learning in the 50 States: A Brief on Findings from CASEL's Experience*, by Linda Dusenbury and Roger P. Weissberg, April 2016, Collaborative for Academic, Social, and Emotional Learning, www.casel.org/wp-content/uploads/2016/08/CASELBrief-DevelopmentandImplementationofSELStandardsinthe50States-April2016.pdf; *Literature Review: A Trauma-Sensitive Approach for Children Aged 0–8 years*, by Women's Health Goulburn North East, 2012, www.whealth.com.au/documents/work/trauma/LiteratureReview.pdf; "Case Studies: What Are Case Studies?" 2015, Carnegie Mellon University, Eberly Center, www.cmu.edu/teaching/designteach/teach/instructionalstrategies/casestudies.html.

15. *How to Raise an Adult: Break Free of the Overparenting Trap and Prepare Your Kid for Success*, by Julie Lythcott-Haims (New York, NY: Henry Holt, 2016).

16. See "Antonio Machado: 1875–1939," 2016, Poetry Foundation, www.poetryfoundation.org/poems-and-poets/poets/detail/antonio-machado.

Chapter 6

1. "Elastic," (n.d.), The Free Dictionary, www.thefreedictionary.com/elastic.

2. "Cookie Test Yields Secrets of Self-Control Years Later," by Charles Q. Choi, August 29, 2011, Live Science, www.livescience.com/15821-cookie-test-control.html; "What the Marshmallow Test Really Teaches About Self-Control," by Jacoba Urist, September 24, 2014, *The Atlantic*, www.theatlantic.com/health/archive/2014/09/what-the-marshmallow-test-really-teaches-about-self-control/380673/.

3. "Lastic," November 4, 2015, The Caribbean Dictionary, Wiwords, wiwords.com/word/lastic. In patois, *lastic* is a shortened form of *elastic*; see "Definitions of 'Lastic,'" 2016, Jamaican Patwah, jamaicanpatwah.com/term/Lastic/1577#.WAtb6RSIB9Y.

4. *The Convergence of K–12 and Higher Education: Policies and Programs in a Changing Era*, edited by Christopher P. Loss and Patrick J. McGuinn, Educational Innovations Series (Cambridge, MA: Harvard Education Press, 2016).

5. "Documents," 2016, State of Vermont Agency of Education, education.vermont.gov/documents/EDU-Data_High_School_Graduates_Higher_Education_Enrollment_Rate.pdf.

6. "New Data: Vermont Graduation Rate Rising, College Enrollment Lags," by Charlotte Albright, December 17, 2014, VPR, digital.vpr.net/post/new-data-vermont-graduation-rate-rising-college-enrollment-lags#stream/0; "Vermont Students in Low-Income Areas Perform Poorly on Tests," by Tiffany Danitz Pache, September 22, 2016, *VTDigger*, vtdigger.org/2016/09/22/vermont-students-low-income-areas-perform-poorly-tests/.

7. "A Wider Lens on the 'Match' Between Students and Colleges," by Beckie Supiano, August 22, 2016, *The Chronicle of Higher Education*, chronicle.com/article/A-Wider-Lens-on-the/237519; "Five Key Measures of Success in the First Year of College" (blog post), by Lorenzo L. Ester, August 19, 2016, *Completion with a Purpose*, completionwithapurpose.org/2016/08/19/five-key-measures-of-success-in-the-first-year-of-college/; "The Next Equity Challenge?" by Estela Mara Bensimon, August 26, 2016, *Inside Higher Ed*, www.insidehighered.com/views/2016/08/26/work-faculty-members-classroom-next-equity-challenge-essay; "Poverty and Merit," by Paul Fain, January 12, 2016, *Inside Higher Ed*, www.insidehighered.com/news/2016/01/12/high-achieving-low-income-students-remain-rare-most-selective-colleges.

8. *Racing Odysseus: A College President Becomes a Freshman Again*, by Roger H. Martin (Berkeley and Los Angeles, CA: University of California Press, 2010).

9. "I'm First! Scholarship" (n.d.), I'm First, www.imfirst.org/scholarship/; "Team Strive" (n.d.), Strive for College, striveforcollege.org/our-staff/.

10. *Building Authentic Confidence in Children* (electronic book), by Spencer Taintor (n.d.), ibooklibrary.net/BUILDING-AUTHENTIC-CONFIDENCE-CHILDREN-SPENCER.html; *How to Raise an Adult: Break Free of the Overparenting Trap and Prepare Your Kid for Success*, by Julie Lythcott-Haims (New York, NY: Henry Holt, 2016).

11. "Grit: The True Story of Steve Young," by Kevin Doman, April 4, 2014, *Deseret News*, www.deseretnews.com/article/865600232/Grit-The-true-story-of-Steve-Young.html; "Forever Young: It Takes a Neighborhood," by Christopher W. Hunt, February 2, 2013, *Greenwich Time*, www.greenwichtime.com/news/article/Forever-Young-It-takes-a-neighborhood-4241288.php.

12. "Success Program," 2016, Bottom Line, www.bottomline.org/content/success-program.

13. "KIPP Through College," 2016, KIPP, www.kipp.org/our-approach/kipp-through-college.

14. "Call for Help," by Paul Fain, September 4, 2015, *Inside Higher Ed*, www.insidehighered.com/news/2015/09/04/outsourced-employee-style-counseling-can-work-first-generation-college-students.

15. "The Outsourced College: Vendors Provide More Than Just Dining Halls and Parking Lots Now," by Scott Carlson, February 29, 2016, *The Chronicle of Higher Education*, chronicle.com/article/The-Outsourced-College/235445; "Outsourcing Services in Higher Education: Consider the Campus Climate," by David Milstone, March 2010, *The Bulletin*, 78(2), www.acui.org/Publications/The_Bulletin/2010/2010-03/12134/; "New Adventures in Outsourcing," by Sandra R. Sabo, July/August 2014, *Business Officer*, www.nacubo.org/Business_Officer_Magazine/Magazine_Archives/JulyAugust_2014/New_Adventures_in_Outsourcing.html.

16. "Outsourcing Experiment Meets Its End," by Doug Lederman, May 26, 2016, *Inside Higher Ed*, insidehighered.com/news/2016/05/26/akron-abandons-advising-experiment-outside-start-after-1-year; "Chapman Saves $650,000 by Discontinuing InsideTrack," by Taylor Johnson, September 12, 2010, *The Panther*, www.thepantheronline.com/news/chapman-saves-650000-by-discontinuing-insidetrack.

Chapter 7

1. "What Is Phenotypic Plasticity and Why Is It Important?" by Douglas W. Whitman and Anurag A. Agrawal, January 2008, www.eeb.cornell.edu/agrawal/pdfs/whitman-and-agrawal-2009-Ch_1-Phenotypic-Plasticity-of-Insects.pdf; "Scientists Reprogram Brain with a Beam of Light—'Human Brain Is Plastic, Not Hardwired,'" August 24, 2016, *The Daily Galaxy—Great Discoveries Channel*, www.dailygalaxy.com/my_weblog/2016/08/scientists-reprogram-brain-with-a-beam-of-light-human-brain-is-plastic-not-hardwired.html.

2. "Scientists Reprogram Brain with a Beam of Light—'Human Brain Is Plastic, Not Hardwired,'" August 24, 2016, *The Daily Galaxy—Great Discoveries Channel*, www.dailygalaxy.com/my_weblog/2016/08/scientists-reprogram-brain-with-a-beam-of-light-human-brain-is-plastic-not-hardwired.html.

3. "After Blast, New Yorkers Examine Themselves for Psychological Shrapnel," by Michael Wilson, Samantha Schmidt, and Sarah Maslin Nir, September 18, 2016, *The New York Times*, www.nytimes.com/2016/09/19/nyregion/after-blast-new-yorkers-are-feeling-around-for-psychological-shrapnel.html.

4. *Afterwar: Healing the Moral Wounds of Our Soldiers*, by Nancy Sherman (New York, NY: Oxford University Press, 2015).

5. "Why Some Patients Are Unhappy: Part 2, Relationship of Nasal Shape and Trauma History to Surgical Success," by Mark B. Constantian and Chee Paul Lin, 2014, *Plastic and Reconstructive Surgery, 134*(4), 836–851, doi:10.1097/PRS.0000000000000552; "Toxic Stress," 2016, Center on the Developing Child, Harvard University, developingchild.harvard.edu/science/key-concepts/toxic-stress/; "Pediatricians Take On Toxic Stress," by Carol Gerwin, May 30, 2013, Center on the Developing Child, Harvard University, developingchild.harvard.edu/science/key-concepts/toxic-stress/tackling-toxic-stress/pediatricians-take-on-toxic-stress/; "Brain Architecture," 2016, Center on the Developing Child, Harvard University, developingchild.harvard.edu/science/key-concepts/brain-architecture/; "InBrief: The Impact of Early Adversity on Children's Development," 2016, Center on the Developing Child, Harvard University, developingchild.harvard.edu/resources/inbrief-the-impact-of-early-adversity-on-childrens-development/; *Excessive Stress Disrupts the Architecture of the Developing Brain*, by National Scientific Council on the Developing Child, Center on the Developing Child, Harvard University, 2005, updated 2014, 46y5eh11fhgw3ve3ytpwxt9r.wpengine.netdna-cdn.com/wp-content/uploads/2005/05/Stress_Disrupts_Architecture_Developing_Brain-1.pdf; "'Big T' Versus 'Little T' Trauma," by "Alex" Caroline Robboy, 2016, The Center for Growth, www.therapyinphiladelphia.com/tips/big-t-versus-little-t-trauma.

6. "Lifespan Adversity and Later Adulthood Telomere Length in the Nationally Representative US Health and Retirement Study," by Eli Puterman, Alison Gemmill, Deborah Karasek, David Weir, Nancy E. Adler, Aric A. Prather, and Elissa S. Epel, 2016, *Proceedings of the National Academy of Sciences of the United States of America, 113*(42), E6335–E6342, doi:10.1073/pnas.1525602113.

7. "Epistemic Trust, Psychopathology, and the Great Psychotherapy Debate," by Peter Fonagy, Patrick Luyten, Chloe Campbell, and Liz Allison, December 2014, The Society for the Advancement of Psychotherapy, societyforpsychotherapy.org/epistemic-trust-psychopathology-and-the-great-psychotherapy-debate/; *Mitigating the Impact of Toxic Stress and Trauma Through Healthy Social Emotional Development*, by Julie A. Larrieu (n.d.), Tulane University School of Health, www.wismhi.org/-wismhi-files/PDF/ECCS-/LarrieuMitigatingToxicStress41715Handout.pdf; *The Impact of Trauma and Toxic Stress on Infant and Toddler Development* (n.d.), eclkc.ohs.acf.hhs.gov/hslc/tta-system/ehsnrc/docs/000886-impact-trauma-toxic-stress.pdf.

8. "Dr. Herbert Benson" (n.d.), Massachusetts General Hospital, Benson Henry Institute for Mind Body Medicine, oasis.lib.harvard.edu/oasis/deliver/~med00061.

9. "Tiger Teacher: Shocking Moment New York Educator at High-Pressure 'Success' School Is Secretly Recorded Ripping Up Homework and Berating First-Grader for Getting Math Problem Wrong," by Valerie Edwards, February

13, 2016, *Daily Mail.com*, www.dailymail.co.uk/news/article-3446147/Shocking-moment-New-York-teacher-secretly-recorded-ripping-homework-berating-grader-getting-math-problem-wrong.html; "Disturbing Video of Teacher Ripping Up Homework" (n.d.), Gawker, gawker.com/disturbing-video-of-teacher-ripping-up-homework-and-ber-1758717361.

10. *The Short and Tragic Life of Robert Peace: A Brilliant Young Man Who Left Newark for the Ivy League*, by Jeff Hobbs (New York, NY: Scribner, 2014).

11. "Beating the Odds: An Approach to the Topic of Resilience in Children and Adolescents," by Katrin Skala and Thomas Bruckner, 2014, *Neuropsychiatrie: Psychiatrie, Psychotherapie, Public Mental Health und Sozialpsychiatrie, 28*(4), 208–217, doi:10.1007/s40211-014-0125-7.

12. "Public Policy and Resilience: How We Can Change Our Policies to Help Disadvantaged Kids Cope and Thrive," by Bari Walsh, March 23, 2015, Usable Knowledge, www.gse.harvard.edu/news/uk/15/03/public-policy-and-resilience.

13. "Compassionate Schools Project," 2016, Compassionate Schools Project, www.compassionschools.org/program/; *The Heart of Learning and Teaching: Compassion, Resiliency, and Academic Success*, by Ray Wolpow, Mona M. Johnson, Ron Hertel, and Susan O. Kincaid, 2016, Washington State Office of Superintendent of Public Instruction (OSPI) Compassionate Schools, www.k12.wa.us/compassionateschools/pubdocs/TheHeartofLearningandTeaching.pdf; "Compassionate Schools: The Heart of Learning and Teaching," updated July 30, 2015, State of Washington Office of Superintendent of Public Instruction, www.k12.wa.us/compassionateschools/.

14. "Who's Really Skipping School?" by Emily Richmond, August 29, 2012, *The Atlantic*, www.theatlantic.com/national/archive/2012/08/whos-really-skipping-school/261725/; "Chronic Absenteeism Plagues More Than Poor Urban Districts," by Tara García Mathewson, September 7, 2016, Education Dive, www.educationdive.com/news/chronic-absenteeism-plagues-more-than-poor-urban-districts/425850/; "Who's Really Skipping School?" by Emily Richmond, August 29, 2012, *The Atlantic*, www.theatlantic.com/national/archive/2012/08/whos-really-skipping-school/261725/; "How to Keep Children from Skipping School," by Robert Balfanz and Leslie Cornfeld, June 9, [2016], *The Washington Post*, www.washingtonpost.com/opinions/how-to-keep-children-from-skipping-school/2016/06/09/0cb8cc90-2dc3-11e6-9de3-6e6e7a14000c_story.html; "Do US Laws That Punish Parents for Truancy Keep Their Kids in School?" by Nadja Popovich, June 23, 2014, *The Guardian*, www.theguardian.com/education/2014/jun/23/-sp-school-truancy-fines-jail-parents-punishment-children.

15. "Do US Laws That Punish Parents for Truancy Keep Their Kids in School?" by Nadja Popovich, June 23, 2014, *The Guardian*, www.theguardian.com/education/2014/jun/23/-sp-school-truancy-fines-jail-parents-punishment-children; "One Answer to School Attendance: Washing Machines," by Mimi Kirk,

August 22, 2016, *CityLab*, www.citylab.com/cityfixer/2016/08/school-attendance-washing-machines/496649/.

16. "How to Keep Children from Skipping School," by Robert Balfanz and Leslie Cornfeld, June 9, [2016], *The Washington Post*, www.washingtonpost.com/opinions/how-to-keep-children-from-skipping-school/2016/06/09/0cb8cc90-2dc3-11e6-9de3-6e6e7a14000c_story.html.

17. *A Restorative Approach to Truancy*, by Jodi Martin and Gail Spolar (n.d.), ccyj.org/wp-content/uploads/2015/04/A-Restorative-Approach-to-Truancy.pdf; "Restorative Justice: A Different Approach to Discipline," by WeAreTeachers Staff, June 4, 2013, We Are Teachers, www.weareteachers.com/restorative-justice-a-different-approach-to-discipline/.

18. "What's So Special About Mirror Neurons?" (blog post), by Ben Thomas, November 6, 2012, *Scientific American*, blogs.scientificamerican.com/guest-blog/whats-so-special-about-mirror-neurons; "Mirror Neurons in Education," by Amber Nicole Dilger, June 2, 2016, Center for Educational Improvement, www.edimprovement.org/2016/06/6627/; "Contagious Emotions and Responding to Stress," by Lori Desautels, March 31, 2016, Edutopia, www.edutopia.org/blog/contagious-emotions-responding-to-stress-lori-desautels.

19. "Do US Laws That Punish Parents for Truancy Keep Their Kids in School?" by Nadja Popovich, June 23, 2014, *The Guardian*, www.theguardian.com/education/2014/jun/23/-sp-school-truancy-fines-jail-parents-punishment-children.

20. "A Case That Shook Medicine," by Barron H. Lerner, November 28, 2006, *The Washington Post*, www.washingtonpost.com/wp-dyn/content/article/2006/11/24/AR2006112400985.html.

Chapter 8

1. "Why Do Teenagers Make Bad Choices? One Word: Science," by Danica Davidson, March 4, 2015, MTV News, www.mtv.com/news/2094754/one-bad-choice-teenage-brains/; "Ten Wise Choices: Elementary Level," 2016, Project Wisdom, www.projectwisdom.com/ERS/Resource_Public.asp?key=TenWiseE.

2. *Framing the Message: Using Behavioral Economics to Engage TANF Recipients*, by Mary Farrell, Jared Smith, Leigh Reardon, and Emmi Obara, March 2016, MDRC, www.mdrc.org/sites/default/files/Framing_the_Message_FR.pdf; "Making Decisions: Suggestions for Schools and Early Childhood Services" (n.d.), Kids Matter, www.kidsmatter.edu.au/mental-health-matters/social-and-emotional-learning/making-decisions/suggestions-schools-and-early; "Students as Decision-Makers," March 31, 2015, SoundOut, soundout.org/students-as-decision-makers/; "Ten Wise Choices: Elementary Level," 2016, Project Wisdom, www.projectwisdom.com/ERS/Resource_Public.asp?key=TenWiseE; "Why Don't People Take Free Cash?" by Syon Bhanot and Antonia Violante, January 22, 2016, *The Psych Report*, thepsychreport.com/science/why-dont-people-take-free-cash/.

3. "Elementary Students Encouraged to Set College Goals," by Cara-lee J. Adams, October 28, 2016, *Education Week*, www.edweek.org/ew/articles/2010/12/08/14colleges_ep.h30.html; "Why Third Grade Is So Import-ant: The 'Matthew Effect,'" by Annie Murphy Paul, September 26, 2012, *Time*, ideas.time.com/2012/09/26/why-third-grade-is-so-important-the-matthew-effect/; "Great Teaching," by Raj Chetty, John N. Friedman, and Jonah E. Rock-off, 2012, *Education Next, 1*(3), educationnext.org/great-teaching/; *Measuring the Impacts of Teachers I: Evaluating Bias in Teacher Value-Added Estimates*, by Raj Chetty, John N. Friedman, and Jonah E. Rockoff, 2013, Working Pa-per 19423, National Bureau of Economic Research, doi:10.3386/w19423; *First Generation Students: College Aspirations, Preparedness, and Challenges*, by Kara Balemian and Jing Feng, July 13, 2013, College Board, research.col-legeboard.org/sites/default/files/publications/2013/8/presentation-apac-2013-first-generation-college-aspirations-preparedness-challenges.pdf; "Family Class-es Tied to Better School Performance for Poor Kids," by Lisa Rapaport, October 3, 2016, Reuters, www.reuters.com/article/us-health-children-prekindergarten-idUSKCN12326T.

4. "Michael Oher Biography," 2016, Bio, www.biography.com/people/michael-oher-547478; "Michael Oher Wants to Tell a New Story," by Thomas George, February 3, 2016, SB Nation, www.sbnation.com/nfl/2016/2/3/10903876/michael-oher-blind-side-carolina-panthers-left-tackle; "Michael Oher's Inspiring Journey," by Kari Forsee, November 18, 2009, Oprah.com, www.oprah.com/entertainment/Michael-Ohers-Inspiring-Journey-The-Blind-Side; "The Olympic Gymnast Who Overcame a Drug-Addicted Mother," by Alice Park, June 3, 2016, *Time*, time.com/4352599/simone-biles-next-generation-leaders/; "Little Girl with Drug-Addict Mother and Abandoned by Father Is Adopted by Christian Grandpar-ents, Becomes Best Athlete in the World," by Benny Johnson, 2016, *Independent Journal Review*, ijr.com/2016/08/668422-unwanted-child-abandoned-by-father-and-drug-addict-mother-adopted-by-christian-texas-family-becomes-best-athlete-in-the-world/; "Simone Biles Clears Up an Adoption Misconception in 8 Simple Words," by Taylor Pittman, updated August 12, 2016, *Huffington Post*, www.huffingtonpost.com/entry/simone-biles-clears-up-an-adoption-misconception-in-8-simple-words_us_57ac9704e4b06e52746f723a; *The Blind Side: Evolution of a Game*, by Michael Lewis (New York, NY: Norton, 2006); *Courage to Soar: A Body in Motion, a Life in Balance*, by Simone Biles, Michelle Burford, and Mary Lou Retton (Grand Rapids, MI: Zondervan, 2016).

5. "Case Studies: What Are Case Studies?" 2015, Carnegie Mellon Univer-sity, www.cmu.edu/teaching/designteach/teach/instructionalstrategies/casestudies.html; "Asking Effective Questions," by Brandon Cline, 2016, Chicago Center for Teaching, the University of Chicago, teaching.uchicago.edu/teaching-guides/asking-effective-questions/.

6. *One L: The Turbulent True Story of a First Year at Harvard Law School*, by Scott Turow (London: Pan Books, 2014); "The Socratic Approach to Character Education," 2016, GoodCharacter.com, www.goodcharacter.com/Socratic_method.html.

7. "Ask Questions: The Single Most Important Habit for Innovative Thinkers," by Paul Sloane, 2013, Innovation Management.se, www.innovationmanagement.se/imtool-articles/ask-questions-the-single-most-important-habit-for-innovative-thinkers/; "Emphasis on Teaching," by Marshall Brain, 1998, BYG, www.bygpub.com/eot/eot2.htm; "5 Ways to Help Your Students Become Better Questioners," by Warren Berger, updated August 17, 2015, Edutopia, www.edutopia.org/blog/help-students-become-better-questioners-warren-berger; "Teach Students to Ask Their Own Questions," 2016, Right Question Institute, rightquestion.org/education/.

8. "Marlboro College Makes Campus Governance Everyone's Job," by Jarrett Carter, October 3, 2016, Education Dive, ww.educationdive.com/news/marlboro-college-makes-campus-governance-everyones-job/427454/.

9. "Including Student Voice," by Bill Palmer, March 29, 2013, Edutopia, www.edutopia.org/blog/sammamish-2-including-student-voice-bill-palmer; "8 Ways to Empower Student Voice in Your Classroom," by Jennifer Snelling, April 20, 2016, ISTE, www.iste.org/explore/articleDetail?articleid=719&category=In-the-classroom&article=.

10. *No Vehicles in the Park*, by David K. Trevaskis (n.d.), Pennsylvania Bar Association, www.pabar.org/scjap/SCJAP-NoVehicles.pdf.

Chapter 9

1. "Reciprocity" (n.d.), Oxford Dictionaries, www.oxforddictionaries.com/us/definition/american_english/reciprocity

2. "Student-Centered Learning," last updated May 7, 2014, edglossary.org/student-centered-learning/; "Student-Centered Learning: It Starts with the Teacher," by John McCarthy, September 9, 2015, Edutopia, www.edutopia.org/blog/student-centered-learning-starts-with-teacher-john-mccarthy.

3. "Have You Used Trigger Warnings in the Classroom?" (blog post), by Andy Thomason, August 26, 2016, *The Chronicle of Higher Education*, www.chronicle.com/blogs/ticker/have-you-used-trigger-warnings-in-the-classroom/113779; "U. of Chicago's Condemning of Safe Spaces and Trigger Warnings Reignites Debate" (blog post), by Andy Thomason, August 25, 2016, *The Chronicle of Higher Education*, www.chronicle.com/blogs/ticker/u-of-chicagos-condemning-of-safe-spaces-and-trigger-warnings-reignites-debate/113760; "University of Chicago Strikes Back Against Campus Political Correctness," Richard Pérez-Peña, Mitch Smith, and Stephanie Saul, August 26, 2016, *The New York Times*, www.nytimes.com/2016/08/27/us/university-of-chicago-strikes-back-against-campus-political-correctness.html.

4. "Hey, University of Chicago: I Am an Academic. I Am a Survivor. I Use Trigger Warnings in My Classes. Here's Why," by Erika D. Price, August 25 (no year), Medium, medium.com/@erikadprice/hey-university-of-chicago-i-am-an-academic-1beda06d692e#.vtp28hl9l.

5. *Remembering Denny*, by Calvin Trillin (New York, NY: Farrar, Straus and Giroux, 1993).

6. "Patient Involvement in Health Care Decisionmaking: A Review," by Shaghayegh Vahdat, Leila Hamzehgardeshi, Somayeh Hessam, and Zeinab Hamzehgardeshi, January 5, 2014, NCBI, www.ncbi.nlm.nih.gov/pmc/articles/PMC3964421/; "Empowering Patients as Partners in Health Care" (blog post), by Susan Edgman-Levitan and Tejal Gandhi, July 24, 2014, *Health Affairs*, healthaffairs.org/blog/2014/07/24/empowering-patients-as-partners-in-health-care/.

7. *Racing Odysseus: A College President Becomes a Freshman Again*, by Roger H. Martin (Berkeley and Los Angeles, CA: University of California Press, 2010); *Nickel and Dimed: On (Not) Getting By in America*, by Barbara Ehrenreich (New York, NY: Henry Holt).

8. "20 Things Students Say Help Them Learn" (blog post), by Anne Curzan, October 11, 2016, *The Chronicle of Higher Education*, www.chronicle.com/blogs/linguafranca/2016/10/11/20-things-students-say-help-them-learn/.

Chapter 10

1. "From Trash to Triumph: The Recycled Orchestra" (blog post), by Anastasia Tsioulcas, September 14, 2016, *Deceptive Cadence*, www.npr.org/sections/deceptivecadence/2016/09/14/493794763/from-trash-to-triumph-the-recycled-orchestra; "Why First-Generation Students Need Mentors Who Get Them," by Jennine Capo Crucet, September 20, 2016, *PBS NewsHour*, www.pbs.org/newshour/bb/first-generation-students-need-mentors-get/.

2. "Remedial Education: The Cost of Catching Up," by Laura Jimenez, Scott Sargrad, Jessica Morales, and Maggie Thompson, September 28, 2016, Center for American Progress, www.americanprogress.org/issues/education/report/2016/09/28/144000/remedial-education/; "Teacher Expectations Reflect Racial Biases, Johns Hopkins Study Suggests," by Jill Rosen, March 30, 2016, *The Hub*, hub.jhu.edu/2016/03/30/racial-bias-teacher-expectations-black-white/; "How to Simplify the Scholarship Application Process," by Karen Gross, May/June 2016, *The Aspen Journal of Ideas*, aspen.us/journal/editions/mayjune-2016/how-simplify-scholarship-application-process; "Kids Can't Learn from Teachers They Don't Like" (blog post) (n.d.), *Education Shift*, www.educationshift.net/2013/06/kids-cant-learn-from-teachers-they-dont.html; "Building Self-Esteem: Children 1–8 years," by Raising Children Network, last updated or revised November 21, 2012, raisingchildren.net.au/articles/self-esteem_different_ages.html; "Why the Teacher's Pet Resembles the Teacher," by Anya Kamenetz, February 24, 2015,

ww2.kqed.org/mindshift/2015/02/24/why-the-teachers-pet-often-resembles-the-teacher/; "Personality Similarity Between Teachers and Their Students Influences Teacher Judgement of Student Achievement," by Tobias Rausch, Constance Karing, Tobias Dörfler, and Cordula Artelt, 2016, *Educational Psychology, 36*(5), 863–878, doi:10.1080/01443410.2014.998629.

3. An exercise is described in *Dancing in the Rain: Leading with Compassion, Vitality, and Mindfulness in Education*, by Jerome T. Murphy (Cambridge, MA: Harvard Education Press, 2016) in which a jar is filled with golf balls, then glass stones, then sand, then water. Murphy observes that leaders (I'd include teachers) need to remember themselves (the golf balls represent them) and not get mired in all the details of the job (stones/sand). I beg to differ. Think of the sand and glass as day-to-day issues that matter, even if small.

4. "How Native Students Can Succeed in College: 'Be as Tough as the Land That Made You,'" by Claudio Sanchez, September 26, 2016, NPR Ed, www.npr.org/sections/ed/2016/09/26/493112553/how-native-students-can-succeed-in-college-be-as-tough-as-the-land-that-made-you.

5. "Molly Stark to Use Karen Gross' 'Lady Lucy's Quest' for Year-Long Study," by Makayla McGeeney, August 30, 2016, *Bennington Banner*, www.benningtonbanner.com/ci_30305062/molly-stark-use-gross-lady-lucys-quest-year (syllabus available for review; visit www.ladylucysquest.com); "First, Discover Their Strengths," by Thomas Armstrong, 2012, *EL: Educational Leadership, 70*(2), 10–16, www.ascd.org/publications/educational-leadership/oct12/vol70/num02/First,-Discover-Their-Strengths.aspx.

6. "8 Ways to Empower Student Voice in Your Classroom," by Jennifer Snelling, April 20, 2016, ISTE, www.iste.org/explore/articleDetail?articleid=719&category=In-the-classroom&article=; "What Is Genius Hour?" by Chris Kesler, March 29, 2013, Genius Hour, www.geniushour.com/what-is-genius-hour/.

7. *Using Students' Strengths to Support Learning Outcomes: A Study of the Development of Gardner's Intrapersonal Intelligence to Support Increased Academic Achievement for Primary School Students*, by Maura Sellars (Saarbrücken, Germany: VDM Verlag Dr. Müller, 2008); "The Marshmallow Challenge: Team Bonding and Building for Student Journalists," by Aaron Ramponi (n.d.), www.schooljournalism.org/wp-content/uploads/2013/09/The-Marshmallow-Challenge-Team-Bonding-and-Building-for-Student-Journalists.pdf.

8. "When a C Isn't Good Enough," by Kasia Kovacs, September 23, 2016, *Inside Higher Ed*, www.insidehighered.com/news/2016/09/23/students-who-earn-cs-gateway-courses-are-less-likely-graduate-new-data-show.

9. *The Pact: Three Young Men Make a Promise and Fulfill a Dream*, by Sampson Davis, George Jenkins, and Rameck Hunt (New York, NY: Riverhead Books, 2003).

Chapter 11

1. "Whys and Hows of Assessment" (n.d.), Carnegie Mellon University, Eberly Center, www.cmu.edu/teaching/assessment/assesslearning/conceptmaps. html; see *Reflective Teaching and Learning: A Guide to Professional Issues for Beginning Secondary Teachers*, edited by Sue Dymoke and Jennifer Harrison (Los Angeles, CA: Sage, 2008), p. 57.

2. "Installation Art" (n.d.), *Encyclopedia of Art*, www.visual-arts-cork. com/installation-art.htm; "Identity Tapestry" (n.d.), Mary Corey March, www. marymarch.com/Identity_Tapestry.html; "SVC Installs 'Identify Tapestry,'" September 16, 2013, *Vermont Biz*, www.vermontbiz.com/news/september/svc-installs-identify-tapestry; *The Chronicle*, Fall 2015, issuu.com/southern-vermont-college/docs/chroniclefall2015.

3. "College Tour Fail: Why Can't Admissions Offices Tell It Like It Is?" by Simon Kuh, September 7, 2016, *Los Angeles Times*, www.latimes.com/opinion/op-ed/la-oe-kuh-college-tour-advice-20160907-snap-story.html.

4. "7 Hidden Messages in These World-Famous Company Logos," by Alex Kosoian, July 14, 2016, *Business Insider*, www.businessinsider.com/hidden-messages-company-logos-toyota-bmw-yamaha-fedex-cisco-2016-6; "Charges Dropped Against Yale Dishwasher Who Broke 'Racist' Calhoun Stained Glass," by Emily Zanotti, July 25, 2016, *Heat Street*, heatst.com/culture-wars/yale-rehires-worker-who-broke-priceless-stained-glass-calhoun-window/.

5. "Meaning of the Olympic Rings" (n.d.), Olympics.mu, www.olympics.mu/meaning-olympic-rings.html.

6. "4,000+ New Clemson Students Make Tiger Paw in Death Valley" (video), September 21, 2015, www.youtube.com/watch?v=64zUHZ4D1SQ; "Freshmen Form Human 'Paw' in Clemson's Memorial Stadium," updated August 18, 2015, WYFF, www.wyff4.com/news/freshmen-form-human-paw-in-clemsons-memorial-stadium/34782806.

7. "Helping HBCUs Get the Attention and Attendance They Deserve" (blog post), by Tyler Carrillo-Waggoner, Karen Gross, Pierce Huff, Aria Killough-Miller, and Jessica Zeng, September 21 (no year), *MSIs Unplugged*, msisunplugged.com/2016/09/21/helping-hbcus-get-the-attention-and-attendance-they-deserve/; "College Scorecard Needs Improvement in Promoting HBCUs" (blog post), by Tyler Carrillo-Waggoner, Karen Gross, Pierce Huff, Aria Killough-Miller, and Jessica Zeng, September 27 (no year), *MSIs Unplugged*, msisunplugged.com/2016/09/27/college-scorecard-needs-improvement-in-promoting-hbcus/; "High School Counselors and Their College Knowledge: A Sad State of Affairs for HBCUs" (blog post), by Tyler Carrillo-Waggoner, Karen Gross, Pierce Huff, Aria Killough-Miller, and Jessica Zeng, October 4 (no year), *MSIs Unplugged*, msisunplugged.com/2016/10/04/high-school-counselors-and-their-

college-knowledge-a-sad-state-of-affairs-for-hbcus/; "Developing a Coordinated Social Media Campaign to Garner Attention for HBCUs" (blog post), by Tyler Carrillo-Waggoner, Karen Gross, Pierce Huff, Aria Killough-Miller, and Jessica Zeng, October 11 (no year), *MSIs Unplugged*, msisunplugged.com/2016/10/11/developing-a-coordinated-social-media-campaign-to-garner-attention-for-hbcus/.

Chapter 12

1. *Our Compelling Interests: The Value of Diversity for Democracy and a Prosperous Society*, edited by Earl Lewis and Nancy Cantor (Princeton, NJ: Princeton University Press, 2016), p. 15.

2. "Why Are Fewer College Presidents Academics?" by Laura Mckenna, December 3, 2015, *The Atlantic*, www.theatlantic.com/education/archive/2015/12/college-president-mizzou-tim-wolfe/418599/; "College Presidents with Business-World Ties," March 1, 2016, *The New York Times*, www.nytimes.com/roomfordebate/2016/03/01/college-presidents-with-business-world-ties; "Drowned Bunnies: Part 2," by Scott Jaschik, January 25, 2016, *Inside Higher Ed*, www.insidehighered.com/news/2016/01/25/mount-st-marys-board-blames-faculty-furor-over-presidents-metaphor-and-plans.

3. "Six Components of a Great Corporate Culture," by John Coleman, May 6, 2013, *Harvard Business Review*, hbr.org/2013/05/six-components-of-culture; "10 Examples of Companies with Fantastic Cultures," by Sujan Patel, August 6, 2016, *Entrepreneur*, www.entrepreneur.com/article/249174; "The 25 Most Enjoyable Companies to Work For," by Julie Bort, August 22, 2014, *Business Insider*, www.businessinsider.com/25-best-corporate-cultures-2014-8.

4. See "Charges Dropped Against Yale Dishwasher Who Broke 'Racist' Calhoun Stained Glass," by Emily Zanotti, July 25, 2016, *Heat Street*, heatst.com/culture-wars/yale-rehires-worker-who-broke-priceless-stained-glass-calhoun-window/.

5. "Hiring for Cultural Fit? Here's What to Look For," by Paula Fernandes, February 14, 2016, *Business News Daily*, http://www.businessnewsdaily.com/6866-hiring-for-company-culture.html; "Recruiting for Cultural Fit," by Katie Bouton, July 17, 2015, *Harvard Business Review*, hbr.org/2015/07/recruiting-for-cultural-fit; "10 Examples of Companies with Fantastic Cultures," by Sujan Patel, August 6, 2016, *Entrepreneur*, www.entrepreneur.com/article/249174.

6. "Mountain Day" (n.d.), Smith College, www.smith.edu/about-smith/college-events/mountain-day; "Suicide Is Not a Laughing Matter," by Joe Katz, February 6, 2007, *The Chicago Maroon*, www.chicagomaroon.com/2007/02/06/suicide-is-not-a-laughing-matter/.

7. "Challenges: Newest Challenges" (n.d.), Challenge.gov, www.challenge.gov/list/; "Developing a Coordinated Social Media Campaign to Garner Attention for HBCUs" (blog post), by Tyler Carrillo-Waggoner, Karen Gross, Pierce Huff, Aria Killough-Miller, and Jessica Zeng, October 11 (no year), *MSIs Unplugged*,

msisunplugged.com/2016/10/11/developing-a-coordinated-social-media-campaign-to-garner-attention-for-hbcus/.

8. *The Tipping Point: How Little Things Can Make a Big Difference*, by Malcolm Gladwell (New York, NY: Little, Brown, 2013).

Chapter 13

1. "Half of Teachers Leave the Job After Five Years. Here's What to Do About It," by Alexandria Neason, July 18, 2014, *The Hechinger Report*, hechingerreport.org/half-teachers-leave-job-five-years-heres/; "Teacher Attrition Costs United States up to $2.2 Billion Annually, Says New Alliance Report" (press release), July 17, 2014, Alliance for Excellent Education, all4ed.org/press/teacher-attrition-costs-united-states-up-to-2-2-billion-annually-says-new-alliance-report/; "Research: Teacher-Retention Rates Higher Than Previously Thought" (blog post), by Stephen Sawchuk, May 1, 2015, *Teacher Beat*, blogs.edweek.org/edweek/teacherbeat/2015/05/research_teacher-retentions_ra.html.

2. "TFA Teachers: How Long Do They Teach? Why Do They Leave?" by Morgaen L. Donaldson and Susan Moore Johnson, October 28, 2016, *Education Week*, www.edweek.org/ew/articles/2011/10/04/kappan_donaldson.html.

3. "Teacher Turnover Affects All Students' Achievement, Study Indicates" (blog post), by Stephen Sawchuk, March 21, 2012, *Teacher Beat*, blogs.edweek.org/edweek/teacherbeat/2012/03/when_teachers_leave_schools_ov.html.

4. "Why Looping Is a Way Underappreciated School-Improvement Initiative," by Justin Minkel, June 17, 2015, *Education Week Teacher*, www.edweek.org/tm/articles/2015/06/17/looping-a-way-underappreciated-school-improvement-initiative.html; "10 Pros and Cons of Looping in Education," May 15, 2015, *TeachThought*, www.teachthought.com/learning/10-pros-and-cons-of-looping-in-education/.

5. "Revolving Doors: The Impact of Multiple School Transitions on Military Children," by S. Beth Ruff and Michael A. Keim, 2014, *The Professional Counselor, 4*(2), 103–113, doi:10.15241/sbr.4.2.103.

6. "Revolving Doors: The Impact of Multiple School Transitions on Military Children," by S. Beth Ruff and Michael A. Keim, 2014, *The Professional Counselor, 4*(2), 103–113, doi:10.15241/sbr.4.2.103; "Addressing the High Costs of Student Mobility: Military-Connected Schools Show How to Ease the Burden of Frequent Moves," by Linda Jacobson, 2013, *Harvard Education Letter, 29*(2), hepg.org/hel-home/issues/29_2/helarticle/addressing-the-high-costs-of-student-mobility_563; "Second Lady Calls for More Research to Help Military Children," by Karen Jowers, April 17, 2016, *MilitaryTimes.com*, www.militarytimes.com/story/military/family/2016/04/17/jill-biden-children-military-research-education/82997858/; "Visiting Fort Knox: Of Songs, Symbols, and Gold" (blog post), by Karen Gross (n.d.), *Home Room*, blog.ed.gov/author/kgross/; "Resilience Among Military Youth," by M. Ann Easterbrooks, Kenneth

Ginsburg, and Richard M. Lerner, 2013, *Military Children and Families, 23*(2), The Future of Children, futureofchildren.org/publications/journals/journal_details/index.xml?journalid=80.

7. "Thematic Instruction," April 14, 2011, www.funderstanding.com/educators/thematic-instruction/; *Transformational Teaching: A Team Approach*, by Rachel Pleasants McDonnell, October 2016 (Boston, MA: Jobs for the Future), www.jff.org/sites/default/files/publications/materials/Transformational%20Teaching%20091516.pdf.

Chapter 14

1. "Learning Money's Language," by Karen Gross, March 1, 2005, *UB: University Business*, www.universitybusiness.com/article/learning-moneys-language; "Portraits of Grief: A Focus on Survivors," by Karen Gross, March 20, 2003, *New York Law School Law Review*, www.nylslawreview.com/wp-content/uploads/sites/16/2013/11/46-3.4.Gross_.pdf; "Symbolic Meaning of Money, Self-Esteem, and Identification with Pancasila Values," by Juneman Abraham, Eko A. Meinarno, and Wahyu Rahardjo, 2012, *Procedia: Social and Behavioral Sciences, 65*, 106–115, doi:10.1016/j.sbspro.2012.11.099.

2. "How Students Missed Out on $2.7 Billion in Free FAFSA College Aid" (blog post), by Victoria Simons and Anna Helhoski, January 27, 2016, *NerdWallet*, www.nerdwallet.com/blog/loans/student-loans/college-students-fafsa-money/; "States Vary on FAFSA Completion Rates," by Owen Phillips, March 7, 2014, New America, www.newamerica.org/education-policy/edcentral/filling-fafsas/.

3. "What Colleges Can Do Right Now to Help Low-Income Students Succeed," by Sara Goldrick-Rab, August 28, 2016, *The Chronicle of Higher Education*, www.chronicle.com/article/What-Colleges-Can-Do-Right-Now/237589; "Navient Chief: There Are 56 Options for Repaying Federal Student Loans. It's Time to Simplify," by Jack Remandi, August 26, 2016, *The Washington Post*, www.washingtonpost.com/news/grade-point/wp/2016/08/26/navient-chief-there-are-56-options-for-repaying-federal-student-loans-its-time-to-simplify/#comments; "Why Don't Americans Claim Their Earned Income Tax Credit?" by Katie Blackley and Essential Pittsburgh, January 28, 2016, WESA, wesa.fm/post/why-dont-americans-claim-their-earned-income-tax-credit#stream/0; *Paying the Price: College Costs, Financial Aid, and the Betrayal of the American Dream*, by Sara Goldrick-Rab (Chicago, IL: University of Chicago Press, 2016).

4. "Why Don't People Take Free Cash?" by Syon Bhanot and Antonia Violante, January 22, 2016, *The Psych Report*, thepsychreport.com/science/why-dont-people-take-free-cash/; "Too Many Choices: A Problem That Can Paralyze," by Alina Tugend, February 26, 2010, *The New York Times*, www.nytimes.com/2010/02/27/your-money/27shortcuts.html.

5. "Student Loans I: Yes, Something Is Wrong," by Karen Gross, March 21, 2014, *Inside Higher Ed*, www.insidehighered.com/views/2014/03/21/we-need-right-solutions-student-debt-problem-essay; "How to Simplify the Scholarship Application Process," by Karen Gross, May 1, 2016, *The Aspen Journal of Ideas*, www.aspeninstitute.org/aspen-journal-of-ideas/how-to-simplify-the-scholarship-application-process/.

6. "Six Components of a Great Corporate Culture," by John Coleman, May 6, 2013, *Harvard Business Review*, hbr.org/2013/05/six-components-of-culture; "The Rich-Poor Divide on America's College Campuses Is Getting Wider, Fast," by Jon Marcus and Holly K. Hacker, December 17, 2015, *The Hechinger Report*, hechingerreport.org/the-socioeconomic-divide-on-americas-college-campuses-is-getting-wider-fast/.

7. *Practice for Life: Making Decisions in College*, by Lee Cuba, Nancy Jennings, Suzanne Lovett, and Joseph Swingle (Cambridge, MA: Harvard University Press, 2016); "Why Students Don't Attend Office Hours," by Maryellen Weimer, January 21, 2015, *Faculty Focus*, www.facultyfocus.com/articles/teaching-professor-blog/students-dont-attend-office-hours/.

8. "Spoof of Drug Ad for Real Teaching Issue," by Scott Jaschik, September 1, 2016, *Inside Higher Ed*, www.insidehighered.com/news/2016/09/01/arizona-state-uses-spoof-drug-ad-encourage-students-use-office-hours.

Chapter 15

1. "Why You Should Care About Parental Leave (Whether or Not You Have Kids)," by Whit Barringer, May 31, 2016, Earn Spend Live, earnspendlive.com/2016/05/care-parental-leave-whether-not-kids/; *Failing Its Families: Lack of Paid Leave and Work-Family Supports in the US*, by Janet Walsh, 2011, Human Rights Watch, www.hrw.org/report/2011/02/23/failing-its-families/lack-paid-leave-and-work-family-supports-us.

2. "Prenatal Substance Abuse: Short- and Long-Term Effects on the Exposed Fetus," by Marylou Behnke and Vincent C. Smith, 2013, *Pediatrics*, *131*(3), 1009–1023, doi:10.1542/peds.2012-3931; "Maternal, Infant, and Child Health," October 27, 2016, HealthPeople.gov, www.healthypeople.gov/2020/topics-objectives/topic/maternal-infant-and-child-health.

3. "How Important Is Physical Contact with Your Infant?" by Katherine Harmon, May 6, 2010, *Scientific American*, www.scientificamerican.com/article/infant-touch/.

4. "Poverty and Language Development: Roles of Parenting and Stress," by Suzanne C. Perkins, Eric D. Finegood, and James E. Swain, 2013, *Innovations in Clinical Neuroscience*, *10*(4), 10–19, www.ncbi.nlm.nih.gov/pmc/articles/PMC3659033/; "The Thirty Million Word Gap," by Betty Hart and Todd R.

Risley, 2003, School Literacy and Culture, literacy.rice.edu/thirty-million-word-gap; "Tackling the Vocabulary Gap Between Rich and Poor Children" (blog post), by Christopher Bergland, February 16, 2014, *The Athlete's Way*, www.psychologytoday.com/blog/the-athletes-way/201402/tackling-the-vocabulary-gap-between-rich-and-poor-children.

5. *Early Warning! Why Reading by the End of Third Grade Matters*, by the Annie E. Casey Foundation, 2010, www.ccf.ny.gov/files/9013/8262/2751/AECFReporReadingGrade3.pdf; "Why Third Grade Is So Important: The 'Matthew Effect," by Annie Murphy Paul, September 26, 2012, *Time*, ideas.time.com/2012/09/26/why-third-grade-is-so-important-the-matthew-effect/; "Teacher Expectations Reflect Racial Biases, Johns Hopkins Study Suggests," by Jill Rosen, March 30, 2016, *The Hub*, hub.jhu.edu/2016/03/30/racial-bias-teacher-expectations-black-white/; "The Alarming Effect of Racial Mismatch on Teacher Expectations," by Seth Gershenson, August 18, 2015, Brookings, www.brookings.edu/blog/brown-center-chalkboard/2015/08/18/the-alarming-effect-of-racial-mismatch-on-teacher-expectations/; "Building Self-Esteem: Children 1–8 Years," by Raising Children Network, last updated or revised November 21, 2012, raisingchildren.net.au/articles/self-esteem_different_ages.html; "Why the Teacher's Pet Resembles the Teacher," by Anya Kamenetz, February 24, 2015, MindShift, ww2.kqed.org/mindshift/2015/02/24/why-the-teachers-pet-often-resembles-the-teacher/.

6. "Stop the Summer Slide," by Nina Rees, June 15, 2015, *U.S. News & World Report*, www.usnews.com/opinion/knowledge-bank/2015/06/16/summer-slide-is-bad-for-students; "Low-Income Students Stand to Lose More with Summer Learning Loss," by Caroline Bauman, June 17, 2015, *Chalkbeat*, www.chalkbeat.org/posts/tn/2015/06/17/low-income-students-have-more-to-lose-with-summer-learning-loss/#.V81t0zeIB9Y.

7. *Our Kids: The American Dream in Crisis*, by Robert D. Putnam (New York, NY: Simon and Schuster, 2015).

8. "Great Teaching," by Raj Chetty, John N. Friedman, and Jonah E. Rockoff, *Education Next*, educationnext.org/great-teaching/; *Measuring the Impacts of Teachers I: Evaluating Bias in Teacher Value-Added Estimates*, by Raj Chetty, John N. Friedman, and Jonah E. Rockoff, 2013, Working Paper 19423, National Bureau of Economic Research, www0.gsb.columbia.edu/faculty/jrockoff/papers/w19423.pdf.

9. "Teacher Expectations Reflect Racial Biases, Johns Hopkins Study Suggests," by Jill Rosen, March 30, 2016, *The Hub*, hub.jhu.edu/2016/03/30/racial-bias-teacher-expectations-black-white/; "The Alarming Effect of Racial Mismatch on Teacher Expectations," by Seth Gershenson, August 18, 2015, Brookings, www.brookings.edu/blog/brown-center-chalkboard/2015/08/18/the-alarming-effect-of-racial-mismatch-on-teacher-expectations/; *Betraying the College Dream: How Disconnected K–12 and Postsecondary Education Systems Undermine*

Student Aspirations, by Andrea Venezia, Michael W. Kirst, and Anthony L. Antonio (n.d.), Bridge Project, Stanford Institute for Higher Education Research, web. stanford.edu/group/bridgeproject/betrayingthecollegedream.pdf; "Redoing Application Reading," by Rick Seltzer, September 23, 2016, *Inside Higher Ed*, www. insidehighered.com/news/2016/09/23/demographic-changes-prompt-changes-application-reading.

10. "Effective Counseling in Schools Increases College Access," 2006, *Research to Practice Brief* (1), www.careerladdersproject.org/wp-content/uploads/2013/02/Effective-Counseling.pdf; "Helping HBCUs Get the Attention and Attendance They Deserve" (blog post), by Tyler Carrillo-Waggoner, Karen Gross, Pierce Huff, Aria Killough-Miller, and Jessica Zeng, September 21 (no year), *MSIs Unplugged*, msisunplugged.com/2016/09/21/helping-hbcus-get-the-attention-and-attendance-they-deserve/.

11. "Don't Wait to Address Summer Melt: The Time Is Now," by Karen Gross, April 14, 2015, *Diverse: Issues in Higher Education*, diverseeducation. com/article/71621/; "4 Simple Ways to Stop Summer Melt" (blog post), by Bethany Showers, August 11, 2016, *Brazen Blog*, www.brazen.com/blog/universities/4-simple-ways-to-stop-summer-melt/.

12. "Overcoming Long Odds," by Paul Bradley, June 9, 2016, *Community College Week*, ccweek.com/article-5209-overcoming-long-odds.html; "Go to College to Get an Education, Not Just a Degree," by Ransom Patterson, last updated September 6, 2015, College Info Geek, collegeinfogeek.com/degree-plus-education/; "Who Can Help First Gen Students: Not Just First Gen Administrators!" by Karen Gross, May 19, 2015, LinkedIn, www.linkedin.com/pulse/who-can-help-first-gen-students-just-administrators-karen-gross; "Supporting First-Gen College Students," by Ioanna Opidee, February 25, 2015, *UB: University Business*, www. universitybusiness.com/article/supporting-first-gen-college-students.

13. "Family Classes Tied to Better School Performance for Poor Kids," by Lisa Rapaport, October 3, 2016, Reuters, www.reuters.com/article/us-health-children-prekindergarten-idUSKCN12326T.

14. *Checklists to Improve Patient Safety*, by American Hospital Association, June 2013, Signature Leadership Series, www.hpoe.org/Reports-HPOE/CkLists_PatientSafety.pdf; "A Simple Checklist That Saves Lives," by Ellen Barlow, Fall 2008, Harvard T. H. Chan School of Public Health, www.hsph.harvard.edu/news/magazine/fall08checklist/; "Improve Performance" (blog post), by Dennis Sparks, June 14, 2010, *Dennis Sparks on Leading and Learning*, dennissparks.wordpress. com/2010/06/14/475/; *The Checklist Manifesto: How to Get Things Right*, by Atul Gawande (New York, NY: Henry Holt, 2011).

15. "The Power and Uses of Checklists for Teachers and Administrators" (blog post), by Dennis Sparks, April 25, 2013, *Dennis Sparks on Leading and Learning*, dennissparks.wordpress.com/2013/04/25/the-power-and-uses-of-checklists-for-teachers-and-administrators/.

16. *Generation on a Tightrope: A Portrait of Today's College Student*, by Arthur Levine and Diane R. Dean (San Francisco, CA: Jossey-Bass, 2012), pp. xii, xiii.

17. *Practice for Life: Making Decisions in College*, by Lee Cuba, Nancy Jennings, Suzanne Lovett, and Joseph Swingle (Cambridge, MA: Harvard University Press, 2016), p. 20.

18. "Universities' Messages About Socioeconomic Diversity Can Affect Academic Confidence," December 14, 2015, EurekAlert, www.eurekalert.org/pub_releases/2015-12/nu-uma121415.php; "Understanding Microaggressions: Seeing the Invisible," by Karen Gross, December 19, 2015, LinkedIn, www.linkedin.com/pulse/understanding-microaggressions-seeing-invisible-karen-gross.

19. See nicholaschristakis.net.

Chapter 16

1. "Jabberwocky" (from *Through the Looking-Glass and What Alice Found There*, 1872), by Lewis Carroll, www.jabberwocky.com/carroll/jabber/jabberwocky.html; "A Short Analysis of 'Jabberwocky' by Lewis Carroll," January 22 (no year), Interesting Literature, interestingliterature.com/2016/01/22/a-short-analysis-of-jabberwocky-by-lewis-carroll/; "The Jabberwocky," by Cathy Dean, last updated March 25, 1998, www.design.caltech.edu/erik/Misc/Jabberwock.html.

2. "Predicting New Words," January 3, 2008, Visual Thesaurus, www.visualthesaurus.com/cm/dictionary/predicting-new-words/; "How to Get a Word into the Dictionary," Dictionary.com, blog.dictionary.com/getting-words-into-dictionaries/.

3. "Where Does the Phrase 'Pull Yourself Up by Your Bootstraps' Actually Come From?" by Sarah Alvarez, April 7, 2015, State of Opportunity: Can Kids in Michigan Get Ahead? stateofopportunity.michiganradio.org/post/where-does-phrase-pull-yourself-your-bootstraps-actually-come.

Additional Relevant Readings

Best, J., & Best, E. (2014). *The student loan mess: How good intentions created a trillion-dollar problem*. Berkeley, CA: University of California Press.

Bowen, W. G., & McPherson, M. S. (2016). *Lesson plan: An agenda for change in American higher education*. Princeton, NJ: Princeton University Press.

Conrad, C., & Gasman, M. (2015). *Educating a diverse nation: Lessons from minority-serving institutions*. Cambridge, MA: Harvard University Press.

Craig, R. (2015). *College disrupted: The great unbundling of higher education*. New York, NY: St. Martin's Press.

Crow, M. M., & Dabars, W. B. (2015). *Designing the new American university*. Baltimore, MD: Johns Hopkins University Press.

Dweck, C. (2006). *Mindset: The new psychology of success*. New York, NY: Random House.

Feldman, D. B., & Kravetz, L. D. (2015). *Supersurvivors: The surprising link between suffering and success*. New York, NY: HarperWave.

Forward, S. (2002). *Toxic parents: Overcoming their hurtful legacy and reclaiming your life*. New York, NY: Bantam.

Gabriel, K. F., & Flake, S. M. (2008). *Teaching unprepared students: Strategies for promoting success and retention in higher education*. Sterling, WV: Stylus.

Gasman, M., & Commodore, F. (Eds.). *(2014)*. *Opportunities and challenges at historically Black colleges and universities*. New York, NY: Palgrave Macmillan.

Gazzaniga, M. S. (2015). *Tales from both sides of the brain: A life in neuroscience* (Enhanced ed.). New York, NY: HarperCollins.

Lahey, J. (2015). *The gift of failure: How the best parents learn to let go so their children can succeed*. New York, NY: Harper/HarperCollins.

Menasche, D. (2014). *The priority list: A teacher's final quest to discover life's greatest lessons*. New York, NY: Touchstone.

Mettler, S. (2014). *Degrees of inequality: How the politics of higher education sabotaged the American dream*. New York, NY: Basic Books.

Perna, L. W., & Jones, A. (2013). *The state of college access and completion: Improving college success for students from underrepresented groups*. New York, NY: Routledge.

Pryor, L. (2016). *Look at you now: My journey from shame to strength*. New York, NY: Random House.

Shay, J. (2010). *Achilles in Vietnam: Combat trauma and the undoing of character*. New York, NY: Simon & Schuster.

Shonkoff, J. P., & Phillips, D. A. (Eds.). (2000). *From neurons to neighborhoods: The science of early childhood development*. Washington, DC: National Academies Press.

Taintor, S. (2016). *Building authentic confidence in children*. Waukesha, WI: Reji Laberje.

Tinto, V. (2012). *Completing college: Rethinking institutional action*. Chicago, IL: University of Chicago Press.

Schroff, L., & Tresniowski, A. (2011). *An invisible thread: The true story of an 11-year-old panhandler, a busy sales executive, and an unlikely meeting with destiny*. New York, NY: Howard Books.

Index

Note: Page numbers followed by "n" indicate numbered endnotes.

About the Author

Karen Gross is a higher education consultant based in Washington, DC. Gross currently serves as senior counsel for Finn Partners and sits on the advisory council of the Penn Center for Minority Serving Institutions at the University of Pennsylvania Graduate School of Education.

As the president for 8 years of Southern Vermont College, where more than 65% of students are the first in their families to go to college and approximately 50% are Pell Grant eligible, Gross spoke frequently on student access and success and, with her team, implemented innovative teaching and learning practices, measurably increasing the success rates of vulnerable students.

In her role as senior policy adviser at the U.S. Department of Education during the administration of President Barack Obama, Gross worked closely with the Departments of Defense, Veterans Affairs, and Labor and the Domestic Policy Council to improve transition to civilian life for service members and their families and helped implement the president's 2020 initiative to increase college access and success.

Prior to this, Gross was a tenured law professor for more than 2 decades and sat on nonprofit boards, including those of Campus Compact (a national service learning organization), the Sage Colleges, and the Association of Vermont Independent Colleges.

A frequent voice on education issues across the pre-K–20 pipeline, she has been published in numerous publications, among them *The Washington Post*, *Change: The Magazine of Higher Learning*, *Huffington Post*, *The Hechinger Report*, *The New England Journal of Higher Ed*, *Diverse*, *Road2College*, *National Journal*, *InsideHigherEd*, and *The Chronicle of Higher Education*.

She is the author of the award-winning book *Failure and Forgiveness* (Yale University Press); a children's book series, titled *Lady Lucy's Quest*; and *Teach Your Children Well*, about the lessons learned from the signs of the 2017 Women's March.